# VALENCE
## AND THE
## STRUCTURE OF ATOMS
## AND
## MOLECULES

By GILBERT NEWTON LEWIS, *1875-1946*

*With a New Introduction by*
*KENNETH S. PITZER*
*President, Rice University*

DOVER PUBLICATIONS, INC., NEW YORK

Published in Canada by General Publishing Com-
pany, Ltd., 30 Lesmill Road, Don Mills, Toronto,
Ontario.
Published in the United Kingdom by Constable
and Company, Ltd., 10 Orange Street, London
W. C. 2.

This Dover edition, first published in 1966, is
an unaltered and unabridged republication of the
work originally published by The Chemical Catalog
Company, Inc., in 1923. This edition contains a new
Introduction by Kenneth S. Pitzer.

*Library of Congress Catalog Card Number: 66-17120*

Manufactured in the United States of America
Dover Publications, Inc.
180 Varick Street
New York, N. Y. 10014

To my colleagues and students of the University of California, without whose help this book would not have been written. In our many years of discussion of the problems of atomic and molecular structure, some of the ideas here presented have sprung from the group rather than from an individual; so that in a sense I am acting only as editor for this group.

# INTRODUCTION TO THE DOVER EDITION

Gilbert N. Lewis not only made chemical discoveries of the greatest significance, but also described them in an unusually lucid style. He steered a masterful course between unnecessary approximations on one side and an excessively formal and abstruse presentation on the other. Consequently, even forty or more years later, many of his writings are among the clearest statements on these subjects. In the case of his book on thermodynamics (*Thermodynamics and the Free Energy of Chemical Substances*, 2nd ed., New York, 1961), Professor Leo Brewer and I were given the opportunity to preserve the Lewis presentation of the fundamental principles while modernizing those sections in which great advances had been made in recent years. Thus, it is with great pleasure that I write these few words to accompany a new printing of another Gilbert N. Lewis classic. This reprinting is especially interesting in view of the first sentence of Professor Lewis' Preface in which he states that this book "belongs to the ephemeral literature of science."

One historical point will be of interest to current readers. Professor Lewis developed most of his key ideas concerning valence and the chemical bond before he was drawn into World War I as the officer advising General Pershing on chemical warfare. These ideas were initially presented in 1916 in a single paper in the *Journal of the American Chemical Society*. Irving Langmuir was stimulated primarily by Lewis' 1916 paper to extend and refine the basic concepts in two papers written [and published in the above journal (Vol. 41, 1919)] while Lewis was on military duty. *Valence and the Structure of Atoms and Molecules* constituted Lewis' delayed presentation of material that would presumably have appeared several years earlier had it not been for the war.

At the time this book was written (1923), quantum theory was still in a nebulous state. With the refinement of quantum theory, many details of valence theory have been revised and put into

3

much more definite form than was possible in 1923.   But the concept of the chemical bond comprising a pair of electrons shared between two atoms remains the keystone of valence theory.   Also, we note that Lewis correctly stated that the "tendency to form pairs is not a property of free electrons, but rather . . . it is a property of electrons within the atom" (see p. 81).

It is helpful in understanding the nature of science to follow the development of the major theories through successive stages of refinement.   The renewed availability of this book will contribute toward such an understanding of valence theory.

*Houston, Texas*                                    KENNETH S. PITZER
*September, 1965*

# GENERAL INTRODUCTION

## American Chemical Society Series of Scientific and Technologic Monographs

By arrangement with the Interallied Conference of Pure and Applied Chemistry, which met in London and Brussels in July, 1919, the American Chemical Society was to undertake the production and publication of Scientific and Technologic Monographs on chemical subjects. At the same time it was agreed that the National Research Council, in coöperation with the American Chemical Society and the American Physical Society, should undertake the production and publication of Critical Tables of Chemical and Physical Constants. The American Chemical Society and the National Research Council mutually agreed to care for these two fields of chemical development. The American Chemical Society named as Trustees, to make the necessary arrangements for the publication of the monographs, Charles L. Parsons, Secretary of the American Chemical Society, Washington, D. C.; John E. Teeple, Treasurer of the American Chemical Society, New York City; and Professor Gellert Alleman of Swarthmore College. The Trustees have arranged for the publication of the American Chemical Society series of (a) Scientific and (b) Technologic Monographs by the Chemical Catalog Company of New York City.

The Council, acting through the Committee on National Policy of the American Chemical Society, appointed the editors, named at the close of this introduction, to have charge of securing authors, and of considering critically the manuscripts prepared. The editors of each series will endeavor to select topics which are of current interest and authors who are recognized as authorities in their respective fields. The list of monographs thus far secured appears in the publisher's own announcement elsewhere in this volume.

The development of knowledge in all branches of science, and especially in chemistry, has been so rapid during the last fifty years and the fields covered by this development have been so varied that it is difficult for any individual to keep in touch with the progress in branches of science outside his own specialty. In spite of the facilities for the examination of the literature given by Chemical Abstracts and such compendia as Beilstein's Handbuch der Organischen Chemie, Richter's Lexikon, Ostwald's Lehrbuch der Allgemeinen Chemie, Abegg's and Gmelin-Kraut's Handbuch der Anorganischen Chemie and the English and French Dictionaries of Chemistry, it often takes a great deal of time to coördinate the knowledge available upon a single topic. Consequently when men who have spent years in the study of important subjects are willing to coördinate their knowledge and present it in concise, readable form, they perform a service of the highest value to their fellow chemists.

It was with a clear recognition of the usefulness of reviews of this character that a Committee of the American Chemical Society recommended the publication of the two series of monographs under the auspices of the Society.

Two rather distinct purposes are to be served by these monographs. The first purpose, whose fulfilment will probably render to chemists in general the most important service, is to present the knowledge available upon the chosen topic in a readable form, intelligible to those whose activities may be along a wholly different line. Many chemists fail to realize how closely their investigations may be connected with other work which on the surface appears far afield from their own. These monographs will enable such men to form closer contact with the work of chemists in other lines of research. The second purpose is to promote research in the branch of science covered by the monograph, by furnishing a well digested survey of the progress already made in that field and by pointing out directions in which investigation needs to be extended. To facilitate the attainment of this purpose, it is intended to include extended references to the literature, which will enable anyone interested to follow up the subject in more detail. If the literature is so voluminous that a complete bibliography is impracticable, a critical selection will be made of those papers which are most important.

The publication of these books marks a distinct departure in the policy of the American Chemical Society inasmuch as it is a serious attempt to found an American chemical literature without primary regard to commercial considerations. The success of the venture will depend in large part upon the measure of coöperation which can be secured in the preparation of books dealing adequately with topics of general interest; it is earnestly hoped, therefore, that every member of the various organizations in the chemical and allied industries will recognize the importance of the enterprise and take sufficient interest to justify it.

## AMERICAN CHEMICAL SOCIETY

### BOARD OF EDITORS

# PREFACE

I take it that a monograph of this sort belongs to the ephemeral literature of science. The studied care which is warranted in the treatment of the more slowly moving branches of science would be out of place here. Rather with the pen of a journalist we must attempt to record a momentary phase of current thought, which may at any instant change with kaleidoscopic abruptness.

It is therefore not unlikely that some of the things said in this book may soon have to be unsaid, but I trust that these may be matters of detail rather than of essence. During the seven years that have elapsed since my previous publication concerning the structure of the molecule and the nature of the chemical bond, I have found little need of subtracting from the views there set forth, although there is now much to add. So in this present work I shall hope that there are no serious sins of commission. That there are sins of omission I am already only too well aware. To attempt to keep pace with the rapid developments in so many ramifications of science, all of which contribute to our knowledge of the atom and the molecule, is, especially for one who is at best a slothful reader, an impossible task.

Nevertheless it is the same atom and the same molecule that is being studied by the organic chemist, the inorganic chemist and the physicist; the marvellously exact conclusions of the spectroscopist, the far more vague but equally difficult and important generalizations of the student of the carbon compounds, must contribute, each in due measure, to our knowledge of that microcosmos which appears to us the more mysterious as its nature becomes more nearly revealed to us. It was with this thought in mind that I have devoted several of the earlier chapters to an attempt to bring to the better acquaintance of chemists some of the astounding accomplishments of modern physics.

GILBERT N. LEWIS

# CONTENTS

# VALENCE AND THE STRUCTURE OF ATOMS AND MOLECULES.

## Chapter I.

## The Atomic Theory.

### The Discontinuity of Matter.

There has been much debate among historians of chemistry as to the order of discovery of Dalton's two great generalizations. Which came first, the atomic theory or the law of multiple proportions? The fact probably is that in Dalton's mind the two ideas were essentially one. The concept of a granular structure of matter had been a favorite among philosophers for centuries, and at the beginning of the nineteenth century it was prevalent among scientists and laymen. "Pound St. Paul's church into atoms, and consider any atom . . ." Boswell quoted Johnson as saying a decade earlier.

Moreover, many of those who held this philosophical doctrine regarded the atoms of any one simple substance as equivalent to one another, like building bricks. The idea that a simple substance is composed of small particles, all similar one to another, must therefore be presumed to have been a part of the intellectual heritage of that period.

What Dalton saw (1808) was the possibility of a crucial scientific test of this hypothesis. If elements and compounds are made up of discrete and characteristic particles, each particle of a compound substance must contain an integral number of particles of its component elements. In fact Dalton found, in the two hydrocarbons which we call ethylene and methane, a given amount of hydrogen combined with twice as much carbon in the former as in the latter. In the two oxides of carbon he found the ratio of oxygen to carbon to be twice as great in one as in the other. When he also discovered a similar integral relationship among the oxides of nitrogen, he felt justified in announcing the general law of multiple proportions. The crudity of the experiments upon which he based this law, and the fact that his analysis of one of the oxides of nitrogen was entirely erroneous, indicate a strong predisposition toward the conclusion which he reached.

The law of multiple proportions converted a philosophic speculation into a working theory of science. The theory of atoms and molecules not only became the basis of stoichiometry, but later again proved its great fertility in the development of the mechanical theory of heat.

At the end of the last century a short period of scepticism as to the reality of atoms and molecules was abruptly terminated through the rapid advance of scientific discovery. It became possible to count the atoms. The ultramicroscope in the hands of Perrin (1908) permitted the observation of particles moving about in exact accord with the predictions of molecular theory. In the processes of radioactivity heavy atoms were found to be disintegrating into lighter atoms, and it was shown by Rutherford and Soddy (1903) that each atom of helium emitted by a radioactive substance produces a scintillation upon a screen of barium platino-cyanide, so that in a sense we see the individual atoms.

Thus the atoms have been counted, analyzed, decomposed. Even the secrets of the innermost nucleus are being brought to light. But such familiarity has tended to produce over-confidence. For a time it seemed that the structure and the behavior of the atom could be interpreted without essential change in the modes of thought which had been found adequate in dealing with the massive bodies of everyday experience. However, this feeling of confidence has received a rude shock as we have encountered one by one the mysteries and paradoxes which have led to the quantum theory of the present day.

Through the work of Dalton the conception of matter as a continuum was definitely displaced by the conception of discrete quanta of matter, and we are now beginning to see that this was but the first stage in a great revolution against the theory of the continuum. Step by step we are being forced to "quantize" physico-chemical phenomena. How far this revolution will go, and how much of our former belief in the continuity of nature will remain, we cannot now predict; but it is already evident that many of our best established principles of science are under fire, and we may be sure that the theory of atoms is but one of many phases of the coming theory of discontinuity in nature.

## The Unity of Matter.

There is another philosophic belief which at all times has been widely held. This is the idea that all of the various substances known to us are merely different manifestations of a single basic substance. Just as Dalton saw the scientific implications of the atomic theory, so Prout (1815) saw a possible scientific consequence of the theory of the unity of matter.

He noted that the weights of the several atoms appeared to be multiples of the weight of hydrogen, and advanced the idea that all other atoms are composed of hydrogen atoms. This proposal, which was vigorously contested, received the adherence of some of the best minds of the period. The experimental evidence was conflicting. Atomic weights had been but roughly determined, and while accidental errors would not on the average bring atomic weights nearer to whole numbers, an instinctive tendency toward the rounding off of uncertain figures seemed adequate to account for the rule discovered by Prout.

Continual refinement of method led to an increasing accuracy in analytical results, and for over a century the determination of atomic weights has been one of the favorite occupations of chemists. It soon became apparent that the atomic weights in general were not exact multiples of that of hydrogen, and Prout's theory gradually fell into disrepute. Nevertheless it was occasionally pointed out that the majority of atomic weights were much nearer to whole numbers than would be expected from the laws of chance.

For example, Rydberg (1897) showed that the chance of the atomic weights of the first twenty-two elements falling as near to whole numbers as they do would be less than one in one billion. It therefore seemed reasonable to ascribe the close approximation of atomic weights to whole numbers, not to pure chance, but rather to some such fundamental principle as that of Prout, perhaps modified by some factors of a secondary nature. Indeed we are now nearly convinced that Prout's theory was correct, and that the deviations of atomic weights from integral numbers are due to two separate causes.

The first of these causes was foreseen in a remarkable prophecy made by Marignac in 1860. He says: "Could one not, for example, while preserving the fundamental principle of this law (of Prout) make the following supposition, to which I do not attach importance except in so far as to show that one might explain the discordance which appears to exist between the results of observation and the immediate consequences of this principle? Might one not suppose that the cause, which is unknown but probably differs from the physical and chemical agencies that we recognize, and which has determined certain groupings of the atoms of the single primordial matter to give birth to our simple chemical atoms, and to impose upon each of these groups a special character and particular properties, has also been able to exercise an influence upon the way in which these groups of atoms obey the law of universal attraction, such that the weight of each of them is not exactly the sum of the weights of the primordial atoms which constitute them?" Since the advent of relativity we know that the mass of a body varies with its energy, so that if two atoms combine with a certain evolution of energy there is a proportional loss in mass. This is one of the reasons for the deviations from the rule of Prout.

The second cause which we now recognize as responsible for some of the large deviations from the rule of Prout is that many of the elements are mixtures of one or more isotopes which can be separated only with the greatest difficulty. Such elements have atomic weights that depend upon the relative amounts of the several isotopes which they contain. The separate isotopes, studied by the method of positive ray analysis developed by J. J. Thomson (1913) and by Aston (1920), for the most part show atomic weights which are very close to whole numbers.

The problem of isotopes is one which concerns what is now called the nucleus of the atom, and it would carry us too far from the main purpose of this work to discuss in any detail the many important observations which concern the structure and the disintegration of that nucleus.

## Theories of Chemical Affinity.

In the earliest experiments on electricity it was found that different substances, brought into contact and then separated, remain charged, one with vitreous and the other with resinous electricity, or in Franklin's nomenclature, with positive and negative electricity. Different substances appeared to exercise different degrees of attraction for the electric fluid or fluids.

In the course of the brilliant experiments of Davy (1807) concerning the effect of the electric current upon various chemicals, he was led to the idea that the particles of substances become electrified when they meet dissimilar particles, and that the attraction between the opposite charges, so produced, is the cause of chemical union. This idea was developed by Berzelius (1819) into the electrochemical theory, which remained for many years the dominant theory of chemistry.

All kinds of chemical union were explained in accordance with this theory. Thus it was considered, when an atom of zinc comes in contact with an atom of oxygen, that a flow of electricity occurs which leaves the former positive and the latter negative. Although sulfur also would be negative toward zinc it is positive toward oxygen and becomes the positive part of a molecule such as sulfur trioxide. Thus each of the molecules, zinc oxide and sulfur trioxide, was regarded as held together by the electric forces operating between the oppositely charged parts. But these two molecules when brought together would also not remain neutral. Zinc oxide as a whole being positive with respect to sulfur trioxide, these two molecules would in turn be held together by electric forces to produce a molecule of zinc sulfate. Soon the theory was extended to apply not only to simple compounds but even to the most complex bodies known to mineralogy.

When the electrochemical or dualistic theory was first proposed it was not known that some of the firmest chemical compounds are composed of two like atoms, as $H_2$ or $N_2$. The existence of such types of union presented an apparently insuperable objection to the theory. Also the study of organic chemistry drew attention to a class of compounds which seemed to fit inadequately into the dualistic scheme of Berzelius. Especially it was pointed out that electronegative chlorine could be substituted for electropositive hydrogen, in numerous compounds, without appearing to produce any pronounced change in properties. In consequence of these discoveries the dualistic theory was largely abandoned.

Then continued the great development of structural organic chemistry, from the work of Kekulé (1858) on the chemical bond and on the spatial arrangement of the atoms, to the work of LeBel (1875) and of van't Hoff (1875) on stereoisomerism. No generalization of science, even if we include those capable of exact mathematical statement, has ever achieved a greater success in assembling in simple form a multitude of heterogeneous observations than this group of ideas which we call structural theory. The graphical formula is far more than a mere theory of atomic arrangements; it has become a remarkable shorthand method of representing a great variety of chemical knowledge.

In all this development of structural chemistry the electrochemical properties of the elements seemed to play but a subordinate rôle. But, after the great wave of enthusiasm for the synthesis and analysis of complex organic substances was spent, attention once more reverted to substances of the saline type. Faraday (1833) had shown that the law of definite and multiple proportions is valid not only for the chemical elements but also for electricity. Thus a gram of copper carries just twice as much electricity in the electrolysis of a cupric salt as in the electrolysis of a cuprous salt. It is singular that so many years elapsed after the announcement of Faraday's law before it was realized that this law implies a discontinuity of electricity in the same degree that Dalton's law implied a discontinuous structure of ordinary matter. By the same reasoning electricity occurs in quanta that are all alike, and capable of combining with atoms and groups of atoms only by integral numbers. It was Helmholtz in his celebrated Faraday lecture of 1881 who first pointed out this deduction of the atom of electricity, or as it is now called, the electron.

Our knowledge of the atom of negative electricity, the electron, is largely due to the brilliant investigations of J. J. Thomson and of those whom he has inspired. The proof that free electricity is negative electricity; the determination of the ratio between the charge and the mass of an electron; and the study of the physical and chemical effects produced by moving electrons, comprise one of the most fascinating chapters of modern science.

The study of saline substances was greatly fostered by the electrolytic dissociation theory of Arrhenius (1887) which clarified in so remarkable a manner our ideas concerning salt solutions. This theory through a generation of criticism has fully justified its essential accuracy. We are fully convinced that, in a dilute aqueous solution of sodium chloride, this salt is separated into two distinct parts, one of which has a negative charge, equal to the charge of an electron, while the other is positively charged in equal amount. Thus we have full demonstration of a phenomenon which was assumed in the dualistic theory.

Again chemists were tempted to revert to the electrochemical theory as an explanation of all chemical union, and again they met the difficulty of explaining by such means the properties of substances like methane and diatomic hydrogen. There obviously is a wide gap between extreme types: on the one hand an extremely "polar" substance like sodium chloride, in which presumably there is at all times a considerable displacement of electricity from the sodium to the chlorine, and which sometimes completely dissociates into sodium and chloride ions; on the other hand a relatively non-polar substance like diatomic hydrogen which gives no *a priori* reason for, nor shows any evidence of, such electric displacement. Must we conclude that there are two distinct types of chemical union, one a completely polar and the other a completely non-polar type, and must we assume that a substance which appears to have intermediate properties, and to be slightly polarized electrically, is merely a mixture of polar and non-polar molecules? Or can we find some means of ascribing all the most varied types of chemical union to one and the same fundamental cause, differing only in the nature and degree of its manifestation? These are questions which will occupy our attention in later chapters.

# Chapter II.

## The Periodic Law and the Chemist's Picture of the Atom.

Even before the advent of the atomic theory it was known that the elements form natural groups or families, and as soon as Dalton's theory was established it became a matter of interest to see what relations might exist between the properties of similar atoms and their atomic weights. About the same time that Prout announced the hypothesis which gave such an impetus to the accurate determination of atomic weights it was discovered by Döbereiner (1816) that in a number of "triads" of related elements the atomic weight of a certain element of the triad was approximately the mean of the atomic weights of the other two. We now know many of the elements, which he studied, to be mixtures of isotopes, and yet these coincidences pointed out by Döbereiner are still evident in our present table of atomic weights and have not as yet been explained.

The periodic relations between the atomic weights and the properties of the elements could hardly be discovered during the period in which many elements were assigned atomic weights which were multiples or sub-multiples of their true values, but after the introduction of the modern system of atomic weights by Cannizzaro (1858) many chemists began to discern such periodic relations. Probably the first to publish anything like our present periodic table was de Chancourtois (1863), who arranged the elements in a spiral in the order of their atomic weights, and made the significant remark, "The properties of substances are the properties of numbers." Similar observations were made by Newlands (1863) and more fully by Lothar Meyer (1870), but it is to Mendeléeff (1869) that we owe the fullest recognition of the periodic law and its consequences. It is unnecessary to recite here the achievements of the periodic law of Mendeléeff, which for fifty years has been the guiding principle of systematic chemistry. The confidence in this principle was not shaken but rather strengthened by the discovery of a completely new family of the elements, the gases of the argon type.

However, we must call attention to a certain error in the original statement of the principle. The idea that the properties of the elements vary in a regular manner with the atomic weights is untenable, for in spite of many efforts no quantitative relations have been found between the atomic weight of an element and its chemical properties.

If we glance at the table of the elements we see that there is a difference of 3.4 units in atomic weight between sulfur and chlorine, while there is a difference of only 0.7 between selenium and bromine. It is therefore not altogether surprising to find that iodine has an atomic weight actually below that of tellurium. If the elements were to be arranged strictly in the order of increasing atomic weights, iodine would be forced into the group of oxygen and sulfur, while tellurium would fall among the

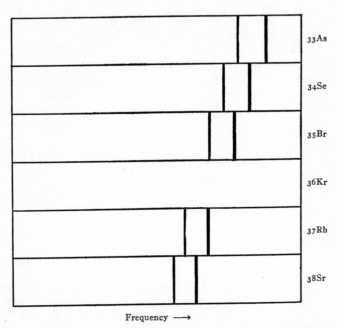

Frequency ⟶

Fig. 1.—X-Ray Emission Lines.

halogens. So also the positions of argon and potassium and of cobalt and nickel would be reversed.

It was Rydberg (1897, 1914) who first comprehended the underlying truth in the periodic classification. The properties of an element are determined by a single "independent variable" which is not, however, the atomic weight. In the second of his remarkable papers in which Rydberg gave the ordinal number of each element, he was obliged to decide upon the exact placing of all the elements of the rare earths, upon the number of elements still remaining undiscovered, and upon the exact position of these vacancies in the periodic table. In all of these difficult tasks he was completely successful, and his table of ordinal numbers is identical with our present table of atomic numbers, except that he assumed the existence of two elements between hydrogen and helium. If we reduce all of his numbers, except the

## ATOMIC NUMBERS.

| | | | | | |
|---|---|---|---|---|---|
| Hydrogen | 1 | Germanium | 32 | Europium | 63 |
| Helium | 2 | Arsenic | 33 | Gadolinium | 64 |
| Lithium | 3 | Selenium | 34 | Terbium | 65 |
| Beryllium | 4 | Bromine | 35 | Dysprosium | 66 |
| Boron | 5 | Krypton | 36 | Holmium | 67 |
| Carbon | 6 | Rubidium | 37 | Erbium | 68 |
| Nitrogen | 7 | Strontium | 38 | Thulium | 69 |
| Oxygen | 8 | Yttrium | 39 | Ytterbium | 70 |
| Fluorine | 9 | Zirconium | 40 | Lutecium | 71 |
| Neon | 10 | Columbium | 41 | .... | 72 |
| Sodium | 11 | Molybdenum | 42 | Tantalum | 73 |
| Magnesium | 12 | .... | 43 | Tungsten | 74 |
| Aluminum | 13 | Ruthenium | 44 | .... | 75 |
| Silicon | 14 | Rhodium | 45 | Osmium | 76 |
| Phosphorus | 15 | Palladium | 46 | Iridium | 77 |
| Sulfur | 16 | Silver | 47 | Platinum | 78 |
| Chlorine | 17 | Cadmium | 48 | Gold | 79 |
| Argon | 18 | Indium | 49 | Mercury | 80 |
| Potassium | 19 | Tin | 50 | Thallium | 81 |
| Calcium | 20 | Antimony | 51 | Lead | 82 |
| Scandium | 21 | Tellurium | 52 | Bismuth | 83 |
| Titanium | 22 | Iodine | 53 | Polonium | 84 |
| Vanadium | 23 | Xenon | 54 | .... | 85 |
| Chromium | 24 | Cesium | 55 | Niton | 86 |
| Manganese | 25 | Barium | 56 | .... | 87 |
| Iron | 26 | Lanthanum | 57 | Radium | 88 |
| Cobalt | 27 | Cerium | 58 | .... | 89 |
| Nickel | 28 | Praseodymium | 59 | Thorium | 90 |
| Copper | 29 | Neodymium | 60 | .... | 91 |
| Zinc | 30 | .... | 61 | Uranium | 92 |
| Gallium | 31 | Samarium | 62 | | |

first, by two we obtain the accompanying table, which gives the atomic numbers that are now adopted.

The problem was also being attacked by the physicists. Rutherford (1911) had been led by experiments on the rebounding of alpha particles from other atoms to conclude that there lies in the center of each atom a small nucleus, with a positive charge which can be neutralized by the presence of an integral number of negative electrons. It was proposed by van den Broek (1913) that the integral number which represents the positive charge on the nucleus of an atom represents also

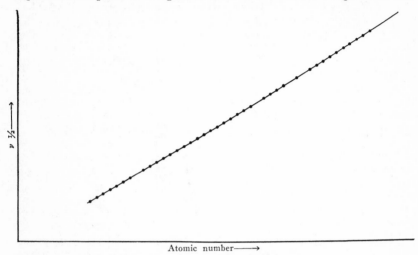

Fig. 2.—Atomic Number and X-Ray Frequency.

the ordinal number which determines the position of the element in the periodic table.

This idea was brought into sharp relief by the extraordinary results of the experiments of Moseley (1913, 1914) on the X-ray spectra of the several elements. Moseley found that when the various elements are bombarded by electrons in an X-ray tube each element emits a characteristic spectrum composed of a number of high frequency lines. These lines are arranged in groups which appear to be identical in form in neighboring elements, except that they are shifted step by step with the atomic number. Thus Figure 1 shows the wave lengths of a pair of lines of the highest frequency, the $K_a$ and $K_\beta$ lines, of the elements arsenic, selenium, bromine, rubidium and strontium. The evident gap between bromine and rubidium shows a missing element, which in this case is not unknown, but is the element krypton which cannot be made the target in an X-ray tube.

The way in which the position of any one line changes from element to element is shown in Figure 2, in which the atomic numbers of the elements are plotted against the square root of the frequency of a given line, the $K_\alpha$ line; the points falling, within the very small limits of experimental error, upon a continuous curve which is nearly a straight line.

In obtaining his ordinal numbers, Rydberg concluded that there were 32 elements in the group beginning with cesium and ending with niton. It had previously been supposed that a larger number, probably 36, would be found in this period. This new conclusion, which is entirely verified by the work of Moseley, led Rydberg to a simple arithmetical rule, which he called the rule of "quadratic groups." Since he assumed the existence of two unknown elements between hydrogen and helium, he arranged the elements in the following periods: H — (?), 2; (?) — He, 2; Li — Ne, 8; Na — A, 8; K — Kr, 18; Rb — X, 18; Cs — Nt, 32; (?) — (?), 32. This gives two periods of 2, two of 8, two of 18, and two of 32, and the numbers 2, 8, 18, 32 are equal to $2 \times 1^2$, $2 \times 2^2$, $2 \times 3^2$ and $2 \times 4^2$.

Now Rydberg was unquestionably wrong in assuming the two atomic numbers between those of hydrogen and helium. This seems to be entirely demonstrated by the relations between the spectrum of hydrogen and the enhanced spectrum of helium, which we shall discuss in the next chapter. Moreover, although only a few members of the last period of the elements are known, the first part of this period does not seem to be analogous to the period of 32 just preceding, but rather shows great resemblance to the period before that, which is one of 18. Thus thorium is more like zirconium than like cerium, while uranium, the sixth member of the last period, belongs definitely in the same family as molybdenum (which is the sixth member of the last period of 18) and seems to bear no resemblance to neodymium (which is the sixth member of the period of 32). While therefore the facts do not substantiate Rydberg's theory in full, nevertheless we shall see later that his series of quadratic numbers plays an important rôle in our present theory of atomic structure.

We may summarize the essential features of the periodic classification as follows: (a) The properties of the elements are periodic functions of the atomic numbers. (b) When the elements are arranged by atomic number they fall into one period of 2 elements, two periods of 8, two of 18, one of 32, and a fragmentary period which as far as it is known seems to resemble a period of 18. (c) Elements which occupy corresponding positions in the several periods have similar properties.

Countless attempts have been made to express the periodic relationships of the elements in the form of a table, a diagram, or a space model. Of these none can be regarded as thoroughly satisfactory. Some fail to show all the interesting relationships which exist, others suggest non-existing or merely formal relationships. On the whole it seems best to employ a simple table which tells less than the whole truth rather than more. Such a table, for which I am largely indebted to Professor Bray, is given below. It brings out the essential relations between the elements, although not all the interesting ones.

## PERIODIC TABLE.

| | | | | | | | | | | | | | | | | | | |
|--|--|--|--|--|--|--|--|--|--|--|--|--|--|--|--|--|--|--|
| | | | | | | | | | | | | H | He | | | | | |
| | | | | | | | | | N | O | F | Ne | Li | Be | B | C | |
| | | | | | | | | | P | S | Cl | A | Na | Mg | Al | Si | |
| V | Cr | Mn | Fe | Co | Ni | Cu | Zn | Ga | Ge | As | Se | Br | Kr | K | Ca | Sc | Ti | |
| Cb | Mo | — | Ru | Rh | Pd | Ag | Cd | In | Sn | Sb | Te | I | X | Rb | Sr | Y | Zr | |
| Ta | W | — | Os | Ir | Pt | Au | Hg | Tl* | Pb* | Bi* | ★ | — | Nt* | Cs | Ba | La | Ce | Pr |
| ★ | U* | | | | | | | | | | | | | — | Ra* | ★ | Th* | |

(A single vertical line stands between the Ni·Pd·Pt group and the Cu·Ag·Au group; a double line stands between the He·Ne·A·Kr·X·Nt* group and the Li·Na·K·Rb·Cs group. Pr is followed by "(continued below)".)

Continuation of row 5:

Nd — Sm Eu Gd Tb Dy Ho Er Tu Yb Lu —

(The asterisks mark the position of the chief radioactive elements.)

Thus the relation of magnesium to zinc is not clearly indicated, and hydrogen might equally well be placed above lithium as above the halogens, although this is a matter to which we shall recur.

### Some Atomic Models.

In the year 1902 (while I was attempting to explain to an elementary class in chemistry some of the ideas involved in the periodic law) becoming interested in the new theory of the electron, and combining this idea with those which are implied in the periodic classification, I formed an idea of the inner structure of the atom which,

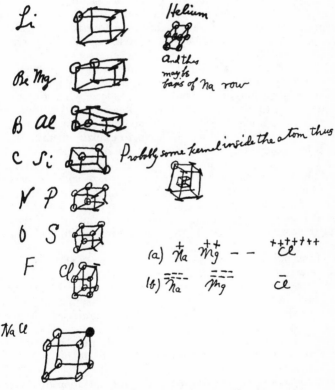

Fig. 3.—Lewis: Memorandum of 1902.

although it contained certain crudities, I have ever since regarded as representing essentially the arrangement of electrons in the atom. In Figure 3 is reproduced a portion of my memorandum of March 28, 1902, which illustrates the theory.

The main features of this theory of atomic structure are as follows:

(1) The electrons in an atom are arranged in concentric cubes.

(2) A neutral atom of each element contains one more electron than a neutral atom of the element next preceding.

(3) The cube of 8 electrons is reached in the atoms of the rare gases, and this cube becomes in some sense the kernel about which the larger cube of electrons of the next period is built.

(4) The electrons of an outer incomplete cube may be given to another atom, as in $Mg^{++}$, or enough electrons may be taken from other atoms to complete the cube, as in $Cl^-$, thus accounting for "positive and negative valence."

In accordance with the idea of Mendeléeff, that hydrogen is the first member of a full period, I erroneously assumed helium to have a shell of eight electrons. Regarding the disposition of the positive charge which balanced the electrons in the neutral atom, my ideas were very vague; I believe I inclined at that time toward the idea that the positive charge was also made up of discrete particles, the localization of which determined the localization of the electrons.

These hypotheses regarding the arrangement of electrons in the atom, while they were discussed freely with my colleagues and in my classes, were given no further publicity. Indeed while this theory of structure seemed to offer a remarkably simple and satisfactory explanation of the process which occurs when sodium combines with chlorine to form sodium chloride, it did not seem to explain chemical combinations of a less polar type, such as occur in the hydrocarbons.

Yet I could not bring myself to believe in two distinct kinds of chemical union. It seemed rather that the union of sodium and chlorine and the union of hydrogen and carbon must represent extreme types of a method of combination which ultimately would be found to be common to all kinds of compounds. However, it was many years before I found it possible to reconcile this idea entirely with the idea of the cubical atom.

The first publication which recognized the stability of the group of eight electrons was by Abegg (1904), whose paper on "Valence and the Periodic System; Attempt at a Theory of Molecular Compounds" ends with the significant remark, "The sum 8 of our normal and contra-valences possesses therefore simple significance as the number which for all atoms represents the points of attack of electrons; and the group-number or positive valence indicates how many of the 8 points of attack must hold electrons in order to make the element electrically neutral."

The next important contribution to the interpretation of the periodic law was made by J. J. Thomson (1904) who considered the mathematical consequences of the assumption that the atoms of the elements consist of a number of electrons "enclosed in a sphere of uniform positive electrification." He was thus led to conclude that a ring of electrons, equally spaced and revolving about a positive center, would be stable until the number of electrons in the ring exceeded a certain number, and would then break into two concentric rings. Thus, if the number of electrons in the outer ring is increased, a limit is reached where another ring is formed, and so on. As an illustration of the various types of stability, he showed that if a number of small magnets are floated by corks upon a surface of water, so that all of the north poles point upward, and if the south pole of a larger magnet is brought near the surface, the small magnets will orient themselves about the larger one in concentric rings. Thomson recognized that under certain circumstances electrons would arrange themselves not in rings in a certain plane but in polyhedral figures about the center, but the difficulty of mathematical calculation in such cases led him to restrict his attention to the arrangements in a single plane, and this decision may have been partly responsible for some later theories which assume a co-planar arrangement of electrons in atoms.

Thomson saw immediately the analogy between his arrangement of electrons and the periodic system of Mendeléeff. "Thus if we consider the series of arrangements of corpuscles (electrons) having on the outside a ring containing a constant number of corpuscles, we have, at the beginning and end, systems which behave like the atoms of an element whose atoms are incapable of retaining a charge of either positive or negative electricity; then (proceeding in the order of increasing number of corpuscles) we have first a system which behaves like the atom of a monovalent electropositive element, next one which behaves like the atom of a divalent electropositive element, while at the other end of the series we have a system which behaves like an atom with no valency, immediately preceding this, one which behaves like the atom of a monovalent electronegative element, while this again is preceded by one behaving like the atom of a divalent electronegative element.

"This sequence of properties is very like that observed in the case of the atoms of the elements. Thus we have the series of elements:

| He | Li | Be | B  | C  | N | O | F  | Ne |
| Ne | Na | Mg | Al | Si | P | S | Cl | A  |

"The first and last element in each of these series has no valency, the second is a monovalent electropositive element, the last but one is a monovalent electronegative element, the third is a divalent electropositive element, the last but two a divalent electronegative element, and so on.

"When atoms like the electronegative ones, in which the corpuscles are very stable, are mixed with atoms like the electropositive ones, in which the corpuscles are not nearly so firmly held, the forces to which the corpuscles are subject by the action of the atoms upon each other may result in the detachment of corpuscles from the electropositive atoms and their transference to the electronegative. The electronegative atoms will thus get a charge of negative electricity, the electropositive atoms one of positive, the oppositely charged atoms will attract each other, and a chemical compound of the electropositive and electronegative atoms will be formed."

It is evident that Thomson's picture of the union of two atoms is entirely similar to the one offered by Abegg, although unlike the latter Thomson considered his results as partly deducible from certain laws of force, corresponding to his assumption of a sphere of positive electrification in which the electrons were supposed to be imbedded. Such an idea regarding the positive part of the atom soon proved to be untenable. Rutherford's study of the scattering of alpha rays by various substances seems explicable only on the assumption that the positive part of an atom is concentrated in a very small region at the atomic center, and he therefore proposed what may be called the planetary theory of atomic structure, according to which the electrons were assumed to be revolving in orbits about the small positive nucleus, and subject to the same laws of force (the inverse square law) that governs the motion of the planets about the sun. This theory of the planetary atom will be further discussed in the next chapter.

In 1915 Parson published a very interesting paper entitled "A Magneton Theory of the Structure of the Atom." Here the electron was regarded as a rotating ring of negative electricity which therefore possesses a magnetic moment [1] and could be called a magneton. As in Thomson's theory, the electrons or magnetons were assumed to lie inside a large sphere of uniform positive electrification, and Parson believed that the magnetic forces between the magnetons would cause them to arrange themselves in cubes (not concentric, but lying alongside one another in the large positive sphere).

There is one feature of Parson's theory which is now generally regarded as erroneous, and for which I am afraid that I am in part responsible. When Mr. Parson first showed me his magneton theory he considered his rings of electricity capable of various degrees of velocity, sometimes even exceeding the velocity of light. It was at my suggestion that he attributed a fixed magnetic moment to his magneton so as to make it in a sense the elementary unit of magnetism as the electron is also the unit of electric charge. This idea has not proved fruitful, and it seems unlikely, although perhaps not impossible, that an electron possesses any magnetic properties except when it is a part of an atom or a molecule. It is, however, to be observed that in the Bohr theory, which we shall discuss in the next chapter, and which offers a more satisfactory picture of the motion of electrons within the atom than Parson's theory, there appears again a definite unit of magnetic moment.

Parson's paper was largely devoted to a discussion of the stability of the groups of eight electrons and the tendency to form such groups in various types of chemical union, and he showed that those compounds in which these complete groups of eight cannot be assumed are the ones whose magnetic properties show that the molecule possesses a large magnetic moment.

In March and in April 1916 there appeared two papers, one by

---

[1] A brief description of some of the elementary principles of magnetism will be given in the next chapter.

Kossel, "Über Molekülbildung als Frage des Atombaus," and one by myself on "The Atom and the Molecule." These two papers offered closely parallel pictures of the structure of the atoms and of those molecules of the more polar sort, where each atom may be regarded as existing in the state of an ion. In both papers the electrons of an atom were regarded as surrounding the small positive nucleus in concentric groups, the first being a group of two, the second a group of eight, the third a group of eight, and then other groups of somewhat indeterminate character, but always ending in an outer group of eight electrons in the atoms of the rare gases, as also in simple elementary ions.

Kossel assumed these successive groups to occur in concentric rings about the nucleus, while I (in accordance with my early views ex-

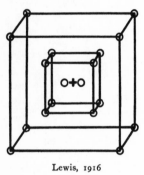
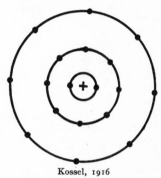

Lewis, 1916                                        Kossel, 1916

FIG. 4.—Two Models of the Argon Atom.

pressed in Figure 1) assumed these groups to constitute concentric shells forming a three-dimensional structure about the central atom. Figure 4 shows the two pictures of the argon atom side by side.

In both theories the electron groups were supposed to reach the highest degree of symmetry and stability in the atoms of the several rare gases; helium with its group of two, neon with its groups of two and eight, argon with its groups of two, eight and eight, and so on. Other atoms were conceived as having a strong tendency either to give up electrons or to take up electrons in such manner as to ape the structure of the nearest rare gas.

In this connection I emphasized the peculiarity of hydrogen which, by giving off an electron, can become the simplest of positive ions, consisting solely of an atomic nucleus, while by taking on one electron it can complete the group of two, characteristic of the helium atom. This process seemed so nearly like the taking on of one electron by fluorine or by chlorine to form F⁻ or Cl⁻, with structures corresponding to neon and argon, that I felt justified in regarding hydrogen as belonging, in this respect at least, to the halogens; and therefore predicted that the metallic hydrides would prove to have the character of salts, consisting of metal ion and hydride ion, and further that electrolysis of a hydride should produce hydrogen at the anode. This prediction has been entirely verified in the work of Bardwell (1922) who succeeded in electrolysing a melt containing calcium hydride, and obtaining hydrogen at the anode in amount corresponding to Faraday's law.

Aside from this one case, atoms show a very marked tendency to form an outer group of eight electrons, and this tendency furnishes a very simple interpretation of a large class of the more polar chemical compounds, as shown in the several papers of Parson, Kossel and myself. My paper went further and attempted to furnish an equally simple explanation of compounds of the less polar type, but this will be the subject of a later chapter.

# Chapter III.

## Spectral Series and the Physicist's View of the Atom.

As soon as the kind of light emitted or absorbed by a substance was recognized to be peculiar to that substance, the study of characteristic spectra became one of the important methods of chemical analysis. It was Kirchhoff and Bunsen (1860, 1861) who showed the great power of the new method, not only in the detection of existing elements, but also in the discovery of new elements. The heavy alkali metals, rubidium and cesium, were thus discovered by them.

Indeed when metallic salts are placed in a flame the bright spectral lines which are obtained seem ordinarily to be characteristic of the metal rather than of the particular compound which is used. It has long been recognized that the various emission spectra, whether from arc, or spark, or Geissler tube, or flame, fall into two classes, which are technically known as line spectra and band spectra, and there has been no occasion to abandon the view, first suggested by Helmholtz, that while the band spectra are characteristic of molecules, the line spectra are due to atoms which have been set free under the conditions which give rise to the emission of light.

Now it is evident that the characteristic spectral lines of the elements, which are so readily studied, and whose wave lengths can be determined with an accuracy which is hardly attained in any other type of physico-chemical measurement, should furnish information of great value concerning the inner structure and behavior of the atom. But before this information can be utilized we must have some theory of the way in which light is emitted or absorbed by a substance.

The undulatory theory of light strengthened the analogy between light and sound. Monochromatic light is characterized by its frequency, or wave length, just as a musical tone is characterized by its frequency, or wave length in air. The emission of a musical tone is due to something which is vibrating, like a tuning fork. So, according to what we may call the classical theory of light emission, light is due to the vibration of something within the molecule or atom, and after the adoption of Maxwell's electromagnetic theory, it was assumed that the something vibrating carried an electric charge.

According to this classical theory the elementary vibrators or resonators obey the familiar laws of elastic bodies and thus possess a natural frequency or period, independent of the amplitude of vibration if such amplitude is small. These vibrators, set in motion by thermal action or by electric discharge, are then the source of light; and the emission of a bright spectral line is due to the preponderance of vibrators possessing some one natural frequency.

Conversely when light falls upon a substance containing such vibrators the latter are supposed to acquire energy of vibration at the expense of the light, and especially of that part of the light which has a frequency corresponding to the natural frequency of the vibrators. The energy of vibration thus acquired is then converted into thermal energy. This is the classical theory of light absorption.

Now this theory of the emission and absorption of light through the vibration of charged parts of the molecule or atom has furnished a very satisfactory explanation of a large number of phenomena. It is therefore with some regret that we now find ourselves obliged to give up in large part, if not wholly, this simple picture of the inter-action between matter and light.

Some evidence of the inadequacy of the classical theory is furnished by the occurrence of spectral lines in groups or series. Now by analogy to a musical instrument that sends out a series of tones and over-tones it was to be expected that the elementary vibrators, especially if they exert a mutual influence one upon another, might emit not one but a series of bright lines, and the discovery that a single element does emit a whole series of spectral lines seemed at first to support such an analogy. But the quantitative relation between the frequencies of the several lines of an elementary spectrum proved to be very differ-ent from anything that was to be expected from the analogy to musical tones.

Various attempts to express in a simple numerical formula the several lines in a single spectral series were unsuccessful until Balmer (1885) obtained for the important hydrogen series a formula which thenceforth became the prototype of all formulæ for series of line spectra. This formula of Balmer, although containing but a single arbitrary constant, reproduced with marvellous accuracy the positions of the lines of the hydrogen series as they had been observed, not only in the laboratory, but also in the spectrum of sun and stars. Balmer expressed the series of lines by the formula

$$\lambda = A \frac{n^2}{n^2 - 4}, \tag{1}$$

where $\lambda$ is the wave length and $n$ is any one of the whole series of integers from 3 to 8. Each integral value thus corresponds to a single line of an infinite series in which the lines become closer as $n$ increases, and converge at a limiting value known as the head of the series, where $\lambda = A$.

The frequency of a given line (in reciprocal seconds) is equal to $c/\lambda$, and therefore the equation may be written

$$v = \frac{c}{A} \left( 1 - \frac{4}{n^2} \right), \tag{2}$$

or in alternative form,

$$v = \frac{4c}{A} \left( \frac{1}{4} - \frac{1}{n^2} \right). \tag{3}$$

Modern refinements of the methods of spectroscopy have greatly increased the accuracy of the determination of spectral lines. Twenty lines of the Balmer series have been obtained in the laboratory and thirty from stellar observation, and the frequencies of these lines do not on the average differ from those calculated from the formula by more than one part in a million.

One of the most significant discoveries relating to spectral series was made by Pickering (1897) in observing the spectrum of the star ζ-Pupis. Here a series was found, every alternate line of which appeared to coincide with a line of the Balmer series. The whole series was accurately represented by the formula

$$\lambda = A \frac{n^2}{n^2 - 16}. \tag{4}$$

This formula gives lines identical with those of the Balmer formula when $n = 6$, 8, etc., and gives the additional lines of the Pickering series when $n = 5$, 7, etc. These new lines were originally ascribed to hydrogen in some peculiar form, but we shall see that Bohr has shown this series to be due to helium, and the similarity between the Balmer and Pickering series thus furnishes a remarkable illustration of the intimate inter-relationship between the line spectra of different elements.

## The Work of Rydberg.

Until ten years ago the great accumulation of exact spectroscopic data regarding line series had led to the discovery of only two fundamental generalizations, both of which were made by Rydberg (1890), whose wonderful perspicacity we have already recognized in his discovery of the significance of the atomic numbers.

His first discovery was that a certain number appeared in the arithmetical expression for the line spectra of a number of elements. This number, $N_0$, which he announced as "a constant common to all series and to all elements," is now recognized as a universal constant of great significance. This constant of Rydberg (except for a very small correction) is the coefficient which appears in the second member of Equation 3.

Another equally important generalization of Rydberg has become known as the combination principle. When an element exhibits two or more different line series, the lines of one series and those of another are simply related to one another. According to the combination principle, as it is now usually stated, the frequency of each of the many spectral lines obtained from the same atomic species may be obtained by taking the several differences between a relatively small number of basic frequencies.  In order to illustrate this point we may consider the complete spectrum of monatomic hydrogen.

In addition to the Balmer series there are a number of other important spectral lines which are ascribed to free hydrogen atoms.  One important series has been obtained by Lyman (1904, 1906) in the ultra-violet, another by Paschen (1909) in the ultra-red, and very recently a few lines of a fourth series have been obtained by Brackett (1922) in the extreme ultra-red.  The formulæ which reproduce the several series are as follows:

$$\text{(Lyman)} \qquad \nu = N_0\Big(\frac{1}{1^2} - \frac{1}{n^2}\Big),$$

$$\text{(Balmer)} \qquad \nu = N_0\Big(\frac{1}{2^2} - \frac{1}{n^2}\Big),$$

$$\text{(Paschen)} \qquad \nu = N_0\Big(\frac{1}{3^2} - \frac{1}{n^2}\Big),$$

$$\text{(Brackett)} \qquad \nu = N_0\Big(\frac{1}{4^2} - \frac{1}{n^2}\Big).$$

The first three of these series are represented in Figure 5, where only a few of the lines of each series are shown (together with the head of the series, represented by a dotted line).

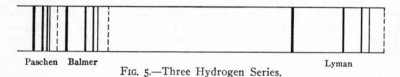

Paschen  Balmer                                                   Lyman

Fig. 5.—Three Hydrogen Series.

Now it is evident that a line of any one of these series may be expressed by the formula

$$\nu = N_0\Big(\frac{1}{n'^2} - \frac{1}{n^2}\Big), \qquad (5)$$

therefore the frequency of every line can be regarded as the difference between some one pair of the basic frequencies

$$\nu_1{}^* = \frac{N_0}{1^2}; \ \ \nu_2{}^* = \frac{N_0}{2^2}; \ \ \nu_3{}^* = \frac{N_0}{3^2}; \ \ \dots \qquad (6)$$

Thus the second line of the Balmer series is $\nu_2{}^* - \nu_4{}^*$, the third line of the Lyman series is $\nu_1{}^* - \nu_4{}^*$, and the first line of the Paschen series is $\nu_3{}^* - \nu_4{}^*$.

It is customary to express the combination principle graphically as in Figure 6, where again frequencies are plotted from left to right.  The vertical lines represent the values of $\nu^*$, the basic frequencies, and the length of the horizontal lines terminating at these vertical lines represent the frequencies of three spectral lines that we have just mentioned.

When we turn to other elements than hydrogen we find a condition of far greater complexity. As a rule it is no longer possible to express either the frequencies of the series lines, or the basic frequencies, by any such simple formulæ as sufficed in the case of hydrogen. The equations which have been most useful in expressing these series require several arbitrary constants, and appear to be of only approximate validity. Nevertheless we find also in these more complex cases that the observed frequencies are once more obtainable as exact

$$0 \quad \frac{No}{5^2} \frac{No}{4^2} \frac{No}{3^2} \qquad \frac{No}{2^2} \qquad\qquad\qquad\qquad No$$

Fig. 6.—Basic Frequencies of Hydrogen.

differences between certain basic frequencies, in complete accordance with the combination principle.

These ideas, which originated with Rydberg, have become the foundation of the theory of spectral series which has been so rapidly developed during the past decade. Before discussing these recent advances, it will be necessary to give brief consideration to that revolution in scientific thought which is known as the quantum theory.

## The Quantum Theory.

It was one of the foremost deductions of the kinetic theory of gases that the molecules of all gases should possess the same average kinetic energy of translation at a given temperature. This idea was carried over by analogy to liquids and solids, and it was assumed that every particle would have the same average kinetic energy at a given temperature. This is known as the Law of the Equipartition of Energy.

This principle led Boltzmann to the explanation of the law of Dulong and Petit. If the atoms of a solid possess the same kinetic energy as the atoms of a monatomic gas, and if they vibrate about fixed positions in accordance with Hooke's law, so that (as in the case of any simple vibration) the average potential energy equals the average kinetic energy, then the total thermal energy of the atoms in a solid would be twice as great as that of an equal number of atoms of a monatomic gas; and the energy would increase twice as rapidly with the temperature for the former as for the latter. But Dulong and Petit's law is only true as a limiting law at high temperatures. Many substances at ordinary temperatures and all substances at low temperatures show a very much smaller change of energy with the temperature than that law requires. If we plot the energy against the absolute temperature, as in Figure 7, the dotted line expresses Dulong and Petit's law, while the behavior of an actual substance is indicated by the continuous curve, which has the same slope as the dotted line only at high temperatures.

The theory of equipartition appears to give a very satisfactory explanation of the thermal energy of a monatomic gas. But the atom of such a gas is by no means the ultimate particle. By the equipartition law each of the several particles which compose such an atom should acquire its quota of energy. On the contrary we are convinced that a monatomic gas acquires no appreciable thermal energy

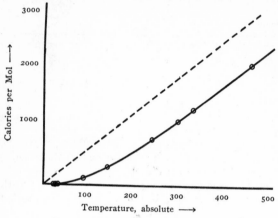

FIG. 7.—Heat Content of Copper.

except that which is due to the translational motion of its molecule as a whole.

In spite of the obvious falsity of the equipartition law, it nevertheless seems to be a direct consequence of accepted mechanical principles. Perhaps its deduction from these principles by the methods of statistical mechanics has never been made in a manner entirely free from objection, but it is generally believed that such a deduction is possible. Thus we are led to the inference that the mechanics of atoms differ in some respect from the known mechanics of massive bodies.

The equipartition law fails not only in its application to the thermal energy of ordinary bodies, but also when it is applied to the distribution of energy in the spectrum of radiation emitted by a black body. In such radiation we presumably have light of all frequencies from zero to infinity, and we may speak of the amount of radiant energy which is comprised between two chosen frequencies $v_1$ and $v_2$. It was shown by Rayleigh (1900) to be a consequence of the equipartition law that the energy comprised between two such fixed limits of frequency must be proportional to the absolute temperature, as shown by the dotted line in Figure 8. The continuous curve of that figure represents the actual facts as brought out by Wien (1896) and more fully by Planck (1901). This curve approaches a straight line, as demanded by the equipartition law, only at high temperatures.

Planck, seeing that his equation for the distribution of radiant energy was incompatible with the deductions from accepted mechanics and electromagnetics, announced a hypothesis of unusual boldness which, together with the mass of new laws and hypotheses which have grown out of it, is known as the quantum theory. Planck assumed in the first instance that bodies contain electrical oscillators which can absorb or emit radiation, not in a continuous manner, but by finite

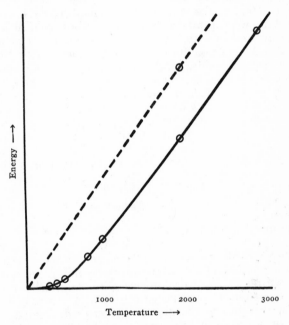

FIG. 8.—Density of Radiant Energy (Between Two Given Frequencies).

amounts; and that each of these finite amounts of energy is proportional to the natural frequency of the oscillator. He further assumed the proportionality factor to be the same for all oscillators and therefore a universal constant, which is denoted by $h$ and known as the Planck constant. According to this theory, an oscillator whose natural frequency is $v$ can possess energy only in the amount $hv$ or some multiple of $hv$.

Einstein (1907) suggested that we go further, and regard the energy, $hv$, emitted by an oscillator, as a quantum or corpuscle of radiant energy which, preserving a certain degree of individuality, could only be reabsorbed as a whole. This idea has not been widely accepted because of the difficulty of its reconciliation with the phenomenon of the interference of light. However, it led Einstein to one of the most important deductions from quantum theory, namely, his photoelectric equation. According to this equation, when a substance is subjected to monochromatic light of frequency $v$, the maximum energy which can be acquired by one of its electrons is $hv$.

It was also Einstein who saw the connection between the two types of deviation from the equipartition law, of which we have spoken. If a solid body is supposed to be composed of atoms which are analogous to the hypothetical oscillators of Planck, and therefore capable of acquiring energy only in finite increments, the energy would not be the linear function of the temperature required by the law of Dulong and Petit. At low temperatures many atoms would be unable to acquire the energy $hv$, and therefore would possess no energy at all. Thus, from the Planck radiation formula, Einstein obtained his equation for the specific heats of solids, which qualitatively, although not quantitatively, is in accord with the numerous measurements of specific heats that have since been made at low temperatures.

Once in the early days of quantum theory Professor Einstein remarked to me that the quantum theory was not really a new theory, but merely a recognition of the falsity of previous theories. This remark remains true. Some scientists have been inclined to give up such fundamental ideas as the laws of conservation of momentum and of energy, and to replace them by analogous theorems which are only valid in a statistical sense. Others have gone so far as to conclude that the continuum of space and of time must be replaced by a discontinuum.

For the moment we need only conclude that in giving up the continuous theory of matter, and replacing it by the theory of discrete centers which we call atoms (or electrons and nuclei), we have somehow failed in consistency. A race with more limited sense perceptions than our own might study the properties of sand and conclude these properties to be due to the existence of grains, but would they then be justified in regarding the grains as composed of sand? Yet this is the kind of inference that modern science has sanctioned. The properties of electricity have been explained by assuming it to be composed of electrons, after which we naïvely consider the electrons as made up of electricity, and speculate concerning the distribution of electricity about the electron center. We also have regarded the atoms as possessing properties similar to those of the larger bodies which they compose. The various phenomena which are grouped under the title of quantum theory are the new data in the light of which we must construct the new geometry and the new mechanics which are valid in the immediate vicinity of electrons and nuclei. Quantum theory has been criticized for furnishing no adequate mechanism, but presumably the root of our present problem lies deeper than this, and it is hardly likely that any mechanism based on our existing modes of thought will suffice for the explanation of the many new phenomena which the study of the atom is disclosing.

## A Partial Statement of Bohr's Theory.

Out of the chaos of spectroscopy with its scarcity of guiding principles and its abundance of almost uncorrelated data, order and simplicity were achieved at a single stroke through the brilliant theory proposed by Bohr (1913). To this theory, which has so justly captivated the minds of physicists, we must now give our attention. It

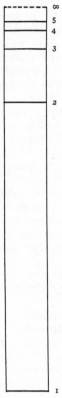

FIG. 9.—Energy Levels in the Hydrogen Atom.

will be presented in a somewhat different manner from that employed originally by Bohr himself, in order to separate that part of the theory which may be stated independently of any atomic model from the part which deals with his model.

Considering the simplest case of an atom like monatomic hydrogen, which is composed solely of a nucleus and one electron, it is first postulated that the electron may assume any one of a whole series of states, so that each state may be spoken of as an energy level. Thus in Figure 9 we may represent these levels by a series of lines, such that the distance between two lines is equal to the energy difference in the atom between the two corresponding states. The lowest level represents the smallest energy and therefore the most stable state of the atom.

These levels form an infinite series, and the energy at the limit of this series (indicated by the dotted line) is assumed to represent the energy of the system when the nucleus and the electron are completely separated from one another. The difference between the energy of the $n$th level and this limiting energy can be designated by $E_n*$ (a negative quantity). For convenience, the value of the limiting energy may be taken as zero, and we may then say that the energy of the first level is $E_1*$, that of the second level $E_2*$, and so on. All of these values of $E*$ are now negative.

The second assumption made by Bohr is that the energy at any level, when divided by $h$, the Planck constant, gives the negative of one of those fundamental frequencies which we have discussed in a preceding section, and from which the various spectral lines of the element may be obtained. In other words, it is assumed that

$$\frac{E_n*}{h} = -\nu_n*. \tag{7}$$

The third assumption is that the atom emits light only when the electron falls from one level to another (or absorbs light only when the electron is raised from one level to another). The energy of the emitted light is equal to the difference between the energies of the two levels, and the frequency of the light is this energy difference divided by $h$. Thus

$$\nu = \frac{E_n* - E_{n'}*}{h} = \nu_{n'}* - \nu_n*. \tag{8}$$

So the second line of the Balmer series, which is $\nu_2* - \nu_4*$, is supposed to be produced when the electron falls from the fourth to the second level of the atom of hydrogen, and the other lines of the Balmer series are obtained when an electron drops from the several upper levels to the second level; while the lines of the Lyman series are produced when the electron drops from various levels to the first and most stable level.

Without going more fully into the complex spectra of the elements than has been possible in this brief summary, it is impossible to show what a wonderful insight into the significance of spectral series is furnished by Bohr's theory. Nor does this partial statement of his theory alone do justice to that brilliant generalization, for when we consider Bohr's atomic model we shall see that an equally simple set of assumptions leads to more far-reaching conclusions than can be drawn from the assumptions which we have so far discussed.

However, it will be seen that the theory as we have developed it so far contains the two essential elements of the quantum theory. The first of these is that monatomic light of frequency ν can change the energy of an electron by the amount $h\nu$. The second is Planck's idea that there is a mechanism in the atom whose energy can vary, not continuously, but only by finite increments.

## The Interpretation of X-Ray Spectra.

The theory of Bohr not only explains the long familiar data of spectroscopy, but by a slight modification gives an equally satisfactory interpretation of the newer data relating to X-ray spectra. Let us consider a heavy element whose atom contains a large number of electrons, and postulate once more that there are certain energy levels, the first being now called the K level, the next the L level, the next the M level, and so on. We may next assume that only a limited number of electrons can be present at each of these levels. Instead of considering these levels as a mere framework, as we do in considering an atom like hydrogen, we may assume that each of the levels—at least each of the lower levels—contains its full quota of electrons. If then by some means an electron from the K level is knocked out of the atom, an electron from the L level may fall in to take its place, thus giving rise to the spectral line designated as $K_\alpha$. If it is an electron from the M level which falls into the vacant place it gives rise to the line $K_\beta$, and electrons dropping from higher levels give a bundle of lines which, if the spectroscopic resolution is not great, are usually observed as a single line, $K_\gamma$. So also an electron may be ejected from the L level, and if its place is filled by an electron from the M level the $L_\alpha$ line results, and so on, for the other lines.

This theory furnishes a beautiful explanation of the peculiar absorption of X-rays. We do not find, as in the case of ordinary spectra, that we have absorption lines corresponding to the several emission lines. The absorption of X-rays at the frequency $K_\alpha$ would indicate an electron being transferred from the K level to the L level, but in the stable atom the L level already has its quota of electrons, and this process is therefore impossible. Absorption cannot begin until the frequency of the X-rays is sufficient to remove the electron entirely from the atom, or at least to one of the outer levels which has not its full quota of electrons. The observed fact is that a continuous absorption band stretches from the higher frequencies down to a frequency a little higher than corresponds to the $K_\gamma$ line and there abruptly terminates.

If the energy at a given level in different elements is supposed to depend primarily upon the charge of the nucleus, we have a new interpretation of the simple relation between the X-ray spectra and the atomic number which Moseley discovered, and which has been illustrated in Figure 2 (Chapter II).

This simple conception has been of the greatest service in accounting for the general characteristics of X-rays, although here as with ordinary spectral lines there are certain complexities, a discussion of which would carry us too far afield. The concept of energy levels requires that the combination principle, which proved so useful in the understanding of ordinary spectra, should hold for X-ray spectra also. Thus if the line $K_\beta$ is determined by the energy difference between the K and M levels, and the $K_a$ line by the difference between the K and L levels, while the $L_a$ line is determined by the difference between the L and M levels, the frequency of the $K_a$ line should be the difference between the frequencies of the other two, and this is an experimental fact.

## Ionization and Resonance Potentials.

In a vacuum tube when the electrons emitted by a hot cathode pass through a potential gradient to an anode, the electrons acquire a kinetic energy corresponding to the difference in potential between the cathode and anode. Also when certain gases are introduced into the tube, the electrons, although meeting and rebounding from the gas molecules, seem to do so in an elastic manner, and finally arrive at the anode with the same kinetic energy which they would acquire in the absence of any gas. This is far from being true of all gases, but there are many in which these collisions between electrons and molecules appear to be completely elastic within the limits of experimental error. In other words, the motion of the electron through the gas can be said to be frictionless.

But even with gases of this type, if the potential difference between cathode and anode is gradually increased, a definite point is reached at which the electron evidently loses energy upon collision. We may say that the slow-moving electron rebounds from the molecule elastically, but that when the kinetic energy of the electron reaches a certain value, a part of its energy is given up to the molecule on collision. This important observation, first made by Franck and Herz (1913), has been confirmed in many investigations.

If the kinetic energy of the electron is increased beyond this first point of inelastic collision, other points become manifest, which indicate new processes by which the energy of the electron is given to some part of the gas molecule. The first of these critical points to be observed is often associated with the sudden emission of light. The frequency of the light is that of one of the characteristic spectral lines of the gas. The potential which suffices to produce this inelastic collision, accompanied by light emission, is known as a resonance potential.

In the simpler cases, the highest of these critical potentials is found to be associated with the sudden appearance of gaseous ionization. It appears therefore that the electron striking the molecule knocks off another electron, so that the two electrons departing leave behind a positively charged ion. The minimum potential required to produce this phenomenon is known as the ionization potential.

Bohr's theory gives an extremely satisfactory qualitative and quantitative explanation of these phenomena. If we consider an atom with an electron in the most stable position, that is, upon the lowest available energy level, the atom can only acquire energy if enough is furnished to raise the electron to one of the higher energy levels. Thus if the atom is struck by an electron which has insufficient energy to produce this result the collision must be elastic. On the other hand, if the bombarding electron possesses just enough energy to raise the electron within the atom to the next energy level, it may lose all its kinetic energy. Then the collision is inelastic, and the electron which has been raised to the second level, or resonated, may a moment later drop back to the first level, emitting the first line of the element's series spectrum. Again, the velocity of the bombarding electron may be great enough to cause the electron of the atom to pass through the whole series of energy levels and become separated altogether from the atom, which therefore becomes ionized. Such is the qualitative explanation of resonance and ionization.

The quantitative explanation is equally satisfactory. The energy required for the first resonance must be equal to $h$ times the frequency of the first line of the spectral series. The energy required for ionization must be $h$ times the limiting frequency of the series (the head of the series). These deductions from the theory have been completely verified by experiments with a large number of elements, within the limits of the experimental accuracy, which unfortunately is not yet all that might be wished.

The phenomenon of resonance and ionization potentials is most sharply evidenced in the metallic vapors. In the case of hydrogen the presence of diatomic molecules complicates the situation, but if we could study pure monatomic hydrogen we should doubtless find the first resonance potential and the ionization potential to be in the ratio of 3 to 4, since the former depends upon the term $\left(\dfrac{1}{1^2} - \dfrac{1}{2^2}\right) = \dfrac{3}{4}$, and the latter upon the term $\left(\dfrac{1}{1^2} - \dfrac{1}{\infty^2}\right) = 1$, thus corresponding to the first line, and to the head, of the Lyman series.

These experiments on resonance and ionization potentials seem to furnish a complete demonstration of the quantum assumption that definite energy levels exist within the atom, and that an electron cannot be lifted above one level unless it receive a sufficient amount of energy to raise it completely to another level.

## Bohr's Atomic Model.

Having seen how exceedingly useful even a partial statement of Bohr's theory can be made, let us turn to his complete theory of the structure of the hydrogen atom. He assumed first a Rutherford atom with a small positive nucleus and an electron revolving about it in a circular orbit. The centripetal force is taken as that given by

Coulomb's law, namely, a force equal to the product of the two charges and inversely proportional to the square of the distance between them. The properties of the system are in this respect identical with those of a system composed of the sun, and a planet moving in a circular orbit.

In conformity with this law of force a continuous series of orbits is possible, the radius of each orbit determining the velocity in the orbit, and the energy (kinetic and potential) of the system. Now Bohr introduced the quantum theory by assuming that not all of these orbits

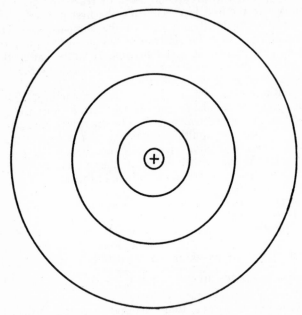

FIG. 10.—Orbits of the Hydrogen Atom (Bohr).

are possible, but only that particular set of orbits in which the angular momentum of the electron is an integral multiple of $h/2\pi$ (Figure 10). The orbit nearest the nucleus is the one in which the angular momentum has this value, the second is one in which it has twice this value, and so on. In conformity with the assumed law of force these orbits must have radii in the ratio of $1:4:9:16$, and so on to infinity, the radius of the first orbit being of the order of $10^{-8}$ cm. His third assumption is the one which we have discussed before, namely, that emission of light occurs when the electron falls from one orbit into an inner orbit, and that the frequency of the emitted light is equal to the difference in energy between the two orbits (or energy levels).

By means of this astonishingly simple assumption, it is possible to obtain quantitatively the whole set of spectral series which we ascribe to atomic hydrogen. Merely from Coulomb's law and the assumption that the angular momentum in each orbit is a multiple of $h/2\pi$, we may calculate the energy of the atom corresponding to any orbit. From this calculation,

$$E_n^* = -\frac{2\pi^2 e^2 e'^2 m}{h^2}\frac{1}{n^2}, \tag{9}$$

where $e'$ is the charge of the nucleus, $e$ the charge on the electron, $m$ the mass of the electron and $h$ the Planck constant.

For the hydrogen atom $e' = e$, and if we use Equation 8 we find for the frequency of any line

$$\nu = \frac{2\pi^2 e^4 m}{h^3}\left(\frac{1}{n'^2} - \frac{1}{n^2}\right). \tag{10}$$

Not only does this equation resemble in form the equation by which we have already expressed the spectral lines of monatomic hydrogen, but the coefficient in the last term of Equation 10 should be equal to the Rydberg constant, and it is so within the narrow limits of error involved in the determination of the several quantities concerned.

Bohr next showed that an atom with a nuclear charge equal to twice that of hydrogen, and possessing a single electron, should give spectral lines according to the formula

$$\nu = 4N_0\left(\frac{1}{n'^2} - \frac{1}{n^2}\right). \tag{11}$$

This formula satisfied the Pickering series, as well as certain other spectral lines which had formerly been ascribed to hydrogen, but which Bohr showed must be due to helium atoms from which one of the two electrons had been ejected, namely, to the ion He$^+$. This inference has since been completely verified by the production of these lines in tubes containing pure helium.

As a matter of fact, the values of Rydberg's constant obtained from the Balmer series and from the "enhanced" helium series are not absolutely identical. Although the difference is small, the methods of spectroscopy have been so refined that it can be measured with some accuracy. This difference was also readily explained, since the mass of an electron is not entirely negligible with respect to the mass of the nucleus of hydrogen or helium, and therefore instead of assuming a system in which the nucleus occupies a fixed position and the electron revolves about it, the two must be considered as revolving about their common center of mass, which is very close to the center of the nucleus. Indeed, by making use of the known masses of the hydrogen and helium atoms and the two values of the constant in the equations for the spectral series, it has been found possible to calculate the mass of an electron with an accuracy which apparently rivals that given by other methods.

It would carry us too far to attempt to describe the many interesting developments and refinements which have been introduced into Bohr's theory by the assumption of elliptical as well as circular orbits, the eccentricity of the orbits varying not continuously but in steps, in accordance with a second application of quantum theory. Many of the more minute observations regarding spectral lines to which we have not been able to give our attention are thus brought into conformity with the Bohr principle.

Altogether we have in this very notable list of quantitative agreements between experiment and the simple assumption of Bohr some very strong reasons for believing that Bohr's model of the hydrogen atom and the singly charged helium atom is something more than a mere working hypothesis, and may represent an ultimate reality. Nevertheless we must be cautious in making such an inference. When the theory of the luminiferous ether was in its prime, several models or mechanical pictures of the ether were offered which represented with some degree of adequacy the properties of the electromagnetic field. We still recognize that the mathematical equations of hydrodynamics are largely identical with the mathematical equations of electromagnetics, but such mechanical pictures of the ether are now thoroughly discredited.

It is to be remarked that while it seems natural to use the same law of force between two charged parts of an atom which is found to hold between two large charged bodies at greater distances from one another, our satisfaction in the success of this experiment is somewhat diminished by the introduction of another assumption which limits the validity of Coulomb's law to certain specific orbits. This is especially true since no suggestion has yet been made regarding the quantitative or even the qualitative laws governing the electron between any two orbits. Indeed the combination of the quantum theory with the Rutherford theory of the atom seems to result in a model which has properties in some sense intermediate between those of an atom whose parts are in rapid motion and those of a static atom, as the following considerations show.

It was predicted from the classical electromagnetic theory that any accelerated charge would emit radiant energy, but the electron in one of the stable orbits of the Bohr theory is subject to constant acceleration toward the center of the atom and yet is supposed to emit no radiation. However, such emission of energy from an accelerated charge does not seem to be an entirely inevitable consequence even of classical theory, and for this reason we may turn our attention to a still more elementary way in which I have attempted to show (1917) the divergence between the properties of the Bohr atom and the properties that would formerly have been assumed for a system containing an electron in motion.

Let us in Figure 11 represent a hydrogen atom according to Bohr with an electron in the first orbit, that is to say in the most stable state, and let us represent by AA' a small wire which may be brought near to the hydrogen atom. Now if the electron in the orbit exerts any sort of electrical force at a distance, when the electron is in position X there will be a slight flow of positive electricity in the wire toward A, and when the electron is at X' there will be a slight flow toward A'. Indeed at any finite distance of the wire from the atom there should be set up in the wire a finite alternating current which would continue indefinitely. Such a current should generate heat, but since the atom is supposed to be in the state of lowest possible energy there appears to be no source from which the heat could originate. In other words, we must conclude either that such an

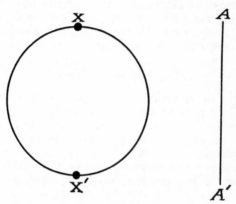

Fig. 11.—Illustrating a Doubtful Point Concerning the Bohr Atom.

alternating current is not produced or that it is produced but meets with no ohmic resistance.

The latter alternative is possible. The electrons in the metal wire may also be presumed to be subject to quantum laws, and since the motion which they would acquire owing to their proximity to the hydrogen atom would be very minute, it might be assumed that their displacement to and fro could occur without frictional loss. Indeed it is perhaps to be predicted that with a perfect crystal at a very low temperature a certain potential gradient will be found to be necessary before the electrons can be sufficiently displaced from their equilibrium positions to give ordinary electrical conduction. But with ordinary metals at ordinary temperatures we have no experimental evidence that Ohm's law would fail even at very small values of the electromotive force, nor does this seem likely on theoretical grounds.

If these considerations are correct, we must conclude that an electron, in a Bohr orbit, exerts upon other electrons no force which depends upon its position in the orbit. In other words it seems as though we should add another assumption to those of Bohr, namely, that while the orbit of one electron may as a whole affect the orbit of another electron, we should look for no effects which depend upon the momentary position of any electron in its orbit. If this idea proves useful it will greatly simplify attempts to secure adequate models of atoms or molecules containing two or more electrons.

The remarkable quantitative success of the Bohr model was limited to the special case of an atomic nucleus accompanied by one electron. Efforts to construct equally complete and adequate models of atoms with two or more electrons have so far failed. In Bohr's original theory of an atom containing a number of electrons, these electrons were supposed to be arranged in successive concentric rings about the central nucleus, the electrons in any one ring being equally spaced and moving with the same velocity. However, this idea has been abandoned and in the next chapter we shall discuss the more recent views of Bohr regarding the structure of such an atom.

### Magnetic Phenomena.

Excepting the observations on spectral lines, there appears to be no method of studying the structure of the atom which is so direct or so promising as the method furnished by the study of magnetism. Unfortunately the experimental difficulties in this field are great, and at present we have very meagre data concerning the magnetic properties of substances. But even the information which we now possess is of the greatest importance to any theory of atomic and molecular structure.

The behavior of substances in a magnetic field is in many respects analogous to that in an electric field. When two plates of an electric condenser in a vacuum are oppositely charged they attract one another, and if any object which has a positive charge at the one end, and a negative charge at the other, is placed between the plates it tends to orient itself so that its positive end approaches the negative plate and its negative end approaches the positive plate. In so doing it diminishes the attraction between the two plates in accordance with the ordinary laws of electric attraction.

So also when the space between the plates, formerly separated by a vacuum, is filled by any substance the attraction diminishes, and the ratio between the original attraction and the attraction now observed is called the dielectric constant of the substance in question. In such cases also it is assumed that the substance contains molecules which are differently charged at the two ends and are therefore called dipoles. The amount of motion of these charges, either through the rotation or stretching of the dipole, or through slight displacements of electrons or nuclei from the equilibrium positions which they normally occupy, is believed to determine the magnitude of the dielectric constant.

The molecular dipoles, which tend to orient themselves strictly in the line of electric force, could not be expected to do so completely, because of thermal agitation, and in accordance with this view it is found experimentally that the dielectric constant of a substance always diminishes with increasing temperature.

A magnet in a magnetic field behaves very much like the dipole in the electric field. Its torque is proportional to what is called its *magnetic moment*. In the case of a simple bar magnet this magnetic moment is proportional to the intensity of magnetization and the distance between the two poles. If the magnet is an electric circuit the moment depends upon the amount of current and the dimensions of the circuit.

Two opposite magnetic poles, separated by a vacuum, exert upon one another an attraction which is diminished if a small magnet is placed between the two poles and is allowed to orient itself in consequence of its magnetic torque, so that its south end approaches the north pole of the magnet, and its north end approaches the south

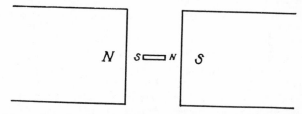

FIG. 12.—Illustrating the Type of Orientation of a Molecular Magnet That Produces Paramagnetism.

pole (Figure 12). As in the analogous case of the electric field, various substances placed between the two magnetic poles diminish the mutual attraction between these poles.

The ratio between the original attraction between the poles and that which is observed after the intervening space has been filled with the substance in question, is known as the permeability of the substance. When the attractive force is thus diminished, the substance is said to be paramagnetic, or in extreme cases, ferromagnetic. It is assumed that the substance contains molecular magnets which tend to orient themselves in the magnetic field, but that the thermal agitation prevents complete orientation. It is an observed fact that the permeability of such paramagnetic substances always diminishes with increasing temperature.

There is, however, another class of substances, having no counterpart in the electrical analogue, that increase the attraction between two magnetic poles, and these substances which have permeability less than unity are called diamagnetic. In a typical diamagnetic substance the permeability is independent of the temperature.

In Langevin's theory of para- and diamagnetism, every molecule contains within it electric circuits or orbital electrons. Each electric circuit is the equivalent of a small magnet, and these elementary circuits or magnets are assumed not to be affected by temperature, nor are they supposed to be free, within the molecule, to orient themselves appreciably in a magnetic field. But if the several elementary magnets which are contained within a molecule have a resultant magnetic moment in one direction, then the molecule as a whole can turn in the magnetic field and produce the phenomenon of paramagnetism.

While the individual electron orbits are not considered free to orient themselves in a magnetic field, it is nevertheless shown to be a consequence of electromagnetic theory that the field will produce a slight change in the orbit itself, and this change is in such a direction as to produce the phenomenon of diamagnetism. Thus according to Langevin's theory every substance exhibits this diamagnetic phenomenon, the effect of which, however, is overshadowed in paramagnetic substances by the large effect of opposite sign which is due to the orientation of the molecular magnets.

Quantitatively Langevin's theory permits a calculation of the dimensions of the electron orbits which seem to be of the expected order of magnitude, although it is now generally believed that the details of his theory must be modified in accordance with quantum theory.

We shall have occasion to return later to the consideration of the magnetic properties of substances, but in the meantime it is evident that, irrespective of any special theory, the mere existence of magnetism in substances appears to imply that the atom contains charged particles in rapid motion. It is conceivable that a stationary electron in a position of asymmetric stress might give rise to a magnetic field, but this suggestion has not hitherto been made, nor does it seem at present capable of useful development. In the present state of science it therefore seems best to regard the existence of magnets as definite evidence of electricity in motion.

# Chapter IV.

# Reconciliation of the Two Views; the Arrangement of Electrons in the Atom.

We have now discussed two distinct views of the internal structure of the atom. According to both views the neutral atom is composed of a central nucleus with a positive charge equal to $Z$, the atomic number, and a group of $Z$ electrons situated about this center.

The view based on the periodic law and the chemical behavior of the elements leads to the picture of a relatively static atom. According to .this picture, the electrons occupy fixed positions which are arranged in concentric shells about the nucleus. It is not implied that the electrons may not be displaced from these positions by the action of heat and light, or driven into new positions when a chemical reaction occurs. Nor is there anything in this view really incompatible with the assumption of an electron in rapid motion, such as the Parson ring electron, so long as the electron as a whole is regarded as occupying a fixed position in the atom. This theory of the static atom obviously abandoned the assumption that the ordinary laws of electrical attraction and repulsion are valid within the atom.

The experiments of physicists led to a quite different view of the atom. The theory of Rutherford assumes the forces between the charged particles within the atom to be the same as those which hold for massive charged bodies. The atom is regarded as a sort of planetary system in which the force of attraction between the nucleus and electrons is balanced by the centrifugal force due to their orbital motion. The electrons are considered to be arranged in successive rings rather than in successive shells.

These two views seemed to be quite incompatible, although it is the same atom that is being investigated by chemist and by physicist. If the electrons are to be regarded as taking an essential part in the process of binding atom to atom in the molecule, it seemed impossible that they could be actuated by the simple laws of force, and travelling in the orbits, required by the planetary theory. The permanence of atomic arrangements, even in very complex molecules, is one of the most striking of chemical phenomena. Isomers maintain their identity for years, often without the slightest appreciable transformation. An organic molecule treated with powerful reagents often suffers radical change in one part of the molecule while the remainder appears to suffer no change. It appears inconceivable that these permanent though essentially unstable configurations could result from the simple law of force embodied in Coulomb's law.

The first step toward removing barriers between the two types of atomic model was made by Bohr when he restricted the application of Coulomb's law to specific states or orbits. I have attempted to show in the preceding chapter that it is the orbit as a whole rather than the particular position of the electron within the orbit that is the thing of essential interest in the Bohr theory. If these orbits are in fixed positions and orientations they may be used as the building stones of an atom which has an essentially static character.

There remained, however, in Bohr's original theory some features which were far from compatible with the chemist's view of the atom. This is essentially true of his models of atoms containing more than one electron. Here he assumed rings of electrons, revolving in a common orbit, which seemed quite irreconcilable with the common phenomena of chemistry.

Also from the side of physics evidence began to accumulate which was opposed to the ring theory. The X-ray spectrographs obtained from crystals seemed to indicate a cubic or some other regular polyhedral structure of the electrons about the atom, as was shown by the investigations of Hull (1917). A like conclusion was reached by Born and Landé (1918) in their searching physico-mathematical investigation of the common physical properties of crystalline substances. These authors, while maintaining the view of the orbital electron, make the orbit small, and make the position of the orbit correspond to the positions assigned to the electrons by Parson and myself.

In his later work Bohr entirely abandoned the ring of electrons. He found that even the phenomena of spectral lines in the visible and in the X-ray regions could not be interpreted in terms of a theory which regards the electrons as associated with one another in joint orbits. He now assigns to each electron its separate orbit and regards these orbits as situated about the atomic center in shells.

It seems to me that by this step Bohr has removed every essential element of conflict between the views of the physicist and the chemist. If we regard as the important thing the orbit as a whole, and not the position of the electron within the orbit, and if each electron is assigned an independent orbit, then we may think of each electron orbit as having a fixed position in space. The average position of the electron in the orbit may be called the position of the electron and will correspond entirely to that fixed position which was assigned in the theory of the static atom.

Let us therefore now attempt to weld these different views into a single theory of atomic structure which, while it certainly can claim no degree of finality, will summarize all of the evidence, chemical and physical, which we now possess regarding atomic structure.

1. First we shall adopt the whole of Bohr's theory in so far as it pertains to a single atom which possesses a single electron. There

are no facts of chemistry which are opposed to this part of the theory, and we thus incorporate in the new model all of the Bohr theory that is strictly quantitative.

2. In the case of systems containing more than one nucleus or more than one electron, we shall also assume that the electron possesses orbital motion, for such motion seems to be required to account for the phenomenon of magnetism; and each electron in its orbital motion may be regarded as the equivalent of an elementary magnet or magneton. However, in the case of these complex atoms and molecules we shall not assume that an atomic nucleus is necessarily the center or focus of the orbits.

3. These orbits occupy fixed positions with respect to one another and to the nuclei. When we speak of the position of an electron, we shall refer to the position of the orbit as a whole rather than to the position of the electron within the orbit. With this interpretation, we may state that the change of an electron from one position to another is always accompanied by a finite change of energy. When the positions are such that no change in position of the several parts of the atom or molecule will set free energy, we may say that the system is in the most stable state.

4. In a process, which consists merely in the fall of an electron from one position to another more stable position, monochromatic radiant energy is emitted, and the frequency of this radiation multiplied by $h$, the Planck constant, is equal to the difference in the energy of the system between two states.

5. The electrons of an atom are arranged about the nucleus in concentric shells. The electrons of the outermost shell are spoken of as valence electrons. The valence shell of a free (uncombined) atom never contains more than *eight electrons*. The remainder of the atom, which includes the nucleus and the inner shells, is called the kernel. In the case of the noble gases it is customary to consider that there is no valence shell and that the whole atom is the kernel.

6. In my paper on "The Atom and the Molecule" I laid much stress upon the phenomenon of the pairing of electrons. I have since become convinced that this phenomenon is of even greater significance than I then supposed, and that it occurs not only in the valence shell but also within the kernel, and even in the interior of the nucleus itself. It has not seemed desirable to discuss in this book the extremely interesting modern ideas concerning the structure of the atomic nucleus, but if we adopt the old hypothesis of Prout it is possible from the atomic weight and the atomic number alone to determine the number of hydrogen nuclei and the number of electrons which compose the nucleus of a given atom. It is a striking fact that with very few exceptions the number of nuclear electrons so calculated is an even number. It is furthermore to be noted that whenever a radioactive atom emits one beta-particle it almost immediately emits another, again illustrating the instability of an unpaired electron within the nucleus. So also we find that in all the more stable states which atoms assume, the

electrons occur in even numbers in the several inner shells. Later we shall show that the valence electrons almost invariably follow the same rule. The simplest explanation of these facts appears to lie in the assumption of a physical pairing of the electrons. There is nothing in the known laws of electric force, nor is there anything in the quantum theory of atomic structure, as far as it has yet been developed, to account for such pairing. However, we have seen that an electron within the atom must be regarded as a magnet, and two such magnets would tend to be drawn together. While the classical theory of magnetism would hardly suffice to account fully for this phenomenon of pairing, there can be no question that the coupling of electrons is intimately connected with the magnetic properties of the electron orbits, and the explanation of this phenomenon must be regarded as one of the most important outstanding problems in quantum theory.

7. We may next consider a very recent idea advanced by Bohr (1921), which is not based so much upon deductions from his atomic model as upon a direct consideration of the experimental data on spectral series. He assumes essentially that the first shell is associated with a single energy level, and that this level can accommodate one pair of electrons, that the second shell contains two energy levels, each of which is capable of holding two pairs of electrons, making a maximum of eight electrons in the second shell. The third shell has three energy levels, each of which can hold three pairs of electrons, so that the maximum number of electrons in the third shell is eighteen. The fourth shell comprises four levels, each capable of holding four electron pairs, making a total of thirty-two electrons, and so on. We shall see the great utility of this conception as we now proceed to consider the arrangement of electrons in the various elements.

## The Inner Structure of the Several Atoms.

In hydrogen the kernel of the atom is the nucleus itself, and there is one valence electron. This single electron should give to the atom a large magnetic moment, and we expect to find that monatomic hydrogen is highly paramagnetic. Unfortunately no one has succeeded in devising an experimental method of ascertaining the susceptibility of the monatomic form, which can only be obtained at very high temperature, or through the agency of a powerful electric discharge.

In a recent investigation of extraordinary interest Stern and Gerlach (1921) have succeeded in studying in a most direct manner the magnetic properties of the silver atom which, like the hydrogen atom, we suppose to have one electron in its outer shell. They find that its behavior is similar to that which would be predicted for the hydrogen atom by the Bohr theory.

(There is of course a possibility that the nucleus of an atom might itself possess a magnetic moment. As a rule, the magnetic properties of substances are found to be largely dependent upon the physical state of an element or its state of chemical combination, so that it may be assumed that the outer electrons, which are the ones chiefly affected in ordinary physical and chemical changes, are the ones that are responsible for magnetic properties. Nevertheless we have no direct evidence that the *nucleus* may not itself be magnetic.)

In diatomic hydrogen and in helium it was originally assumed by Bohr that the two electrons revolved in the same direction in the same orbit. This would produce a large magnetic moment, and the two gases would therefore be expected to be paramagnetic. On the contrary both gases are diamagnetic, and this model is evidently unsatisfactory. A later model in which the two electrons are placed in separate orbits, making an angle with one another, may be criticized on the same grounds, since this arrangement also should lead to paramagnetism. There are two ways in which a pair of magnets can be held

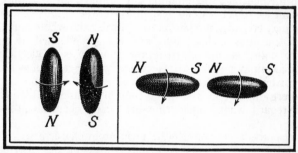

FIG. 13.—Two Ways in Which a Pair of Magnets May Be Drawn Together.

together by their magnetic forces. These are illustrated in Figure 13, in which the magnets are represented either as electric circuits or as the equivalent bar magnets. In the first arrangement the two magnets augment one another and produce a magnetic moment greater than that of either magnet alone. In the second arrangement the two magnetic moments neutralize one another, and the lines of magnetic force are almost entirely confined to the immediate neighborhood of the pair of magnets. Since the phenomenon of diamagnetism is predominant in the great majority of substances, we must assume that the second arrangement more nearly represents the normal condition of an electron pair.

The two electrons of helium are not ordinarily regarded as valence electrons, and therefore we may consider the whole atom of helium as the kernel. In paragraph 7 of the preceding section we have seen that Bohr postulated that the first shell of an atom corresponds to a single energy level and can accommodate two electrons. The pair of electrons in the helium atom constitutes this shell, and a similar pair will appear as the first shell of all atoms of higher atomic number.

The system of nucleus, and first shell of two electrons, forms the kernel of the elements from lithium to fluorine inclusive. The neutral atom of lithium has a nuclear charge of $+ 3$, and one valence electron, which is readily given up by the atom, leaving the kernel, which is the lithium ion. Beryllium has two valence electrons, which are also easily lost, giving the beryllium ion. On the other hand, boron with three valence electrons does not so readily lose these electrons, and the free boron ion is not known to exist. So carbon has four valence electrons, nitrogen five, oxygen six, and fluorine seven. In the last three cases there is an increasing tendency to take up additional electrons to form the stable group of eight, or the octet, which we have shown in Chapter II to be one of the most striking phenomena of chemistry. The nitride ion with three extra electrons probably exists, although this has not been definitely proved. The oxide ion possesses two extra electrons, while fluorine reacts violently with almost all substances in such manner as to take up the one electron necessary to form fluoride ion.

In neon the neutral atom contains this second shell of eight electrons, and forms an extremely stable system. Here again, as in the case of helium, we may consider the kernel to comprise the whole atom, namely, the nucleus, the first shell of two, and the second shell of eight. In terms of the Bohr assumption, the outer group of eight electrons represents the maximum number of electrons which can enter the second shell. According to his idea, four of these electrons are on a somewhat different energy level than the other four, but this is a distinction that we may disregard when considering the purely chemical properties of the atoms.

A kernel entirely resembling the neon atom characterizes all of the elements of the next period. We may represent the distribution of electrons in the successive shells in the following manner: Na, 2-8-1; Mg, 2-8-2; and so on to Cl, in which the distribution is 2-8-7. In each case the last figure gives the number of valence electrons, and, as in the preceding period, the elements with a small number of valence electrons tend to give these up to form positive ions, while those with a greater number tend to take up enough electrons to form negative ions with a complete group of eight in the outer shell.

## The First Long Period.

The distribution of electrons in argon may be represented by 2-8-8, and by analogy to the two preceding periods we might have expected a kernel of this type to characterize the elements of this period, and indeed we find that the chemical properties of the first three elements are in accordance with the arrangements: K, 2-8-8-1; Ca, 2-8-8-2; Sc, 2-8-8-3. But when we come to titanium we see this simple system breaking down. Indeed we have postulated that no atom ever has more than eight valence electrons, and we are dealing with a period of eighteen elements, so that the series cannot proceed from the first to the last element merely by the addition of successive electrons to the outer shell. It is evident that some new phenomenon must occur.

Many years ago I was led to the conclusion that when we speak of an element of variable valence we are including two very different types of phenomena, and that such a change as the oxidation of hydrogen sulfide to sulfurous or sulfuric acid is a very different kind of change from the one which occurs when a ferrous salt is converted into a ferric, or a titanous salt into a titanic. There are numerous reasons for suspecting a fundamental difference between these two types of oxidation. For example, in the first type oxidation and reduction usually occur by steps of two, while the second type more often involves a change of but one step. Substances which undergo the second type of change are usually colored, while those involved in the first type of change are usually colorless. The distinction between the two types was expressed in my paper of 1916 by referring to the atoms which undergo the second type of valence-change as *atoms of variable kernel*.

The properties of the various elements which come before titanium are in accord with the assumption that the electrons which are a part of the kernel do not take part in chemical reactions, but as we now proceed to elements of higher atomic number we shall see that this simple rule is by no means universally valid.

It is a remarkable fact concerning the metals that we have so far discussed that when they form ions they give off simultaneously all of the electrons of the outer shell. When Ca acts as an electrode in electrolysis, its atom never loses a single electron to form the ion $Ca^+$. If it does, this ion must be unstable and react immediately according to the reaction, $2Ca^+ = Ca + Ca^{++}$. It is true that in the ionization of calcium vapor the ion $Ca^+$ is assumed to account for the so-called enhanced spectrum of calcium, but presumably two such ions coming together would undergo the above reaction. Compounds of the type CaCl are unknown. Aluminum does not form the ions $Al^+$ and $Al^{++}$, nor are compounds known of the type AlCl and $AlCl_2$. In other words, when such a metal reacts it uses all of its valence electrons or none. (It is probable that in some atoms of high atomic weight there are exceptions to this rule. It seems likely that in the change from thallous to thallic ion or from aurous to auric ion there is no change in the kernel.)

Now let us see the consequence of applying this rule to the elements in the periodic table which we have now reached. Titanium gives three classes of compounds, one corresponding to the titanous ion, $Ti^{++}$, one to titanic ion, $Ti^{+++}$, and one presumably to the quadripositive ion, $Ti^{++++}$. Now if we are to believe that in each of these ions the atom has given up all its valence electrons, then we must assume that there are three possible states of the titanium atom containing, respectively, two, three, and four valence electrons. Since the total number of electrons must be the same for any state of the neutral atom, this means that the kernel must have one more electron in the first state than in the second, and one more in the second than in the third. If we assume that the extra electrons go into the preceding shell, we can represent the three states of the neutral atom as 2-8-8-4 (quadripositive), 2-8-9-3 (tripositive, titanic), and 2-8-10-2 (bipositive, titanous).

## TABLE.

COMPOSITION OF ATOMIC KERNELS IN ELEMENTS OF THE FIRST LONG PERIOD.

| 2-8-8 | 2-8-9 | 2-8-10 | 2-8-11 | 2-8-12 | 2-8-13 | 2-8-14 | 2-8-15 | 2-8-16 | 2-8-17 | 2-8-18 |
|---|---|---|---|---|---|---|---|---|---|---|
| A | | | | | | | | | | |
| $K^+$ | | | | | | | | | | |
| $Ca^{++}$ | | | | | | | | | | |
| $Sc^{+++}$ | | | | | | | | | | |
| $Ti^{++++}$ | $Ti^{+++}$ | $Ti^{++}$ | | | | | | | | |
| $V^{+++}$ | $V^{++++}$ | $V^{+++}$ | $V^{++}$ | | | | | | | |
| $Cr^{+++}$ | | | $Cr^{+++}$ | $Cr^{++}$ | | | | | | |
| $Mn^{++++}$ | $Mn^{+++}$ | | $Mn^{++++}$ | $Mn^{+++}$ | $Mn^{++}$ | | | | | |
| | | $Fe^{+++}$ | | | $Fe^{+++}$ | $Fe^{++}$ | | | | |
| | | | | | | $Co^{+++}$ | $Co^{++}$ | | | |
| | | | | | | | $Ni^{+++}$ | $Ni^{++}$ | | |
| | | | | | | | | | $Cu^{++}$ | $Cu^+$ |
| | | | | | | | | | | $Zn^{++}$ |
| | | | | | | | | | | $Ga^{+++}$ |
| | | | | | | | | | | etc. |

It will be understood that in writing such formulæ as $Cr^{+++}$ and $Mn^{++++}$ we are not necessarily assuming the existence of these ions, but simply using a shorthand method of expressing the state of chromium in chromates and of manganese in permanganates.

Applying the same idea to the succeeding members of this period of elements of variable kernel, we find the distribution of electrons in the several kernels as shown in the accompanying table. Thus the kernel represented by 2-8-8 is the only one that occurs in argon, potassium, calcium and scandium. It also occurs in titanates, vanadates, chromates and permanganates. Every form of kernel from 2-8-8 to 2-8-18 occurs in the table. Thus the kernel 2-8-11 is contained in vanadous compounds, in chromic compounds, and in manganese dioxide. When we come to the kernel 2-8-18 we find evidence that this composition of the kernel, like the form 2-8-8, appears to possess a higher degree of stability than the transition forms. Thus we find the kernel of copper assuming this form in the cuprous compounds, and all the remaining elements of the period, Zn, Ga, Ge, As, Se and Br, adopt no other form of kernel than 2-8-18.

It is evident that some at least of the electrons in the kernels of the various transition forms between 2-8-8 and 2-8-18 are in a very different state from that which characterizes the electrons of the inner shells of the elements which we have considered hitherto. Simple processes of oxidation or reduction suffice to diminish or to increase the number of electrons in the kernel. That some of these electrons are not tightly held is shown also in the prevalence of color in the compounds of these transition elements. An equally striking characteristic of the transition elements is found in their magnetic properties. To say nothing of the remarkable ferromagnetic properties of the elements themselves, we find that many of the compounds of these metals are strongly paramagnetic.

Indeed we find that pronounced paramagnetism is almost exclusively the property of these elements and of the transition elements of the remaining long periods in which the phenomenon of variable valence also appears. Thus if we inspect the very incomplete data given in the tables of Landolt, Börnstein and Roth, we are struck by the fact that (with the remarkable exception of molecular oxygen, $O_2$) there is listed no elementary or compound substance possessing a higher magnetic susceptibility per gram than $10^{-6}$, except those containing titanium, vanadium, chromium, manganese, iron, cobalt, nickel and cupric copper in the first long period; columbium, rhodium and palladium, which are transition elements in the second long period, and cerium and praseodymium in the third long period.

It is moreover to be noted that the highly paramagnetic character of these elements disappears when the kernel assumes either of the two forms 2-8-8 and 2-8-18. Thus chromates and permanganates are weakly paramagnetic, while cuprous compounds are either slightly paramagnetic or diamagnetic. On the other hand, the most highly magnetic substances are those which occur in the center of the transition group.

In this transition stage which occurs before the completion of the new kernel—and this same process apparently occurs in each of the succeeding periods of the elements—there is a marked departure from the rule which is so generally observed, that electron shells tend to hold an even number of electrons. If we consider the bivalent ions of titanium, vanadium, chromium, manganese, iron, cobalt, nickel, copper, there is no alternation of stability between the forms with even and odd numbers of electrons in the kernel.

While in a stable kernel the electrons, regarded as elementary electric circuits or magnets, seem to be arranged in such manner as to neutralize the magnetic fields and to prevent a resultant magnetic moment, it seems to be quite otherwise in the case of these unstable forms of kernel in the transition group. Without attempting to suggest the actual structure of these unstable kernels, it is perhaps interesting to note that the magnetic properties which have been mentioned would result if, after the kernel has the form 2-8-8, the additional electron orbits (regarded as elementary magnets) entered into the kernel in a row, the north end of one directly toward the south end of the next, so that each additional magnet would increase the total magnetic moment. If

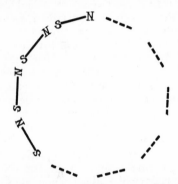

FIG. 14.—A Possible Arrangement of Elementary Magnets in the Transition Metals.

instead of a row we should imagine a ring of ten magnets, as in Figure 14, this ring being built up one magnet at a time, then at the beginning each magnet would increase the resultant magnetic moment, but as the ring approached completion the moment would again diminish, and in the completed ring the magnetic moment would disappear. This may give a crude picture of the way in which the stable and non-magnetic kernel 2-8-8 passes into the stable and non-magnetic kernel 2-8-18, with the highest magnetic moment in the middle of the transition period.

If a metallic ion is merely a kernel which has lost all its valence electrons, and if the structure of this kernel determines the magnetic properties of the ion, then (assuming that the magnetic properties of the ions of the iron group are not much affected or are equally affected by hydration) we might expect a close resemblance between two ions which have precisely the same type of kernel and differ only in the charge of the atomic nucleus. Kossel has called attention to some very remarkable results obtained by Weber (1915) on the atomic susceptibility of such ions. It appears that the paramagnetic susceptibility of the bivalent ions increases from the chromous to the manganous ion and then diminishes to the nickelous ion. He obtained the following figures:

| Ion | $Cr^{++}$ | $Mn^{++}$ | $Fe^{++}$ | $Co^{++}$ | $Ni^{++}$ |
|-----|-----------|-----------|-----------|-----------|-----------|
| $\chi_a$ | 0.011 | 0.015 | 0.013 | 0.010 | 0.004 |

Studying the corresponding trivalent ions, Weber finds $\chi_a = 0.006$ for chromic ion. Manganic ion, which has the same kind of kernel as the chromous ion, has also the same susceptibility, namely, 0.011. Ferric ion, with the same type of kernel as the manganous ion, has its susceptibility, namely, 0.015. (Cobaltic ion was found to have a much lower susceptibility than ferrous ion, but this was very likely due to the difficulty of preparing a pure cobaltic salt.) Such facts show very clearly that in these ions it is the type of kernel that determines the magnetic properties, and that the magnetic susceptibility is at a maximum in the kernel which has five more electrons than are present in the kernel of argon.

All of these facts seem to warrant the assertion that in this first long period we are dealing with a group of elements many of which show the phenomenon of a variable kernel; and that in proceeding through the successive elements from scandium to zinc, ten electrons have been added to the kernel. This is entirely in accordance with Bohr's rule. We have seen that the kernel of the helium type has its first shell fully occupied by the pair of electrons which alone can be accommodated at this energy level. In the kernel of the neon type the second shell also contains its full quota of eight electrons, but in the kernel of the argon type, 2-8-8, the third shell contains only eight of the eighteen which that shell is capable of holding. Therefore we may conclude that, in passing through the transition group from scandium to zinc, the ten electrons which are added to the kernel complete the third shell of eighteen electrons, so that in krypton we have a kernel of the type 2-8-18-8.

## The Remaining Periods.

The fourth atomic shell should be capable of holding thirty-two electrons, and we might expect the next long period, beginning with rubidium, to fill all these places. In fact, however, we find an almost exact duplication of the preceding period. Once more we pass through a series of transition elements, columbium being the first to show a variable kernel. Each of the four preceding elements, rubidium, strontium, yttrium and zirconium, gives but a single ion, and the compounds of these elements are colorless and have a low magnetic susceptibility. The succeeding elements behave very much like those of the first long period, and the final element xenon may be assigned the kernel structure, 2-8-18-18-8.

This kernel of the xenon type persists in the first members of the next period, namely, cesium, barium and lanthanum. In cerium we come to the first element of variable kernel, and now we may assume that the electrons which are added to the kernel complete the fourth shell of thirty-two electrons. Such a process would involve no change in the valence shell from element to element, nor in the next inner shell, and would thus produce only subterranean changes in the atom. Thus we may account for the great similarity in the properties of the rare earths.

The transition process may be assumed to be completed when the fourth shell has its full complement of thirty-two electrons, and the fifth shell eighteen of its possible fifty, so that the kernel of the noble gas, niton, which concludes this period, may be considered to have the structure 2-8-18-32-18-8.

This is essentially the view of the composition of the inner shells which was proposed almost simultaneously by Bohr (1921), who considered the spectroscopic behavior of the elements, and by Bury (1921) who considered their physico-chemical properties. It possesses much verisimilitude and furnishes unquestionably the best picture of the atomic kernel which our existing knowledge permits. Some things which still seem obscure will doubtless be clarified by further study of the ordinary and X-ray spectra of the elements, and of their magnetic properties and ionizing potentials.

In the meantime it must be admitted that the problem is by no means completely solved. Both Bohr and Bury assume that the last fragmentary period of the Mendeléeff table is a period of thirty-two elements, but I have pointed out in a previous chapter that the properties of thorium and uranium indicate a far less resemblance to the preceding period of thirty-two than to the next preceding period of eighteen.

Then again the cause of the stability of certain groups is not yet adequately explained. Presumably the relative energies of the several possible states will determine whether an electron will appear in the outer shell of an atom or enter one of the inner unfilled shells, but while we may grant that the numbers 2, 8, and 18 represent the maximum number of electrons which may enter the first, the second and the third shells of the atom, we have no indication as to why these same groups appear in unfilled shells. We still have no explanation for the extremely significant fact that all of the rare gases (except helium) and all the common elementary ions, such as $S^{--}$, $Cl^-$, $K^+$, $Ba^{++}$ and $Al^{+++}$, contain just eight electrons in the outermost shell.

Neither have we any adequate explanation for the pairing of electrons which seems to characterize all the stable configurations of the kernel. The tendency to form pairs and the tendency to form groups of eight we shall find to be the essential features in the arrangement of valence electrons in compound molecules.

# Chapter V.

# The Union of Atoms; the Modern
## Dualistic Theory.

We have now obtained a view of the structure of the atom which, although perhaps incomplete or even erroneous in some of its details, may safely be regarded as giving us in the main an adequate idea of the arrangement of electrons about the atomic nucleus. Our next task is to ascertain if possible the way in which two or more atoms combine with one another, and thus to obtain a similar intimate picture of the structure of the molecule. In short we must endeavor to interpret the great body of fact and hypothesis comprised in what is commonly known as valence theory.

As I have remarked in another place (1913), "There is always the danger in scientific work that some word or phrase will be used by different authors to express so many ideas and surmises that, unless redefined, it loses all real significance. Thus the term valence has been used in discussing a large number of ideas which have perhaps nothing more in common than the acceptance of Dalton's law of multiple proportions. Even the conception of valence as an integral number has been abandoned by those who speak of 'partial valence.'"

However, to those who have been responsible for the great achievements of structural organic chemistry, the idea of valence has not been ambiguous. The valence of an atom in an organic molecule represents the number of *bonds* which tie this atom to other atoms. Moreover in the mind of the organic chemist the chemical bond is no mere abstraction; it is a definite physical reality, a something which binds atom to atom. Although the nature of such a tie remained mysterious, yet the hypothesis of the bond was amply justified by the signal adequacy of the simple theory of molecular structure to which it gave rise.

The great success of structural organic chemistry led to attempts to treat inorganic compounds in a similar manner, not always happily. I still have poignant remembrance of the distress which I and many others suffered some thirty years ago in a class in elementary chemistry, where we were obliged to memorize structural formulæ of a great number of inorganic compounds. Even such substances as the ferricyanides and ferrocyanides were forced into the system, and bonds were drawn between the several atoms to comply with certain artificial rules, regardless of all chemical evidence. Such formulæ are now believed to be almost, if not entirely, devoid of scientific significance.

67

Such abuse of the structural formula inevitably led to a reaction which found its best expression in the publications of Werner. His "Neuere Anschauungen auf dem Gebiete der anorganischen Chemie" (1905) marked a new epoch in chemistry; and in attempting to clarify the fundamental ideas of valence, there is no work to which I feel so much personal indebtedness as to this of Werner's. While some of his theoretical conclusions have not proved convincing, he marshalled in a masterly manner a great array of facts which showed the incongruities into which chemists had been led by the existing structural formulæ of inorganic chemistry.

Especially Werner called attention to the almost complete analogy between the union of an anhydride with water to give the oxygen acids, and the union of many halides with hydrogen halides to form the halogen acids. Thus the reaction $H_2O + SO_3 = H_2SO_4$ is analogous to the reactions $HF + BF_3 = HBF_4$ and $2HCl + PtCl_4 = H_2PtCl_6$. Now sulfuric acid could be given the structural formula

$$H - O - \overset{\displaystyle O}{\underset{\displaystyle O}{\overset{\|}{\underset{\|}{S}}}} - O - H$$

but no such bonded structure could be given for the two halogen acids. Therefore the latter were said to be molecular compounds. However, there is no such fundamental chemical difference between the two types as would warrant such a distinction, and I believe that anyone who reads all of the facts as assembled by Werner must admit that we must either assign to hydrofluoboric acid a structure not very unlike that of sulfuric, or dispense with structural formulæ altogether.

The growth of such ideas and the success of the electrolytic dissociation theory of Arrhenius once more drew the attention of chemists away from the structural formula and directed it to the electric state of the atoms of a molecule. Thus there came into being what may be called the modern dualistic hypothesis.

The older dualistic theory developed by Davy, and especially by Berzelius, was abandoned largely because it was discovered that the positive element, hydrogen, could be replaced in organic compounds by the negative element, chlorine, without producing any great change in the physical properties of the compound. But later measurements of electrical conductivity showed that, after all, acetic acid and trichloracetic acid are in some respects very different types, and that these differences are readily interpreted on the old assumption that chlorine has a far greater attraction for negative electricity than hydrogen has.

In the theory of Berzelius, electricity was regarded as a fluid which could flow to a greater or less extent from one atom to another, but the recognition of the atomic nature of electricity made it now seem necessary to assume that if the molecule is made up of charged atoms each atom must have an excess or a deficiency of an integral number

THE UNION OF ATOMS; THE MODERN DUALISTIC THEORY 69

of electrons, as compared with the neutral state. Thus the modern dualistic theory regards chemical action as primarily due to the jumping of electrons from atom to atom.

The properties of electrolytes certainly point to such a separation of charges. If sodium and chlorine combine to form aqueous sodium chloride, the sodium atom definitely loses and the chlorine atom gains an electron. It seemed not unnatural to suppose that each molecule of undissociated sodium chloride might also contain the same charged particles, namely, sodium with one electron missing, and chlorine with one additional electron, held together by electric forces. The same theory might then be applied to hydrogen chloride, and then to water, and alcohol, and perhaps eventually to substances like methane and hydrogen.

While the number of different ions which have been shown to exist at high concentrations in aqueous solution is limited, there are many other ions that can be shown to be present in small amount, and there are others which may be assumed to exist in minute amount in order to explain the behavior of various substances. Thus in a solution of sodium aluminate there is an extremely small but perfectly calculable concentration of aluminum ion. It might therefore seem reasonable to regard each aluminum atom, even in the aluminates, as in the same electrical condition, namely, with a positive charge of three units.

In some similar cases the ions have not even been proved to exist, but the hypothetical ion, $Cr^{+++}$, might be considered to represent the actual state of the chromium atom in chromic anhydride or the chromates. By the same method the electrical state of the sulfur atom would be represented by $S^{+++}$ in sulfates, by $S^{++++}$ in sulfites, and by $S^{--}$ in sulfides.

Now such a theory obviously gives a very simple interpretation of those processes in which a given element is said to be oxidized or reduced by a certain number of steps. Thus if manganous ion is oxidized to permanganate ion, it is said that manganese undergoes five units of oxidation, and some other atom or atoms must at the same time be reduced by five units. In the modern dualistic theory this simply means that the manganese atom changes in state from a deficiency of two electrons to a deficiency of seven, that is, from $Mn^{++}$ to $Mn^{++++}$, and that five electrons are taken up by other atoms.

In all chemistry there is no concept which is more fundamental than this one of reduction and oxidation. Under the name of phlogistication and dephlogistication such processes were recognized even before the discovery of oxygen, and this mode of classifying chemical phenomena has ever since been regarded as one of the greatest utility. No one can doubt the desirability of placing in a class by themselves ammonia, alkyl amines and ammonium salts, in another class nitrogen trioxide, nitrous acid, and the nitrites, and in still another class nitrogen pentoxide, nitric acid, and the nitrates. But the question remains as to whether such a classification is an absolute one.

Convenient, and indeed necessary, as it is in the study of many chemical reactions, can this classification be applied without ambiguity to all chemical substances? If it can, it means that we may assign every atom in every compound to a definite oxidation-reduction stage, and this in turn, according to the electrical interpretation, implies a complete acceptance of the modern dualistic theory which ascribes to each atom in a compound an integral number of units of positive or negative charge.

This number, positive or negative (or zero), intended to show the electrical state of each atom, has sometimes been called the positive or negative valence of the atom, but since these terms have also been used to represent the maximum positive or negative charge which the element can assume in a great variety of compounds, rather than the actual charge of the atom in a given compound, Bray and Branch (1913) proposed the better expression, *polar number*. Thus in ferrous sulfate, $FeSO_4$, iron is assigned the polar number $+2$, sulfur the polar number $+6$, and each oxygen $-2$.

It is customary in works on inorganic chemistry to call ferric iron trivalent and ferrous iron bivalent. Now this phraseology is not only out of harmony with that of organic chemistry, but it is essentially bad in that it gives a number without a sign. Thus nitrogen would be said to be trivalent both in ammonia and in nitrous acid. In all cases where the polar number is to be indicated I propose a slightly different mode of expression. Let us say that nitrogen in ammonia is *trinegative,* and that it is *tripositive* in nitrous acid. So also let us say that iron is tripositive in ferric salts and bipositive in ferrous salts.

It is to be noted that these polar numbers may be convenient in a systematic treatment of chemical reactions, even if there is not that definite distribution of atomic charges required by the dualistic theory. To quote from my paper (1913) which was published with that of Bray and Branch, "Oxidation of an element means an increase of its polar number, reduction means a decrease, and this simple system furnishes an adequate method of dealing with all cases of oxidation and reduction. It must be remarked, however, that on account of its very generality this system would apply equally well even if purely fanciful values of the polar number were chosen, provided that the rules required by the fundamental law of the conservation of electricity be observed. Moreover, non-polar compounds may be treated provisionally as polar, and fictitious polar numbers may be assigned without leading to any false conclusions."

Let us consider a very interesting case cited by Bray and Branch. The substance $C_6H_5SO_2OH$ might be regarded as a derivative either of sulfuric or of sulfurous acid, namely, (a) sulfuric acid in which one hydroxyl group is replaced by phenyl, (b) sulfurous acid in which one hydrogen is replaced by phenyl. In accordance with assumption (a) we should assign to sulfur the polar number $+6$ and to phenyl as a whole the polar number — 1. With assumption (b) we should give + 4 as the polar number of sulfur and + 1 as that of phenyl. Now it is taken for granted by the dualists that on hydrolysis a positive radical adds hydroxyl, and that a negative radical adds hydrogen. But when we apply this criterion to the case before us, we find that the substance hydrolyzes in acid solution to give benzene and sulfuric acid, but in a basic medium it gives phenol and sulfurous acid. It was shown by Bray and Branch that in order to preserve intact the idea that every atom must have a definite polar number, it would be necessary to assume the existence of two distinct tautomers in equilibrium with each other, namely, one with the polar numbers $S = +4$ and $C_6H_5 = +1$, and the other with $S = +6$ and $C_6H_5 = -1$.

However, in the papers by Bray and Branch and by myself which have just been cited, it was very definitely shown that many compounds give no evidence of that large separation of electric charge which is required by the modern dualistic theory, and indeed that there are many substances, of the type which we call non-polar, whose properties indicate little or no electric displacement within the molecule. The properties of a substance like sodium chloride differ so radically from those of a substance like molecular hydrogen that it seemed necessary to distinguish in degree if not in kind between the extremely polar and the relatively non-polar types, although I remarked that "It must not be assumed that any one compound corresponds wholly and at all times to either type."

The same idea was very forcefully advanced by J. J. Thomson (1914) who, in addition to a large amount of chemical evidence, adduced physical evidence based on experiments with positive rays and measurements of dielectric constant, to show the great difference between different substances as regards the degree of polarization, or, as he preferred to call it, "intramolecular ionization." This was a radical departure from Thomson's original view in which, in accordance with the views of Abegg, he assumed all chemical action to be due to the transference of electrons from one atom to another. This earlier view had given impetus to an attempt to apply the full theory of electrochemical dualism to organic compounds. Numerous papers by Falk and Nelson (1910), Fry (1911), and others developed the "electron conception of valence," and this theory still has vogue among many organic chemists, as may be seen from a recent interesting paper of Stieglitz (1922). It is to be borne in mind that the assumption employed by these authors is no other than the assumption made by many inorganic chemists that each atom in a molecule exists in a definite oxidation-reduction stage which can be represented by an integral polar number.

Falk and Nelson began their work by quoting from Thomson as follows: "For each valency bond established between two atoms the transference of one (negatively charged) corpuscle from the one atom to the other has taken place, the atom receiving the corpuscle acquiring a unit charge of negative electricity, the other by the loss of a corpuscle acquiring a unit charge of positive. This electrical process may be represented by the producing of a unit tube of electric force between the two atoms, the tube starting from the positive and ending on the negative atom. . . . There is, however, one important difference between the lines representing the bonds and the tubes of electric force. The lines used by the chemist are not supposed to have direction. . . . On the electrical theory, however, the tubes of electric force are regarded as having direction starting from the positive and ending on the negative atom. . . .''

In order to express in the chemical formula the electrical transfer from one atom to another, Falk and Nelson drew an arrow pointing from the atom which had lost an electron to the atom which had gained one. Thus methane, in which each hydrogen atom was assumed to have a positive charge of 1 and the carbon atom to have a charge of — 4; and carbon tetrachloride, in which each chlorine atom was assigned a charge of — 1 and the carbon atom a charge of + 4, were represented by

$$
\begin{array}{cc}
\mathrm{H} & \mathrm{Cl} \\
\downarrow & \uparrow \\
\mathrm{H} \rightarrow \mathrm{C} \leftarrow \mathrm{H} \qquad & \mathrm{Cl} \leftarrow \mathrm{C} \rightarrow \mathrm{Cl} \\
\uparrow & \downarrow \\
\mathrm{H} & \mathrm{Cl}
\end{array}
$$

So methyl alcohol would be represented as

$$
\begin{array}{c}
\mathrm{H} \\
\downarrow \\
\mathrm{H} \rightarrow \mathrm{C} \rightarrow \mathrm{O} \leftarrow \mathrm{H} \\
\uparrow \\
\mathrm{H}
\end{array}
$$

It is evident that the arrows which represented the transfer of an electron were now being used as a substitute for the traditional organic bond.

However, there are numerous objections to such a complete application of the dualistic theory to organic chemistry. Only a few of these need be mentioned.

If the negatively charged chlorine atom in carbon tetrachloride is identical with the chloride ion which comes from electrolytes such as sodium chloride, it might be expected to exert a field of force extending in all directions, and to attract any positively charged atom, but there is nothing in the physical or chemical behavior of carbon tetrachloride to indicate such a state of affairs. Again, the arrow used by Falk and Nelson cannot represent a chemical bond unless it means something more than was stated by the authors (and by Thomson), for as far as they state, the formula for methyl chloride

$$\begin{array}{c} H \\ \downarrow \\ H \rightarrow C \rightarrow Cl \\ \uparrow \\ H \end{array}$$

would merely indicate that each hydrogen has a positive charge, that the chlorine has a negative charge, and that the carbon atom has a charge of — 2. But there is nothing in all this to show from which particular atom a given electron came. We do not think of an electron leaving a trail behind it, as a spider weaves its web, but if not, what is the significance of an arrow?

One of the formulæ proposed by Falk and Nelson for ethylene is

$$\begin{array}{c} H \rightarrow \\ H \rightarrow \end{array} C \begin{array}{c} \rightarrow \\ \leftarrow \end{array} C \begin{array}{c} \leftarrow H \\ \leftarrow H \end{array}$$

They recognize the logical difficulty involved in such a formula when they write, "In those cases where one valence proceeds in one direction and one in the other, it is assumed that the corpuscles which are transferred are localized on the atoms, as otherwise the carbon atoms would become electrically neutral." But even so we might as well indicate that a carbon atom has lost an electron in one part and gained an electron in another part by vertical arrows, as follows:

$$\begin{array}{c} H \rightarrow \\ H \rightarrow \end{array} C \begin{array}{c} \uparrow \\ \downarrow \end{array} \uparrow \ C \begin{array}{c} \leftarrow H \\ \leftarrow H \end{array}$$

Here, however, there is left no indication of a bond holding the two carbon atoms together.

If we adopt the dualistic theory and regard the organic molecule as an assemblage of charged atoms, it would seem impossible to account for the complex structures which often remain unchanged for long periods of time. We should rather expect such a structure to tumble into the particular aggregations which would represent the minimum of electrical energy.

Finally it may be noted that the dualistic theory led to a prediction which has received no verification. W. A. Noyes (see Noyes and Lyon, 1901), who very early considered the possibility that an elementary molecule might be of polar character, has for many years regarded nitrogen trichloride as a compound containing positive chlorine, namely, $N^{---}(Cl^+)_3$. From the dualistic point of view, it was predicted that an isomer of this compound might exist, namely, $N^{+++}(Cl^-)_3$. For many years he has attempted to obtain such isomers, but without success, and the failure of all similar attempts to obtain the isomers predicted by the dualistic theory indicates that there is something illusory in the object of such a quest.

All of these excursions into the theory of valence seemed to lead but to an impasse. Thus the dualistic theory, while offering an adequate explanation of the nature of extremely polar substances, and bringing into relief the electrochemical properties of the elements, proved incompetent to explain the chemical bond and the behavior of the relatively non-polar compounds, especially those of organic chemistry. On the other hand, the pure structural theory gave complete satisfaction in the interpretation of the chief facts of organic chemistry, but seemed little qualified to account for those phenomena of a highly polar type, culminating in the complete division of a molecule into charged ions. Finally the suggestion of two entirely distinct kinds of chemical union, one for polar and the other for non-polar compounds, was repugnant to that chemical instinct which leads so irresistibly to the belief that all types of chemical union are essentially one and the same. Already, however, there were some hints of the way out of this perplexing quandary. If the properties of substances could not be explained by the mere assumption of charged atoms, might they not be explicable if we should no longer regard the atom as a unit, but rather if we might ascertain where the charge or charges resided within the atom itself?

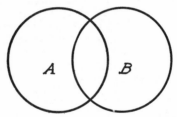

Fig. 15.—Two Overlapping Positive Spheres (Thomson).

It was suggested by J. J. Thomson (1907) that two atoms might be conceived to be held together by electrical forces without electrical polarization. At that time he regarded the positive part of the atom as a sphere in which the electrons were imagined to be imbedded, and he considered the case of two spheres equal in size, overlapping one another (Figure 15), with electrons situated symmetrically in the region of overlapping. He says, "In this case there is no difference in the electrification of the spheres; we cannot say that one is positively, the other negatively electrified; and if the spheres were separated after having been together they would each be neutral. . . . We thus see that it is possible to have forces electrical in their origin binding the two systems together without a resulting charge on either system."

Thomson made no further use of this idea, and his view of the positive sphere has been superseded. Nevertheless, the suggestion that an understanding of chemical affinity must be sought in the localization of the charges within the atom itself contains the germ of the final successful explanation of the chemical bond.

The first [1] to consider the valence electron as attracting simultaneously the positive parts of two different atoms and thus becoming the

---

[1] The idea of shared electrons was foreshadowed by Ramsay in 1908.

agent which binds atoms together, was Stark, who developed this idea very extensively in his "Atomdynamik." At first he con-

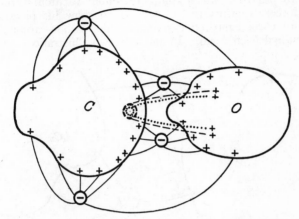

FIG. 16.—Stark's Model of the Carbon Monoxide Molecule.

sidered an electron situated within one atom as sending lines of force to the positive part of that atom and also to the positive part of another atom. Later he allowed such an electron to move out part

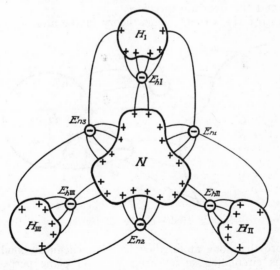

FIG. 17.—Stark's Model of the Ammonia Molecule.

way toward the second atom, and he usually regarded such an electron, situated somewhere between two atoms, as the equivalent of the chemical bond. However, in two cases, namely in the union of carbon to carbon and of hydrogen to carbon, he regarded the chemical bond as due to two electrons which jointly tie atom to atom through their lines of force. Figures 16, 17, 18 and 19 show his pictures of the structure of carbon monoxide, ammonia, the carbon-carbon bond and the carbon-hydrogen bond. In the last two illustrations we see the

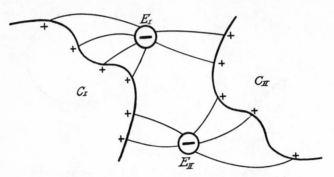

FIG. 18.—Stark's Model of the Carbon-Carbon Bond.

first suggestion of an idea which, as we are going to show in the next chapter, furnishes an extraordinarily simple explanation of the chemical bond, and completely reconciles the divergent views of the structural and the dualistic theories.

Bohr (1913 II), extending his theory of the atom to systems con-

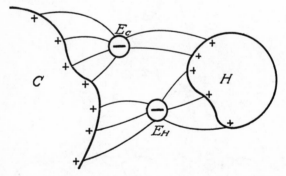

FIG. 19.—Stark's Model of the Carbon-Hydrogen Bond.

taining more than one atom, thought of a chemical bond as a ring of electrons circulating in an orbit with its plane perpendicular to the line joining the atomic centers. Thus he says, "Such considerations suggest a possible configuration for a water molecule, consisting of an oxygen nucleus surrounded by a small ring of four electrons and two hydrogen nuclei, situated on the axis of the ring at equal distances apart from the first nucleus, and kept in equilibrium by help of two rings of greater radius, each containing three electrons. . . ." Each of these rings of three electrons represented a bond. When, however, he considered molecular hydrogen and methane, he concluded that there are two electrons in the ring which constitutes the bond, and thus obtained a picture not unlike that of Stark.

Kossel (1916) employed models of molecules having rings of electrons common to two atoms. Figure 20 shows his picture of the nitrogen molecule.

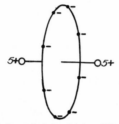

FIG. 20.—Kossel's Model of the Nitrogen Molecule.

Parson (1915) assumed three distinct types of chemical union. One of these types involved a pair of electrons acting jointly to hold two atoms together, as is shown on the right-hand portion of Figure 21, which reproduces his picture of the hydrogen molecule. On the other hand, he assumes a far more complicated process in the union of two atoms of chlorine, as is shown in the left-hand part of the figure, where the dots represent valence electrons and the shaded circles rep-

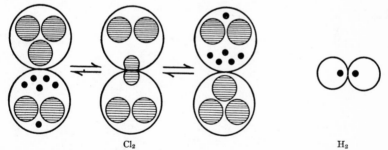

Cl₂ H₂

FIG. 21.—Parson's Models of the Chlorine and Hydrogen Molecules.

resent groups of eight (some of these groups of eight stand for what we now call inner shells).

Thus we see that these authors from very different points of departure arrive at the same conclusion, namely, that two atoms are held together by groups of electrons held in common by the two atoms. Moreover each of these authors occasionally considers that the group of bonding electrons is a group of two, but this was not regarded by any of them as an essential feature of chemical union. We are going to see in the next chapter how far-reaching are the consequences of the simple assumption that the chemical bond is at all times and in all molecules merely a pair of electrons held jointly by two atoms.

# Chapter VI.

## The New Theory of Valence; the Chemical Bond.

At the close of the last chapter we traced the germination of the concept of electrons held in common by two atoms. It is this concept which is going to permit us to harmonize those two main theories of chemical union which formerly seemed so incompatible with one another. In developing this thesis we must now consider the new and somewhat revolutionary ideas regarding valence which were advanced in my paper of 1916 on "The Atom and the Molecule."

We have already noted the preponderating tendency of every atom toward an arrangement of electrons with eight in the outermost shell. This arrangement of outer electrons, which Parson and I called the "group of eight," and which has since been more tersely expressed by Langmuir as the "octet," is attained when atoms lose or gain electrons to form ions.

So when calcium and chlorine unite, the calcium atom by giving off two electrons, and each chlorine atom by acquiring one electron, assume the ionic state in which each atom has the group of eight in its outermost shell. However, we have seen that the assumption of such ionizations as a necessary accompaniment to all chemical combinations, even if it is assumed to be only "intramolecular" ionization, leads to conclusions which are not reconcilable with the facts of chemistry.

The new theory, *which includes the possibility of complete ionization as a special case,* may be given definite expression as follows: Two atoms may conform to the rule of eight, or the octet rule, not only by the transfer of electrons from one atom to another, but also by sharing one or more pairs of electrons. These electrons which are held in common by two atoms may be considered to belong to the outer shells of both atoms.

### The Pairing of Electrons.

The discovery that those electrons which are held jointly by two atoms always occur in pairs led to the realization that the "rule of two" is even more fundamental than the "rule of eight." We see at the beginning of the periodic table that helium with its pair of electrons has the same qualities of stability that characterize the remaining rare gases which possess outer octets. Hydrogen may form hydrogen ion with no electrons, it may form hydride ion by adding one electron and thus completing the stable pair, or finally two hydrogen atoms may unite to form the hydrogen molecule, in which each atom shares with the other this stable pair of electrons.

I called particular attention to the remarkable fact that when we count up the electrons which are comprised in the valence shells of various types of molecules, we find that of some hundred thousand known substances all but a handful contain an even number of such electrons. It is therefore an almost universal rule that the number of valence electrons in a molecule is a multiple of two.

Certain metallic vapors which are produced at high temperatures are exceptions to this rule. Other exceptions which are found at high temperatures are the monatomic forms of hydrogen and the halogens, while at ordinary temperatures we have nitric oxide, nitrogen dioxide and chlorine dioxide, with 11, 17, and 19 valence electrons.

Such molecules which contain an uneven number of valence electrons, and which therefore depart from the simple rule of two, I called *odd molecules*. Until a few years ago, the above mentioned substances were the only ones of known molecular weight which were proved to have odd molecules. Gomberg (1900) discovered a type of odd molecule in triphenylmethyl, and many similar compounds of trivalent carbon have since then been obtained. Analogous compounds of bivalent nitrogen were obtained by Wieland (1911, 1914), who also isolated the interesting substance $(C_6H_5)_2NO$. By analogy I suggested (1916 II) that corresponding compounds of univalent oxygen might be prepared, and investigation has shown that such compounds probably occur, although their existence has not yet been fully demonstrated.

These odd molecules which form an exception to the rule of two may be said in the best sense of the old adage to prove that rule, for they form a class of substances with very singular properties. With the exception of nitric oxide, every one absorbs light in the visible part of the spectrum, and most of them are intensely colored. In so far as they have been investigated, they prove to be highly paramagnetic. They are very reactive and attach themselves to a great variety of substances. Even a substance so little prone to forming addition compounds as hexane, forms a compound with triphenylmethyl.

These odd molecules show a great tendency to combine with other like or unlike odd molecules to form molecules with an even number of electrons, such as $I_2$, $ICl$, $(\varphi_3C)I$, $(\varphi_3C)(N\varphi_2)$, $(\varphi_3C)_2$, $(NO_2)_2$ (where $\varphi$ represents a phenyl or other aryl group). The resulting compounds are usually, though not always, colorless. They do not show the properties indicative of very great "unsaturation" which characterize the odd molecules.

Under other circumstances, and especially in a highly polar environment, instead of a combination of two odd molecules, one loses and the other gains an electron, thus forming the ions with an even number of electrons. Thus pure molten iodine conducts the current, indicating the existence of such ions as $I^+$ and $I^-$. The conductivity of triphenylmethyl dissolved in liquid sulfur dioxide is presumably due to the ions $\varphi_3C^+$ and $\varphi_3C^-$. Chlorine dioxide dissolves in water to some extent to give chlorous and chloric acid. Similarly nitrogen dioxide gives nitrous and nitric acids, and even pure liquid nitrogen tetroxide conducts the current, thus indicating the existence of the ions $NO_2^+$ and $NO_2^-$.

If we could isolate other radicals, such for example as the methyl radical, the peculiarities of odd molecules which we have noted would become even more pronounced. The fact that the few odd molecules which have been studied can be isolated at all shows that they possess to a minimum degree the properties which would be exhibited by free radicals in general.

The simplest explanation of the predominant occurrence of an even number of electrons in the valence shells of molecules is that the electrons are definitely paired with one another. We have suspected such a pairing in the inner shells, and even in the nucleus itself, though that was but a conjecture. The evidence of the pairing of electrons in the valence shell of the typical molecule amounts very nearly to proof. When the gas $NO_2$ polymerizes to form the gas $N_2O_4$, it loses altogether its brilliant color and all the other properties which are characteristic of the odd molecule. The single molecules show all of the properties which we ascribe to a loosely bound electron. In forming the double molecule it seems as though the two odd electrons had been suddenly clamped together by some mechanism.

It is to be supposed that this tendency to form pairs is not a property of free electrons, but rather that it is a property of electrons within the atom. Even within the atom it is not necessary to assume that electrons always exhibit this phenomenon. For example, in the metals of the iron group some of the electrons which seem to be in a condiction of great mobility show no evidence of pairing. In nearly all molecules, however, we must consider the electrons as definitely grouped in pairs. In my first theory of the atom I represented the normal group of eight electrons by a cube with an electron at each corner, but the idea that electrons are coupled leads rather to the view that the stable octet is to be represented rather as a tetrahedron with a pair of electrons at each corner.

The production of a typical electron pair seems to produce and to be indicated by a state of stability in which electrons are firmly bound. We have agreed to consider the electron within the atom as synonymous with the electron orbit or elementary magnet. The pairing of electrons can therefore be regarded as equivalent to a conjugation of two such orbits accompanied by the neutralization of their magnetic fields and the elimination of magnetic moment. We shall later have opportunity to discuss these questions further.

## The Bond.

Two electrons thus coupled together, when lying between two atomic centers, and held jointly in the shells of the two atoms, I have considered to be the chemical bond.  We thus have a concrete picture of that physical entity, that "hook and eye," which is part of the creed of the organic chemist.

When two atoms of hydrogen join to form the diatomic molecule, each furnishes one electron of the pair which constitutes the bond. Representing each valence electron by a dot, we may therefore write as the graphical formula of hydrogen H : H.  So when the atom of hydrogen with its one electron unites with the atom of chlorine with

its seven electrons, they produce the molecule represented by H : C̈l : .

Two chlorine atoms form the molecule : C̈l : C̈l : .

To represent the complete structure of the chlorine molecule with its two nuclei and its thirty-four electrons we might draw such a picture as that shown in Figure 22.  However, such a two-dimensional representation cannot adequately show the spatial configuration of

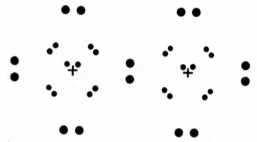

Fɪɢ. 22.—The Arrangement of Electrons in the Chlorine Molecule.  (The Large Circles Represent the Valence Electrons.)

the molecule, nor can we yet locate with any degree of finality the electrons which compose the atomic kernels.  We may be sure, however, that each of the outer shells should be represented by a pair of electrons at each corner of a tetrahedron.  Such a tetrahedron would ordinarily be regular only in the case of a symmetrical atom like that of carbon in methane, or carbon tetrachloride,

$$
\begin{array}{cc}
\text{H} & \qquad \qquad \text{:}\ddot{\text{C}}\text{l:} \\
\text{H : }\ddot{\text{C}}\text{ : H ,} & \quad \text{: }\ddot{\text{C}}\text{l : C : }\ddot{\text{C}}\text{l : .} \\
\ddot{\text{H}} & \qquad \qquad \text{:}\ddot{\text{C}}\text{l:}
\end{array}
$$

It will, however, only rarely be expedient to indicate in the simple graphical formula any distortion of the octet, although we may assume that it often occurs.  Moreover, we must constantly bear in mind, as in the case of ordinary formulæ of organic chemistry, that our two-dimensional representation fails to represent the true stereochemistry of the molecule.  Thus at first sight the formula for water, H : Ö : H, appears symmetrical, although we really regard the two hydrogens as not symmetrically placed with respect to oxygen, but rather at two corners of a more or less distorted tetrahedron. This conclusion has also been drawn from the properties of liquid crystals by Vorländer (1922).

By means of this simple assumption, that the chemical bond is a pair of electrons held jointly by two atoms, I showed how the various types of molecules "ranging from the extremely polar to the extremely nonpolar" could be interpreted. Quoting from my former paper, "Great as the difference is between the typical polar and nonpolar substances, we may show how a single molecule may, according to its environment, pass from the extreme polar to the extreme nonpolar form, not *per saltum,* but by imperceptible gradations, as soon as we admit that an electron may be the common property of two atomic shells." Whether the phrase "imperceptible gradations" is strictly accurate we shall discuss later.

The pair of electrons which constitutes the bond may lie between two atomic centers in such a position that there is no electric polarization, or it may be shifted toward one or the other atom in order to give to that atom a negative, and consequently to the other atom a positive charge. But we can no longer speak of any atom as having an integral number of units of charge, except in the case where one atom takes exclusive possession of the bonding pair, and forms an ion.

For example we may suppose that the normal state of the hydrogen molecule is one in which the electron pair is symmetrically placed between the two atoms. In sodium hydride, on the other hand, we may regard the bonding pair as lying nearer to the hydrogen than to the sodium, making the hydrogen negative; while in hydrochloric acid the bond is shifted toward the chlorine, leaving the hydrogen with a positive charge. In the presence of a polar solvent the chlorine assumes full possession of the bonding pair, and we have complete ionization. I attempted to represent these displacements of electrons by such formulæ as

$$H : H \ , \qquad Na \quad : H \ , \qquad H \quad : \overset{..}{\underset{..}{Cl}} : \ , \qquad \left[ H \right]^{+} + \left[ : \overset{..}{\underset{..}{Cl}} : \right]^{-}$$

Even a symmetrical molecule like that of $H_2$ or $I_2$ may from time to time become polarized in one direction or the other, as a consequence of the disturbance due to thermal motion. When iodine vapor is heated to a high temperature the molecule breaks in such a way as to sever the bonding pair, and forms two uncharged iodine atoms. On the other hand, in liquid iodine a few of the molecules break apart in another manner. The bonding pair remains intact but remains the exclusive property of one atom, forming $I^+$ and $I^-$. These two types of dissociation may be represented as follows:

$$: \overset{..}{\underset{..}{I}} : \overset{..}{\underset{..}{I}} : \ = \ : \overset{..}{\underset{..}{I}} . \ + \ . \overset{..}{\underset{..}{I}} : \ ; \qquad : \overset{..}{\underset{..}{I}} : \overset{..}{\underset{..}{I}} : \ = \ : \overset{..}{\underset{..}{I}} \ + \ : \overset{..}{\underset{..}{I}} : .$$

In other molecules some displacement of electrons may occur without full ionization, thus making the molecule more or less polar.

Bromine, chlorine, fluorine and hydrogen, in the order named, show a diminishing tendency toward either of the above types of dissociation. We say that the bond in the iodine molecule is looser than the bond in the chlorine molecule. We also say that iodine is a more polar substance than bromine.

The two ideas are not synonymous, but as a rule the molecule is less polar the tighter the bond. Professor Branch has called my attention to a certain ambiguity in this regard. When we speak of a polar substance or a polar molecule we imply either that the molecules are largely polarized, or that they are readily capable of polarization. In other words, we imply that the bonding pair is either displaced in one direction or the other, or that it is easily displaceable, in which case we may say that the pair is mobile. The two things ordinarily go together, but this is not invariably so. The molecule of sodium chloride is highly polarized, but the electron pair is so tightly held by the chlorine atom as to possess little mobility.

Let me quote again from my paper. "Let us turn now to a problem in the solution of which the theory which I am presenting shows its greatest serviceability. The electrochemical theories of Davy and Berzelius were overshadowed by the 'valence' theory when the attention of chemists was largely drawn to the nonpolar substances of organic chemistry. Of late the electrochemical theories have come once more into prominence, but there has always been that antagonism between the two views which invariably results when two rival theories are mutually exclusive, while both contain certain elements of truth. Indeed we may now see that with the interpretation which we are now employing the two theories need not be mutually exclusive, but rather complement one another, for the 'valence' theory, which is the classical basis of structural organic chemistry, deals with the fundamental structure of the molecule, while electrochemical considerations show the influence of positive and negative groups in minor distortions of the fundamental form. Let us consider once for all that by a negative element or radical we mean one which tends to draw toward itself the electron pairs which constitute the outer shells of all neighboring atoms, and that an electropositive group is one that attracts to a less extent, or repels, these electrons. In the majority of carbon compounds there is very little of that separation of the charges which gives a compound a polar character, although certain groups, such as hydroxyl, as well as those containing multiple bonds, not only themselves possess a decidedly polar character, but increase, according to principles already discussed, the polar character of all neighboring parts of the molecule. However, in such molecules as methane and carbon tetrachloride, instead of assuming, as in some current theory, that four electrons have definitely left hydrogen for carbon in the first case, and carbon for chlorine in the second, we shall consider that in methane there is a slight movement of the charges toward the carbon so that the carbon is slightly charged negatively, and that in carbon tetrachloride they are slightly shifted toward the chlorine, leaving the carbon somewhat positive. We must remember that here also we are dealing with averages, and that in a few out of many molecules of methane the hydrogen may be negatively charged and the carbon positively.

"In a substance like water the electrons are drawn in from hydrogen to oxygen and we have in the limiting case a certain number of hydrogen atoms which are completely separated as hydrogen ion. The amount of separation of one of the hydrogen atoms and therefore the degree of ionization will change very greatly when the other hydrogen atom is substituted by a positive or negative group. As a familiar example we may consider acetic acid, in which one hydrogen is replaced by chlorine, $H_2ClCCOOH$. The electrons, being drawn toward the chlorine, permit the pair of electrons joining the methyl and carboxyl groups to approach nearer to the methyl carbon. This pair of electrons, exercising therefore a smaller repulsion upon the other electrons of the hydroxyl oxygen, permit these also to shift in the same direction. In other words, all the electrons move toward the left, producing a greater separation of the electrons from the hydrogen of the hydroxyl, and thus a stronger acid. This simple explanation is applicable to a vast number of individual cases. It need only be borne in mind that although the effect of such a displacement of electrons at one end of a chain proceeds throughout the whole chain, it becomes less marked the greater the distance, and the more rigid the constraints which hold the electrons in the intervening atoms."

We have already commented on the interesting substance $C_6H_5SO_2OH$ which sometimes hydrolyzes to give phenol and sometimes to give benzene. It is no longer necessary to consider this substance as a mixture of two tautomeric forms, in one of which the phenyl group has a unit positive charge, and in the other of which it has a unit negative charge, for when we write the formula as follows:

$$\varphi : \overset{\displaystyle : \overset{..}{O} :}{\underset{\displaystyle : \overset{..}{O} :}{\overset{..}{S}}} : \overset{..}{O} : H \quad ,$$

we see that the bonding pair between phenyl and sulfur may be shifted toward the one or the other, and when the molecule is broken at this point, the phenyl group, if it retains possession of the bonding pair, will combine with hydrogen ion, but if it loses possession of the bonding pair will combine with hydroxyl ion.

So also in the case of nitrogen trichloride it is unnecessary to assume the existence of two distinct forms. Rather we must consider that the bonding pairs between nitrogen and chlorine may occupy many positions at varying distances from the nitrogen to the chlorine atoms. All these possibilities are comprised in the formula

$$: \overset{..}{Cl} : \\ : \overset{..}{Cl} : \overset{..}{N} : \overset{..}{Cl} : \quad .$$

These remarks will suffice for the present to show how the pair theory of the chemical bond retains every essential feature of the valence theory which has proved so valuable in the interpretation of organic chemistry, while it also interprets the electrochemical properties of the molecule. The determination of the degree of displacement of electron pairs toward this or that atom is left as a subject for further investigation. We have remarked that the present theory includes as an extreme case the modern dualistic theory; but while that theory required the several electrons to be in all cases the exclusive property of one atom or another, the new theory regards this complete separation of charges as occurring only in some molecules under some conditions.

## Other Features of the New Valence Theory.

In addition to furnishing an explanation of the single bond, and of the double and triple bonds which will be discussed in the next chapter, the new theory which I presented makes several other important changes in our ideas of valence.

It had always been supposed that the atom of oxygen in every one of its compounds is tied to another atom or atoms by two bonds. In applying the new idea of the bonding pair of electrons it became evident that many of the difficulties of the old-fashioned graphical formula, such as Werner pointed out, were at once dispelled if oxygen in many of its compounds, and especially in the oxygen acids, were assigned a single bond. In this way the artificial distinction which had previously been made between the oxygen acids and the halogen acids disappeared. This I showed by writing the following formulæ for the ions of some of the ortho-acids.

$$
\left[\begin{array}{c} :\ddot{O}: \\ :\ddot{O}:\ddot{C}l:\ddot{O}: \\ :\ddot{O}: \end{array}\right]^{-}, \quad
\left[\begin{array}{c} :\ddot{O}: \\ :\ddot{O}:\ddot{S}:\ddot{O}: \\ :\ddot{O}: \end{array}\right]^{--},
$$

$$
\left[\begin{array}{c} :\ddot{O}: \\ :\ddot{O}:\ddot{P}:\ddot{O}: \\ :\ddot{O}: \end{array}\right]^{=-}, \quad
\left[\begin{array}{c} :\ddot{O}: \\ :\ddot{O}:\ddot{S}i:\ddot{O}: \\ :\ddot{O}: \end{array}\right]^{==}.
$$

One is struck by the resemblance between these formulæ and those which we must assign to osmium tetroxide, the ion of hydrofluoboric acid, and carbon tetrachloride, namely,

$$
\begin{array}{c} :\ddot{O}: \\ :\ddot{O}:\ddot{O}s:\ddot{O}: \\ :\ddot{O}: \end{array}, \quad
\left[\begin{array}{c} :\ddot{F}: \\ :\ddot{F}:\ddot{B}:\ddot{F}: \\ :\ddot{F}: \end{array}\right]^{-}, \quad
\begin{array}{c} :\ddot{C}l: \\ :\ddot{C}l:\ddot{C}:\ddot{C}l: \\ :\ddot{C}l: \end{array}.
$$

It was evident from these and similar formulæ that in a large number of elements there is a preponderating tendency for the atom to combine with four other atoms. Thus, giving similar formulæ to ammonium ion and to methane,

$$\left[\begin{array}{c} \text{H} \\ \text{H} : \overset{\cdot\cdot}{\text{N}} : \text{H} \\ \overset{\cdot\cdot}{\text{H}} \end{array}\right]^{+} , \qquad \begin{array}{c} \text{H} \\ \text{H} : \overset{\cdot\cdot}{\text{C}} : \text{H} \\ \overset{\cdot\cdot}{\text{H}} \end{array} ,$$

I stated that "when ammonium ion combines with chloride ion the latter is not attached directly to the nitrogen, but is held simply through electric forces by the ammonium ion." Indeed it seems probable that the nitrogen atom is never attached to other atoms by more than four bonds. The new symmetrical formula for ammonium ion, and the corresponding formulæ for the substituted ammonium compounds, are in complete accord with the stereochemical and other properties of nitrogen compounds discussed by Werner.

These features of the new theory will be more fully discussed in later chapters. In my original paper I contented myself with a brief description of the main results of the theory, intending at a later time to present in a more detailed manner the various facts of chemistry which made necessary these radical departures from the older valence theory. This plan, however, was interrupted by the exigencies of war, and in the meantime the task was performed, with far greater success than I could have achieved, by Dr. Irving Langmuir in a brilliant series of some twelve articles, and in a large number of lectures given in this country and abroad. It is largely through these papers and addresses that the theory has received the wide attention of scientists.

It has been a cause of much satisfaction to me to find that in the course of this series of applications of the new theory, conducted with the greatest acumen, Dr. Langmuir has not been obliged to change the theory which I advanced. Here and there he has been tempted to regard certain rules or tendencies as more universal in their scope than I considered them in my paper, or than I now consider them, but these questions we shall have a later opportunity to discuss. The theory has been designated in some quarters as the Lewis-Langmuir theory, which would imply some sort of collaboration. As a matter of fact Dr. Langmuir's work has been entirely independent, and such additions as he has made to what was stated or implied in my paper should be credited to him alone.

# Chapter VII.

## Double and Triple Bonds.

We have seen that the normal state of a molecule is one in which each atom of hydrogen has its stable pair of electrons, and each other atom has its stable group of eight. We have seen further that in many molecules this result is attained when two atoms share between them the pair of electrons which we have called the chemical bond. There are many cases, however, in which this process of forming single bonding pairs does not suffice to complete the stable shells of the several atoms. Thus for example the atom of oxygen has but six valence electrons, and even if two atoms share an electron pair this does not suffice for the completion of two octets. On the other hand, if two pairs of electrons are shared, then each atom can be said to have its group of eight.

We therefore visualize such a union by considering each atom the center of four electron pairs arranged at the corners of tetrahedra, the two tetrahedra being joined at the two apices. Such a spatial arrangement cannot very well be represented in ordinary type, and for convenience we employ a more schematic representation of the molecule, namely, $: \overset{..}{O} : : \overset{..}{O} :$

This theory is in complete accord with the conventional theory of the double bond as it has been employed in the development of structural organic chemistry. Neither in the old nor in the new theory is the double bond to be regarded as in any sense the equivalent of two single bonds. Organic chemists speak of compounds possessing the double bond as unsaturated, and this term implies much more than a failure to comply with the simplest of valence rules. Unsaturation connotes a set of properties, all of which indicate a looseness of structure and lack of stability. Unsaturated substances as a class are characterized by a high degree of reactivity, by their tendency to change into saturated substances through a rearrangement or through the addition of other substances, and often by the existence of color. The state of unsaturation in a molecule is often manifested by a tendency to form loose complexes with other molecules. When we compare unsaturated with saturated hydrocarbons we note that the former show a marked tendency to form such complexes; thus a substance recrystallized from an unsaturated hydrocarbon frequently carries with it solvent of crystallization. The unsaturated substances are sometimes said to possess residual affinity.

All of the characteristic properties of unsaturated substances indicate that the electrons have not fallen into those positions of symmetry and low energy that they seem to occupy in saturated types. One of the most remarkable properties of ordinary oxygen is its pronounced paramagnetism. This unquestionably is connected in some very intimate manner with the unsaturated state of the oxygen molecule; the double bond does not seem to afford that conjugation of electrons (considered as orbits or magnets) which leads to the self-contained magnetic system existing in saturated molecules.

Ethylene is the typical unsaturated organic compound, and to it we may assign the formula $\overset{\text{H}}{\underset{}{\text{H}:\overset{\cdot\cdot}{\text{C}}::\overset{\cdot\cdot}{\text{C}}:\text{H}}}\overset{\text{H}}{}$ which is entirely analogous to the formula we have assigned to diatomic oxygen. Indeed there is much resemblance between these two substances. While the saturated compounds of organic chemistry are invariably diamagnetic, ethylene is distinctly paramagnetic, and the ethylene bond in any more complicated molecule diminishes the diamagnetism.

Also in their chemical reactions the two substances resemble one another. It is usually assumed that at ordinary temperatures substances oxidize first to form a peroxide. Thus hydrogen set free in the presence of oxygen forms hydrogen peroxide, and substances of the type of triphenylmethyl immediately combine with atmospheric oxygen to produce the corresponding peroxides. Such a process may be regarded as a breaking of one part of the double bond, and the phenomenon is entirely analogous to the addition of hydrogen or bromine to ethylene. In these reactions oxygen and ethylene behave almost as though they had structures represented by the formulæ,

$$\ddot{:}\ddot{\text{O}}:\ddot{\text{O}}:\dot{} , \qquad \overset{\text{H}}{\text{H}}:\overset{\cdot\cdot}{\text{C}}:\overset{\cdot\cdot}{\text{C}}:\text{H} ,$$

in which the molecules are not odd molecules, but each atom is an odd atom, in the sense that it has an unpaired electron. It must not be supposed, however, that such formulæ are anything else than gross exaggerations of the state of affairs which is associated with the double bond. Perhaps they represent extreme states which may occasionally be attained by a few molecules.

The properties of unsaturated organic substances have proved to be in very good accord with the "strain theory" proposed by Baeyer (1895). According to this theory, a bond tends to lie in a straight line joining atom to atom, and the directions of the four bonds emanating from a single carbon atom are those determined by tetrahedral symmetry. Whenever the bonds are forced out of these positions there is supposed to be a state of strain which manifests itself through instability and the general characteristics of unsaturation.

According to this idea it is possible to form a ring of five or six atoms without producing appreciable strain, but rings of three and four members require a considerable distortion of the bonds. In fact ring-compounds such as tetramethylene and trimethylene have many of the characteristics of unsaturated compounds. In the ring of two members, in other words in the double bond, the effect reaches a maximum.

I showed in my paper of 1916 that the precise equivalent of this idea is obtained in terms of the new theory "if we make the simple assumption that all atomic kernels repel one another, and that molecules are held together only by the pairs of electrons which are held jointly by the component atoms. Thus two carbon atoms with a single bond strive to keep their kernels as far apart as possible, and this condition is met when the adjoining corners of the two tetrahedra lie in the line joining the centers of the tetrahedra." Furthermore, if a carbon kernel is attached to four like kernels, these four by their mutual repulsion will assume the form of tetrahedral symmetry.

However we choose to visualize this condition of strain, it is evident that, when two atoms attempt to share not one electron pair but two, the molecule does not settle into an inert condition of high stability and low electron mobility, but rather that the system adjusts itself as it best may under the circumstances, and that in this adjustment either one or both of the bonding pairs remains in a state in which the electrons are neither tightly held nor capable of forming with each other a self-contained magnetic system. Nor can we conclude that this condition is confined to the two pairs of electrons which are supposed to constitute the double bond. The properties of such molecules show very clearly that the remaining bonds are also affected in similar manner, as though their electrons were also drawn away from their positions of greatest stability and rendered more mobile.

Thus the various phenomena which indicate the breaking of a bond—such phenomena as the disruption of a molecule or the rearrangement of radicals—almost invariably occur in the neighborhood of such a seat of unsaturation. If not as an accurate scientific analogy, at least as a metaphor, we may liken the phenomenon to the result of a strain applied to some portion of a mechanical system of elastic bodies. Other portions of the system then yield in such a manner as to reduce the strain at the first point and distribute it more evenly throughout the system. This process continues until some portion of the system, of greater rigidity, fails to take part in, or communicate further, the general yielding movement. So in an organic molecule a condition of strain produced in one atom may communicate itself through a chain of atoms, provided that these all have mobile bonds, but the effect ordinarily is greatly diminished when an atom of the saturated type is reached, that is, an atom of rigid bonds. Thus the whole benzene ring may be considered to be in a state of considerable mobility, but the benzyl radical, $C_6H_5CH_2$, behaves like a methyl radical.

One of the most interesting types of unsaturated molecule is one which contains the so-called conjugated double bonds of the types $-C=C-C=C-$, $-C=C-C=O$. In such systems the condition of unsaturation seems not to be localized at the two double bonds, but seems to be shared by that part of the molecule where the ordinary formula indicates the existence of a single bond. This process of conjugation, whatever it may be, appears to diminish the unsaturation and to increase the stability of the molecule as a whole. Thus we find that when a $\beta$-$\gamma$-unsaturated acid is heated with a base the double bond shifts to the $\alpha$-$\beta$-position as follows:

$$\underset{\underset{R}{|}}{CH} = CH - CH_2 - \underset{\underset{O}{\parallel}}{C} - OH \longrightarrow \underset{\underset{R}{|}}{CH_2} - CH = CH - \underset{\underset{O}{\parallel}}{C} - OH.$$

When such a conjugated molecule undergoes addition, the two added radicals do not necessarily enter on the two sides of a double bond, but more frequently the addition occurs in the 1-4 position as follows:

$$R - CH = CH - CH = CH - R \quad + XY \longrightarrow$$
$$R - CHX - CH = CH - CHY - R.$$

The explanation of "partial valence" given by Thiele (1899) can best be translated into the terms of the present theory by assuming such a molecule as the following with four unpaired electrons:

$$\overset{\text{H}\quad\text{H}\quad\text{H}\quad\text{H}}{H : \overset{..}{\underset{.}{C}} : \overset{..}{\underset{.}{C}} : \overset{..}{\underset{.}{C}} : \overset{..}{\underset{.}{C}} : H}.$$

But here again we must regard such a formula as a highly exaggerated representation, or as a representation of an extreme state of the molecule which only occasionally occurs.

A quite different explanation of the conjugated system may be obtained by considering the arrangement of the atoms in space. This theory, which was first advanced by Erlenmeyer (1901), has been once more brought forward by Huggins (1922), who has developed a

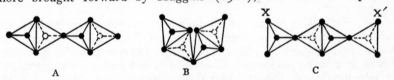

A         B         C

Fig. 23.—Conjugated Double Bonds (Huggins).

number of interesting ideas of organic structure on the basis of the new theory of valence. In Figure 23, A represents the ordinary formula of a conjugated system, while B is the picture suggested by Huggins. The carbon atoms are represented by tetrahedra, the circles showing the positions of electron *pairs*.

It is an essential part of Huggins' theory that a pair of electrons in an unstable condition attracts another similar pair (in such manner, we may suppose, as to diminish mutually their unsaturation, or to neutralize their magnetic fields). Therefore two electron pairs, one from each double bond, approach one another until they come together as in configuration B, in which the distinction between the single and the double bonds has been obliterated. In an addition reaction the two outer atoms may now be attacked, leaving the double bond between the two center atoms, as shown in configuration C.

In accordance with our present theory, it is to be noted that the tetrahedra have no significance except in so far as their corners represent the situation of electron pairs. The positions of the atomic kernels are not indicated, and it seems to me that if we are to adopt such a picture of a conjugated system we might well assume that in such a structure these kernels are pushed out toward the periphery, so that the outermost bonding pairs (being brought nearer into line with the atomic centers) possess more nearly the properties of the single bond. The greater part of the condition of unsaturation is then localized at the center of the molecule. There also it is possible that the condition of unsaturation may be largely diminished if we are willing to admit that two or more unstable bonding pairs, when brought together, tend to neutralize mutually their states of unsaturation.

(We are speaking in vague terms, and although we shall attempt to clarify our ideas somewhat in a later chapter, it seems at present impossible to give very precise definition to the ideas which we express in the term unsaturation. But we apparently imply that a pair of electrons which is unable to reach its normal or stable position is the center of a field of force or "residual affinity" which extends from the atom. It would perhaps be premature to assume that this field

FIG. 24.—Huggins' Model of the Benzene Molecule.

is a magnetic field in the ordinary sense of the term, but it seems to have the general characteristics of such a field, and to be present under circumstances in which experiments indicate that the molecule possesses a magnetic system whose field is not entirely self-contained or self-neutralized. So it is interesting to note that Pascal (1912) finds systems containing conjugated double bonds more diamagnetic than systems containing the same atoms and the same number of double bonds, but unconjugated. This seems to show that there is some process associated with conjugation which diminishes the degree of unsaturation.)

Such views of molecular structure are especially to be judged by their success in interpreting the behavior of the symmetrically conjugated system of benzene. Here Huggins employs a model of the type first suggested by Körner in 1874. It is represented in Figure 24. In this configuration there are three pairs of electrons concentrated at the center of the ring, and if we assume as before that the outer bonding pairs possess nearly the properties of single bonds, we have a picture which goes far toward portraying the benzene molecule as we know it. We must look to further experiments, especially on the possibilities of isomerism in substituted benzene, to determine whether such a configuration is admissible.

It is evident that these models of conjugated systems do not at all conform to the Baeyer strain theory (although it is to be noted that Baeyer himself proposed a benzene structure similar to that shown in Figure 24). Perhaps it could be assumed that as the bonds are distorted from their normal position a position of maximum strain can be reached, beyond which further distortion would produce a greater stability. Whether the assumed force drawing together the unstable electron pairs is sufficient to cause such distortion seems for the present to be a matter of pure conjecture.

However, I am inclined to believe that there is some change of structure of a distinctive character occurring in conjugated systems, and that it is not unlikely that this change is of the character advocated by Huggins,[1] especially if we add to his hypothesis the suggestion which I offered above, namely, that in this change the atomic kernels are displaced in such manner as to give one pair of electrons in each double bond a character more nearly resembling a single bonding pair. Whatever models of molecular structure we may assume, it must always be borne in mind that these models may at best represent the configuration of some molecules some of the time, and that most molecules, especially those with bonds of the weaker sort, are in constant tautomeric change from one configuration to another.

## The Triple Bond.

In accordance with the practice of organic chemists, we should represent a triple bond by three pairs of electrons held in common by two atoms. This is the only way in which we can assign to each carbon atom in acetylene its full quota of eight electrons. Such joining of two carbon tetrahedra at three apices should produce a very high degree of unsaturation according to the Baeyer theory of strains. Indeed it has often been assumed that the triple bond implies a much higher degree of unsaturation than the double bond, but I believe that this view is erroneous. Bromine adds much more rapidly to ethylene than it does to acetylene, and Pascal has shown that the diminution in diamagnetism is far less for the acetylene than for the ethylene linkage. On the whole it would appear that molecules which are ordinarily assigned the triple bond show less unsaturation than those which are assigned the double bond.

Whether, or to what extent, the carbon atoms in acetylene actually share three electron pairs is an open question. It is to be noted that

---

[1] There is one idea which Huggins employs which seems to me to be unsupported by the evidence. This is the idea that occasionally electrons form stable groups of three instead of the normal pairs.

while the partial rupture of an ethylene bond in a symmetrical manner requires the formation of two odd atoms, an acetylene bond may be partly broken in such a manner as to leave only a single bond, while all of the electrons remain paired, but both carbon atoms could no longer retain their complete octets. The properties of acetylene would best be explained by assuming some intermediate form or some tautomeric equilibrium between a number of configurations, such as:

$$H : C : : : C : H \quad \text{and} \quad H : \overset{..}{C} : \overset{..}{C} : H.$$

### Limitation of Multiple Bonds.

Some years ago, while comparing the properties of closely related elements, I was much mystified by the occasional large differences between substances supposed to be analogous. Thus if we compare elements of the two periods which end with fluorine and with chlorine, we see that fluorine and chlorine resemble one another closely in their physical properties, and the differences that exist are such as might be predicted from the general trend in the properties of the halogen group. On the other hand, oxygen and nitrogen differ far more from sulfur and phosphorus, and when we compare carbon and silicon and their compounds we encounter some very curious anomalies.

The tetrachlorides of carbon and silicon are both liquids and closely resemble each other, although the latter has a higher boiling point, as might be expected from its greater molecular weight. On the other hand, two substances could hardly differ more widely than do carbon dioxide and silicon dioxide. The former is a gas, the latter is a solid which does not melt or vaporize except at very high temperatures. The formulæ which have been assigned to these substances are identical, namely, $O = C = O$ and $O = Si = O$, and in no way account for the great dissimilarity in the physical properties of the two substances.

A consideration of a number of such facts led me some years ago to conclude that the ability to form multiple bonds is almost entirely, if not entirely, confined to elements of the first period of eight, and especially to carbon, nitrogen and oxygen. If silicon is incapable of sharing a double bond with oxygen, then in terms of the older valence theory we should be obliged to represent silicon dioxide as

$$- O - \overset{\displaystyle |}{\underset{\displaystyle |}{Si}} - O -$$

and the uncompleted bonds could only be completed by union with other molecules. In terms of the newer theory this would be indicated by some such configuration as

$$\overset{..}{:}\overset{..}{O} : Si : \overset{..}{O} :$$
$$\overset{..}{:}\overset{..}{O} : \overset{..}{Si} : O :$$
$$: \overset{..}{O} : \overset{..}{Si} : \overset{..}{O} : \quad .$$

Such a formula would indicate the existence of unsatisfied valences which could be satisfied only by a process of polymerization which might end in the formation of some complex ring structure with all the valences satisfied, or might lead to an indeterminate molecule, that is, a single molecule which continues to add to itself until all the material is exhausted. It is probable that silica, both in the crystalline state and in the state of a supercooled liquid, possesses such a structure, and that the whole mass may be regarded as one indeterminate molecule. In terms of the theory of electron pairs we should therefore adopt some such picture as that shown above, although this particular picture, having only two-dimensional extension, cannot be supposed to represent the actual configuration of silica.

If sulfur is unable to form a double bond, the molecule could not take the form $: \overset{..}{S} : : \overset{..}{S} :$, but rather would tend to form a continuing molecule in which one of the end atoms would have only three pairs instead of the normal group of eight, such as $: \overset{..}{S} : \overset{..}{S} : \overset{..}{S}$ . This deficiency would, however, be made up, and each atom would have its octet, if a ring were formed. In the formation of such molecules as $S_6$ and $S_8$, and in the formation of polysulfides, we have strong evidence for the correctness of this view of the structure of sulfur molecules. So also the failure to form multiple bonds in phosphorus offers an explanation of the molecule $P_4$, and possibly other complex molecules which may exist in phosphorus vapor.

The indisposition of sulfur to form double bonds is well illustrated in the organic compounds in which the oxygen of a carbonyl group is replaced by sulfur. Such substances, in so far as they have been prepared at all, show evidence of great chemical unsaturation. They are for the most part colored, and show a marked tendency to form associated molecules. The peculiar properties of the carboxyl group, in which the carbon can be replaced by silicon and the oxygen by sulfur, will be discussed at some length in a later chapter.

My observation that it is the elements with kernels of the helium type that form double and triple bonds led Eastman (1922) to a very ingenious theory of multiple bonds. He advanced the idea that the two electrons of the nucleus, which are ordinarily regarded as occupying positions of great stability and taking no part in chemical reactions, might under certain circumstances act as valence electrons in cases where they are only one step removed from the valence shell. He therefore assumed that, in cases where single bonds do not suffice to furnish the full octets, the octets are completed by the entrance of these inner electrons into the valence shell.

This is an interesting theory, and not only offers a new picture of the multiple bond, but affords the only explanation which has so far been offered to account for the existence of the two hydroborons, $B_2H_6$ and $B_4H_{10}$, which appear to be so similar to ethane and butane. Nevertheless, there are some serious objections to the acceptance of Eastman's view, the chief of which is that our X-ray data seem to indicate that the removal of electrons from the inner shell would require a far greater expenditure of energy than is available in ordinary chemical processes. It seems not impossible, however, that a modification of his theory may be useful in which it is assumed that the electrons of the inner shell remain in this position and, while serving as the inner shell of one atom, help fill the outer octet of another atom.

## Résumé

We shall have frequent occasion to discuss the phenomenon of unsaturation, for it is by no means confined to systems containing multiple bonds. Indeed there are many types of electronic arrangement which lead to degrees of unsaturation which may exceed those which occur in our multiple bond systems. Probably in any case it is a mistake to consider the process of forming a multiple bond as one which causes a condition of unsaturation. It is more likely that the reverse is true, and that we should consider the process which forms the structure known as the multiple bond as diminishing the unsaturation which would exist if this process, whatever it may be, were inhibited.

We shall have occasion again to discuss the structure of these multiply-bonded systems, although we shall not find it possible to give any definite and final picture of the electronic configurations of these mobile molecules. For the present it suffices to state that, when there are not enough electrons in a molecule to provide each atom with its stable octet by the process of forming normal bonding pairs, two contiguous atoms may, *to some extent,* share a second or third pair of electrons, although this sharing is by no means so complete or unambiguous as in the single bond; and furthermore that this ability to share a second or third pair is almost entirely limited to carbon, nitrogen and oxygen.

# Chapter VIII.

## Exceptions to the Rule of Eight.

The striking prevalence of molecules in which each atom has its full quota of four electron pairs in the outermost shell has led Langmuir to attempt to make the octet rule absolute, and he even proposes an arithmetical equation to determine, in accordance with this rule, whether a given formula represents a possible chemical substance. I believe that in his enthusiasm for this idea he has been led into error, and that in calling the new theory the "octet theory" he overemphasizes what is after all but one feature of the new theory of valence. The rule of eight, in spite of its great importance, is less fundamental than the rule of two, which calls attention to the tendency of electrons to form pairs.

The electron pair, especially when it is held conjointly by two atoms, and thus constitutes the chemical bond, is the essential element in chemical structure. Even the rule of two has its exceptions in the odd molecules, and such molecules containing an uneven number of electrons obviously cannot conform to the rule of eight. But there are many other exceptions to the octet rule and to my mind these exceptions instead of weakening the fundamental theory, strengthen it; for the reactions of such substances are just such as the great tendency to complete their broken octets would lead us to expect.

The exceptions to the rule of eight may be divided into two classes, one in which an atom has less than four electron pairs in its valence shell, and one in which it has a greater number than four. We shall see that these two types of exceptions are probably very different in character.

In my earliest speculations on this subject in 1902, I thought of the molecule of sodium chloride as produced by the complete transfer of an electron from the sodium atom to a chlorine atom, thus giving to chlorine its valence shell of eight electrons, and leaving sodium only with its inner shell of eight. The two charged particles were supposed to be held together by the electric forces then acting between the sodium ion as a whole and the chloride ion as a whole. This is the view which has been recently entertained by Langmuir in order to maintain the octet rule, which would prevent our ever assigning a chemical bond to an element like sodium. There is no question that elements like sodium do have a very great tendency to give up their electrons and form the ions. When a strong electrolyte is dissolved in water all our evidence seems to indicate that the chemical bond has disappeared, even though we may assume the existence of some un-ionized molecules. But would this be found to be the case if we should study more fully the properties of sodium chloride in the vapor state? In the fused state most typical salts have properties which indicate a completely polarized condition of the molecule, but fused beryllium chloride has a very low electrical conductivity and may be regarded as a weak electrolyte. It is best to assume that the beryllium is tied to the chlorine by definite though possibly very loose bonds. So sodium may form weak electrolytes with other anions. It is very likely that the hydrides of the alkali metals will prove to be weak electrolytes, and when we consider a substance like sodium methyl we find that it possesses no saline properties. Presumably sodium is attached to the methyl group by a chemical bond and thus possesses an uncompleted octet.

The compounds of boron are of much interest in this connection. Our knowledge of these interesting substances has been greatly clarified by the recent work of Stock (1914, 1921). The alkyl compounds of boron have vapor densities corresponding to the simple formula $BR_3$. Thus we may write for boron trimethyl or triethyl the formula

$$R : \overset{..}{\underset{..}{B}} \quad .$$
$$\overset{R}{\underset{R}{}}$$

There seems to be no way in which boron can have more than three electron pairs in its valence shell. And the properties correspond to the above formula, for boron trialkyl is highly reactive toward any substance which is capable of furnishing the electron pair to complete its octet. Thus with ammonia it forms a compound which remains undissociated when dissolved in benzene. This compound may be represented by the formula

$$\begin{matrix} R & H \\ R : \overset{..}{\underset{..}{B}} : \overset{..}{\underset{..}{N}} : H & , \\ R & H \end{matrix}$$

where a free electron pair (or, as Huggins calls it, a lone electron pair) of the nitrogen completes the boron octet. In the older valence theory the formation of such a compound would be unintelligible.

Just after the publication of my paper of 1916, Mr. A. S. Richardson, then a graduate student at Princeton University, called my attention to the great interest attaching to the boron compounds in the light of the new theory of valence, and he undertook an extensive theoretical and experimental study of the compounds of this element. This work, however, was interrupted by the war, and unfortunately has not been resumed. Undoubtedly a further study of the compounds of boron will furnish information of much value, for the compounds of no other element show so clearly the differences between the old and the new valence theories.

In the halides of boron we might allow the possibility of completing the shell of eight about the boron atom, for one of the halogen atoms might share two pairs of electrons with the boron. Indeed our present theory does not exclude the existence of doubly bonded halogens. In iodonium compounds we shall assume that the halogen atom is bonded to two other atoms, and there seems no reason to believe that fluorine might not, at least occasionally, be connected by two bonds to a single atom. But in the present instance the properties of the boron halides are fully explained by assuming a sextet of electrons in the boron shell. Thus water, ammonia, or hydrofluoric acid readily shares one lone electron pair with the boron to complete the latter's octet. The combination of boron trifluoride with hydrogen fluoride to form hydrofluoboric acid is indicated as follows:

$$
\begin{array}{ccc}
:\ddot{F}: & & :\ddot{F}: \\
:\ddot{F}:\ddot{B} \;+\; :\ddot{F}:H \;=\; & :\ddot{F}:\ddot{B}:\ddot{F}:H \;. \\
:\ddot{F}: & & :\ddot{F}:
\end{array}
$$

While molecular weight determinations of the boron trihalides show that they exist as simple molecules, both in the gaseous and in the dissolved states, it is probable that in the solid state the extra electrons of one molecule enter the uncompleted octet of another molecule, thus forming an indeterminate molecule of the type

$$
\begin{array}{cc}
:\ddot{F}: & :\ddot{F}: \\
:\ddot{F}:\ddot{B}:\ddot{F}:\ddot{B} & . \\
:\ddot{F}: & :\ddot{F}:
\end{array}
$$

Professor Hildebrand has called my attention to the probability that in the case of many solids which readily sublime, in other words which pass from the solid to the vapor state without the intervention of the liquid state, there is indication of the formation of such indeterminate or continuing molecules which exist only in the solid phase.

Entirely analogous to the boron trihalides are the corresponding aluminum compounds, and aluminum like boron frequently completes its group of eight by attaching to itself a lone pair belonging to another atom. Thus the compound between aluminum chloride and ether is entirely analogous to that between boron trichloride and water. In such manner we may visualize the various intermediate substances which presumably are formed in the important reactions of Friedel and Craft.

There is great similarity between the physical and chemical properties of boron trifluoride and of sulfur trioxide. Since sulfur does not readily form a double bond, we must write the formula of sulfur trioxide as in the following scheme, which expresses the union of sulfur trioxide and oxide ion to form sulfate ion:

$$\overset{\displaystyle :\overset{..}{O}:}{\underset{\displaystyle :\overset{..}{O}:}{:\overset{..}{O}:\overset{}{S}}} + \left[:\overset{..}{\underset{..}{O}}:\right]^{--} = \left[\overset{\displaystyle :\overset{..}{O}:}{\underset{\displaystyle :\overset{..}{O}:}{:\overset{..}{O}:\overset{}{S}:\overset{..}{O}:}}\right]^{--}.$$

In a similar way sulfur trioxide reacts with ammonia. These are all typical examples of reactions between molecules which have un-bonded electron pairs, and molecules which contain uncompleted octets. Such processes are very much like the one which occurs in the formation of ammonium ion from ammonia and hydrogen ion. Here the nitrogen furnishes the pair of electrons to complete the stable group of hydrogen, which in this case is not a group of eight but a group of two. Thus

$$[H]^+ + \overset{\displaystyle H}{\underset{\displaystyle \overset{..}{H}}{:\overset{..}{N}:H}} = \left[\overset{\displaystyle H}{\underset{\displaystyle \overset{..}{H}}{H:\overset{..}{N}:H}}\right]^+.$$

Our picture of the formation of sulfuric acid from the anhydride and water suggests a possible new type of isomers. The two following formulæ A and B may represent respectively the commoner state of the sulfuric acid molecule, and the state of the molecule when the acid is first formed.

$$(A) \quad \overset{\displaystyle :\overset{..}{O}:}{\underset{\displaystyle :\overset{..}{O}:}{H:\overset{..}{O}:\overset{}{S}:\overset{..}{O}:H,}} \qquad (B) \quad \overset{\displaystyle :\overset{..}{O}: \ H}{\underset{\displaystyle :\overset{..}{O}:}{:\overset{..}{O}:\overset{}{S} \ \ :\overset{..}{O}:H}} \ .$$

Now we shall see numerous cases of this kind in which the opportunities for isomerism are unfulfilled on account of the great mobility of the hydrogen nucleus (hydrogen ion), and its rapid exchange from one electron pair in the molecule to another. This mobility is especially marked when we are dealing with a substance of even the slightest acid properties. Werner has called attention to the possibility of isomers of the type of A and B, but he was still sufficiently under the influence of the older valence ideas to call A a valence compound and B a molecular compound. As we have written the two formulæ we see how unjustifiable such a distinction is. In the rapid tautomerism which we assume to occur between these two forms of sulfuric acid there is no change in the essential distribution of the electron pairs. We merely assume that the two hydrogen nuclei are moving about from one pair of electrons to another, and are only rarely attached to the same atom of oxygen. However, we should expect the mobility to be very greatly diminished if alkyl groups were substituted for hydrogen, and by treating an acid anhydride with an ether it is to be predicted that compounds will be formed which will not immediately rearrange to give the normal esters.

Another type of substance in which we may assume a sextet rather than an octet is represented by metaphosphoric acid. Since we are not inclined to assign a double bond to phosphorus, we may use the following formulæ to represent metaphosphoric acid and its mode of combination with water.

$$\ddot{\text{O}}: \qquad \text{H} \qquad\qquad\qquad :\ddot{\text{O}}\,[:\text{H}]$$
$$\text{H}:\ddot{\text{O}}:\ddot{\text{P}} + :\ddot{\text{O}}:\text{H} = \text{H}:\ddot{\text{O}}:\ddot{\text{P}}:\ddot{\text{O}}:\text{H}$$
$$:\ddot{\text{O}}: \qquad\qquad\qquad\qquad :\ddot{\text{O}}:$$

The resulting molecule corresponds to the formula B given for sulfuric acid. In such forms it is evident that the addition of two hydrogen ions to the same oxygen should produce a highly polar molecule. If we assume that the above transition form in the hydration of metaphosphoric acid is therefore so unstable as to exist only in very small amount, we might thus explain the slowness of hydration of this acid.

Nitric acid and carbonic acid are analogous to metaphosphoric acid. Here we would be more willing to assume a double bond between oxygen and carbon or nitrogen. But it has been pointed out by Latimer and Rodebush (1920) that the crystalline structure of solid nitrates and carbonates seems to indicate that the three oxygens are symmetrically placed with respect to the central atom. If this is also true in the dissolved state we should write, for these ions, formulæ based upon a sextet of electrons, namely,

$$\left[\begin{array}{c} :\ddot{\text{O}}: \\ :\ddot{\text{O}}:\ddot{\text{N}}:\ddot{\text{O}}: \end{array}\right]^{-} , \left[\begin{array}{c} :\ddot{\text{O}}: \\ :\ddot{\text{O}}:\ddot{\text{C}}:\ddot{\text{O}}: \end{array}\right]^{--} .$$

### Atoms with More Than Four Electron Pairs.

We must next consider a group of compounds in which the central atom appears to share pairs of electrons with more than four other atoms. Such substances are $PCl_5$, $SF_6$ and $UF_6$. At the time of the appearance of my first publication, when it became evident that there is no compound of nitrogen in which it is necessary to assume that the nitrogen atom is attached to other atoms by more than four bonds, it seemed possible that other similar apparent exceptions to the rule of eight might be explained away. Dr. E. Q. Adams and I made a full study of the available facts concerning phosphorus pentachloride in order to see whether it might possibly be assigned a formula analogous to that of ammonium chloride, as has since been done by Langmuir, namely,

$$\left[\begin{array}{c} :\ddot{\text{Cl}}: \\ :\ddot{\text{Cl}}:\ddot{\text{P}}:\ddot{\text{Cl}}: \\ :\ddot{\text{Cl}}: \end{array}\right]^{+} \left[:\ddot{\text{Cl}}:\right]^{-} .$$

We concluded, however, that the chemical facts were entirely opposed to any such assumption, and that the five chlorine atoms are directly attached to the phosphorus atom, each by a bonding pair of electrons. In other words, phosphorus is surrounded by a group of ten electrons. So also in the hexafluoride of sulfur we must consider sulfur attached to six bonds and therefore possessing a group of twelve electrons in its shell.

However, the fact that so few compounds of this type are known, and these only when the highly negative elements chlorine and fluorine are present, has suggested to me that the rule of eight may be applied to these substances in a somewhat restricted form if we amplify our ideas of the meaning of the valence shell. We have seen the value of considering a series of energy levels leading outwards from the center of the atom, and we have seen how under some circumstances it is necessary to assume that electrons pass from one level to another. In terms of this theory we may suppose that in addition to the level in which the valence shell normally falls there are outer levels into which the valence electrons may occasionally be drawn. If we call the normal level the first valence shell, it seems probably justifiable to state the universal rule that no atom ever contains more than four pairs of electrons in the first valence shell.

If we adopt this hypothesis, we must state that when an atomic kernel is attached to more than eight electrons, some or all of these electrons have passed into a secondary valence shell. Now such a transfer of electrons to a secondary shell would normally require the expenditure of energy, and therefore such a phenomenon can only be expected to occur when the entrance of these electrons into shells of other atoms provides the necessary energy. The energy released in the completion of the normal valence shell is greater in the more electronegative elements—indeed this is presumably what we mean by an electronegative element—and the maximum energy change in such a process occurs in the completion of the octet of fluorine. We may therefore assume that fluorine and occasionally other electronegative elements are able to draw the electron pairs of other atoms from the primary to the secondary valence shells.

It must, however, be clear that if we eventually find it desirable to adopt this hypothesis of secondary valence shells, it would be irrational to apply it merely to cases in which the valence electrons of an atom exceed eight. On the contrary we should probably wish to apply the same idea to many molecules in which the several atoms possess eight or even fewer electrons, for example, in molecules with double bonds. However, at present we seem hardly ready for any systematic use of this theory of secondary valence shells.

It is interesting to consider whether such substances as sulfate ion or sulfur hexafluoride are little polarized, or whether they are highly polarized but form a multipole of such symmetry as to be subject to no strong orienting forces in an electric field. The hypothesis which has just been suggested favors the latter view. The properties of sulfur hexafluoride are very remarkable. It does not behave at all like a typical polar substance. It is a gas at ordinary temperatures, which shows extraordinarily little chemical reactivity. It neither hydrolyzes with water nor reacts with molten alkali. Nevertheless, if we assume that the six pairs of electrons are drawn out from the primary valence shell of sulfur so that the fluorine atoms have almost complete possession of the electron pairs, it would leave the sulfur atom with a large positive charge. Presumably the atoms of fluorine are arranged about the sulfur atom in positions of much symmetry, perhaps in an octahedral structure, and these atoms of fluorine, which partake almost of the saturated character of fluoride ion, may serve to form a protective layer about the sulfur atom, which guards it from chemical attack.

In the case of phosphorus pentachloride we can hardly assume a condition of great symmetry, and this substance is far more reactive than sulfur hexafluoride, and exhibits an entirely different set of properties. But uranium hexafluoride appears from its physical properties to be a nonpolar substance. For example, it shows a high volatility at ordinary temperatures (although uranium tetrachloride does not volatilize until about 1000° C.), but uranium hexafluoride is highly reactive chemically, and perhaps this may be explained if we consider that the very much larger kernel of uranium is less adequately protected from external attack by the layer of six fluorine atoms.

In addition to the substances which we have been discussing, there is a large class of complex compounds which have been specially studied by Werner, and in which we are led to conclude that an atom is attached to more than four electron pairs. In such compounds as the cobaltic complexes where the ion is apparently bound to six other atoms or radicals by electron pairs, and in the anions such as $SiF_6^{--}$ and $PtCl_6^{--}$, we may eventually assume that the bonding pairs lie in the secondary valence shells of the several central atoms. Such complexes are known involving as many as eight electron pairs attached to the central atom, as in $K_4Mo(CN)_8$. Consideration of these complexes, and of the Werner coordination number, will be continued in the next chapter.

# Chapter IX.

# Valence and Coordination Number.

The normal state of an atom is one in which it possesses four pairs of electrons in the valence shell, these pairs frequently serving as bonds of attachment to other atoms. The rule of eight implies that the maximum number of bonds between a given atom and other atoms is four. Many types of atoms seem to have a tendency to employ this maximum number of bonds, or in other words, to use each electron pair as a bonding pair, but it is possible that this apparent tendency may be due to the need of electrons in order to furnish to other atoms their stable groups of eight (or in the case of hydrogen its stable group of two).

Thus ammonia is a molecule in which each hydrogen has its normal group of two, and the nitrogen atom has its group of eight electrons. This molecule tends strongly to add hydrogen ion and thus complete its four bonds, but this process might equally well be ascribed to the tendency of the hydrogen nucleus (hydrogen ion) to assume its normal group of two. Nevertheless, it seems probable that the stability of ammonium ion and of other like compounds may in part be ascribed to the tetrahedral symmetry of a structure of four bonds attached to a central atom.

In organic chemistry, where the concept of valence has been most definite and most useful, the valence of an atom is defined as the number of bonds which attach it to other atoms, whether these bonds be single or multiple. There appears to be no longer any reason for refusing to make this definition universal, so that it may be applied to inorganic compounds as well. The inorganic chemist's use of the terms positive and negative valence was shown to be misleading in so far as it is implied that we can always ascribe to each atom in a compound a definite polar number or stage of oxidation. When it is expedient to indicate the polar number, this may be done as I have suggested in a previous chapter. Thus instead of saying that cobalt is bivalent in cobaltous compounds, we shall say that it is bipositive. When we speak of its valence we shall refer, as in all other cases, to the number of its bonding pairs. Thus free cobaltous ion has zero valence, but cobaltous ion, which is attached to four molecules of ammonia, is quadrivalent. In general therefore we may define the valence of an atom in any molecule as the number of electron pairs which it shares with other atoms.

It has been proposed by Langmuir to call this number of bonds the covalence, but he has associated this term with an arithmetical equation by which he attempts to predict the existence or non-existence of chemical compounds. By fixing the maximum covalence at four he has been led to regard two compounds like $SiCl_4$ and $PCl_5$ as fundamentally different in character, and it seems to me that his rule brings back some of the arbitrary features of the older graphical formulæ which Werner criticized because they so often create artificial distinctions between entirely analogous substances. We shall therefore employ the old term valence to express the number of bonding pairs of an atom, and just as we found it necessary to conclude that some atoms contain more than eight electrons in their outer shell, so we shall be occasionally required by definition to ascribe to atoms a valence of five or six, or even eight.

However, to most of the elements of small atomic number it is sufficient to ascribe the maximum valence of four. This is the characteristic valence of carbon, and there are few compounds of this element in which it exhibits any other valence, although it has usually been considered bivalent in carbon monoxide, and it forms trivalent compounds, as typified by triphenylmethyl. When an atom of carbon is attached to less than four other atoms we ordinarily assume a sufficient number of double or triple bonds to give to carbon its full quota of four bonds. Usual as this convention is, we may suspect that on some occasions it is a little arbitrary.

Thus when we consider the ortho-acids (in which the central atom is surrounded by four oxygen atoms) we might say that in the silicates the ortho-ion, $SiO_4^{----}$, is the only one which will satisfy the maximum valence of silicon, since this element is not prone to double bond formation. But in the case of carbonic acid we assume that the ortho form can lose water without giving up the quadrivalence of carbon, thus forming ordinary carbonic acid and carbon dioxide to which we assign the formulæ $O = C(OH)_2$, and $O = C = O$. Pursuing the same line of thought with respect to nitric and phosphoric acids we note the existence of the ortho-phosphate ion $PO_4^{---}$, while ortho-nitric acid is unknown. Here we might say that nitrogen maintains its quadrivalence through a double bond, giving to nitrate ion the formula

$$\left[ \begin{array}{c} :\overset{..}{\text{O}}: \\ :\overset{..}{\text{O}}:\overset{..}{\text{N}}::\text{O}: \end{array} \right]^{-}.$$

If, however, the X-ray analysis of crystalline nitrates shows the three oxygens of nitrates to be all alike, this argument may be fallacious, and the corresponding argument regarding carbonic acid would also appear questionable. Whatever the explanation may be, it is evident that the elements of the first period of eight less frequently reach the maximum valence of four than the elements of the second period of eight.

Boron achieves its valence of four at the same time that it obtains its group of eight electrons in such compounds as $HBF_4$ and

$(CH_3)_3BNH_3$. It also appears in some mysterious way to act as a quadrivalent element in the extraordinary compounds $B_2H_6$ and $B_4H_{10}$ which Stock believed to be fully analogous to hexane and butane, $C_2H_6$ and $C_4H_{10}$. This problem we shall discuss again.

Phosphorus, arsenic and antimony, as well as sulfur, selenium and tellurium are quadrivalent in their most highly oxidized acids, and the same thing is true of bromine, chlorine and iodine in the perbromates, perchlorates and periodates, although in the latter case there is evidence of a still higher valence of iodine in salts which seem to be derived from $H_5IO_6$.

When the nitrogen atom in ammonia achieves quadrivalence by adding hydrogen ion to give the molecule

$$\left[ \begin{array}{c} H \\ H : \ddot{N} : H \\ \ddot{H} \end{array} \right]^+ ,$$

we see the prototype, not only of many reactions of nitrogen compounds, but also of compounds containing other atoms which possess lone pairs of electrons. There can be little doubt that the four hydrogens of ammonium ion are symmetrically placed about the nitrogen atom, and the stereochemistry of ammonium derivatives points definitely to conditions entirely similar to those found in carbon compounds, and indicates an arrangement deviating from perfect tetrahedral symmetry only so far as may be due to the differences in the individual radicals which are attached to the nitrogen.

When phosphine is in the presence of hydrogen ion the phosphorus attains the valence of four by adding one hydrogen ion to its lone pair of electrons, forming the symmetrical phosphonium ion $PH_4^+$.

With the exception of the elements of the argon type, every atom which possesses one or more lone pairs of electrons shows a tendency to increase its valence by adding hydrogen ion or some corresponding radical, thus forming a great group of compounds which may for brevity be called the "onium" compounds. Just as the solubility of hydrogen phosphide in water is increased by the addition of an acid, owing to the partial formation of phosphonium ion, so we find that the solubility of hydrogen sulfide in water is increased, although less markedly, by the addition of hydriodic acid. While this fact might be explained without the assumption of chemical combination, the most probable explanation of the increase in solubility is that hydrogen sulfide combines with hydrogen ion forming the first sulfonium ion according to the reaction

$$H : \ddot{S} : H + [H]^+ = \left[ \begin{array}{c} H \\ H : \ddot{S} : H \end{array} \right]^+ .$$

Numerous derivatives of this ion are known, in which organic radicals take the place of hydrogen. To form the second sulfonium ion $(H_4S)^{++}$, in which sulfur would have the valence of 4, would require the addition of another positive ion to a group already positively charged. The formation of such an ion would therefore be opposed by strong electric forces. It is quite possible that in strong acid solutions the second sulfonium ion may be produced in small amounts, but there is no proof of this, nor do we know any of the organic derivatives of this ion.

Just as ammonium ion is more stable than phosphonium ion, so we should expect the ion $OH_3^+$, which may be called the hydronium or the oxonium ion, to be more stable than the corresponding sulfonium ion. The fact that the ordinary reactions of chemistry have been studied largely in aqueous solutions has led us too frequently to ignore the possible complexes between dissolved substances and water. We have far more quantitative evidence regarding the ammonia complexes than we have regarding hydrates. The combination between ammonia and an aqueous acid is unmistakable, and when hydrochloric acid dissolves in liquid ammonia we assume that we have a solution of ammonium chloride. When hydrochloric acid dissolves in water, in all probability a similar though looser complex is formed giving the ions $OH_3^+$ and $Cl^-$. Indeed Latimer and Rodebush (1920) believe that an aqueous solution of hydrochloric acid would have the properties of a weak acid were it not for the formation of this hydronium chloride.

This tendency of oxygen to convert its lone electron pairs into bonds leads to a large number of oxonium compounds, many of which have been definitely proved to exist, while many others have been predicated to explain certain reactions. When ether is added to liquid hydrochloric acid the electrical conductivity of the latter is greatly increased. The only simple explanation of this fact is that diethyl hydronium chloride is formed with the ions

$$\left[\begin{array}{c} R \\ R:\overset{..}{O}:H \\ \phantom{..} \end{array}\right]^+ \text{ and } \left[:\overset{..}{\underset{..}{Cl}}:\right]^-.$$

So also ether and bromine give a conducting solution. In this case we may regard bromine as an extremely weak electrolyte which yields a very small amount of bromous and bromide ions. The bromous ion having an incompleted octet completes its group of eight by means of one of the lone pairs of oxygen, just as the hydrogen ion obtains its stable group of two in the same manner.

This production of a stronger electrolyte from a weak electrolyte by the formation of complexes is a very general phenomenon, first pointed out by Abegg and Bodländer (1899). We now see more clearly the nature of this phenomenon. Methyl chloride is a very weak electrolyte, but, when treated with trimethyl amine, the strong tetramethyl ammonium chloride is produced, namely,

$$\left[\begin{array}{c} R \\ R:\overset{..}{N}:R \\ R \end{array}\right]^+ \quad \left[:\overset{..}{\underset{..}{Cl}}:\right]^-.$$

Here the chloride ion is attached to the complex ion by no chemical bond. The only force holding the two ions together is the electric force due to their charges, and the substance must be a strong electrolyte. (When the hydrogens of ammonium ion are not all replaced by organic radicals there is the possibility of a chemical bond which we shall discuss in a later section.)

The normal halide ions have zero valence, but they readily add hydrogen ion to form the acids, and it is probable that occasionally another hydrogen ion is added to one of the lone pairs. Thus it is possible that such small conductance as is possessed by pure liquid hydrochloric acid may be due to the formation of what might be called chloronium chloride, with the formula $[H_2Cl]^+[Cl]^-$. This, however, is merely a conjecture, and the only compounds of this type whose existence has been demonstrated are illustrated by diphenyl iodonium ion,

$$\left[ \varphi : \ddot{\ddot{I}} : \varphi \right]^+.$$

To form the highest iodonium ion such as $IR_4^{+++}$ it would be necessary to overcome very powerful electric forces, and it is not likely that such a compound will be prepared.

It is to be noted that the formation of the typical "onium" ions is a process which differs in no essential respect from other processes in which hydrogen or other radicals become attached to lone pairs. Thus, starting with oxide ion, the addition of one hydrogen ion produces the ion $OH^-$, the addition of two produces water, and the addition of three produces the hydronium ion. So likewise we may think of nitride ion being converted, by successive additions of hydrogen ion, to imide ion, amide ion, ammonia and ammonium ion.

It very often happens that a molecule contains several atoms capable of attaching hydrogen to form an "onium" compound, and in such cases there are interesting possibilities of rearrangement or tautomerism as the hydrogen is transferred from one atom to another. In the compound of $SO_3$ and HCl the hydrogen may remain with the chlorine or go to the oxygen. So hydroxylamine may be regarded as a mixture of the two tautomers

$$H : \ddot{\ddot{N}} : \ddot{\ddot{O}} : H, \qquad H : \overset{\overset{\textstyle H}{\textstyle\vdots}}{\ddot{N}} : \ddot{\ddot{O}} :$$
$$\overset{\textstyle\cdots}{H} \qquad\qquad\qquad \overset{\textstyle H}{}$$

and while the tautomerism is too rapid to permit the isolation of either of these compounds, when the hydrogen is replaced by the far more immobile alkyl radicals we find isomers of both types, namely, the alkyl hydroxylamines and the amine oxides.

So also phosphorous acid, $H_3PO_3$, may be regarded as a mixture of the two tautomers

$$
\begin{array}{cc}
\overset{\displaystyle H}{\underset{}{:\!\overset{..}{O}\!:}} & \\
H\!:\!\overset{..}{\underset{..}{O}}\!:\!\overset{..}{\underset{..}{P}}\!:\!\overset{..}{\underset{..}{O}}\!:\!H, & 
H\!:\!\overset{..}{\underset{..}{O}}\!:\!\overset{\displaystyle :\!\overset{..}{O}\!:}{\underset{\displaystyle H}{P}}\!:\!\overset{..}{\underset{..}{O}}\!:\!H
\end{array}
$$

Here again organic derivatives of both types are known. We shall later have occasion to discuss further this interesting kind of tautomerism, which indeed is of the same character as the tautomerism which we have recently discussed in the case of sulfuric acid. The fact that only two hydrogens of phosphorous acid are readily replaced by metals, indicates that the second of the above forms is the one which chiefly exists, and that the hydrogen is bound to the phosphorus by a much stronger tie than to the oxygen. So also hypophosphorous acid, $H_3PO_2$, has but one replaceable hydrogen, and the other two hydrogens may be regarded as attached to the phosphorus.

Werner calls attention to the interesting series of compounds from phosphate ion to phosphonium ion. These exhibit in a remarkable way the quadrivalence of phosphorus. With minor changes his formulæ are in complete harmony with our system, according to which this series of compounds may be written as follows. (The next to the last compound is not known as such, but gives organic derivatives, the trialkylphosphine oxides.)

$$
\left[\begin{array}{c}
:\!\overset{..}{O}\!: \\
:\!\overset{..}{O}\!:\!\overset{..}{P}\!:\!\overset{..}{O}\!: \\
:\!\overset{..}{\underset{..}{O}}\!:
\end{array}\right]^{\!-\!-\!-},\quad
\left[\begin{array}{c}
H \\
:\!\overset{..}{O}\!:\!\overset{..}{P}\!:\!\overset{..}{O}\!: \\
:\!\overset{..}{\underset{..}{O}}\!:
\end{array}\right]^{\!-\!-},\quad
\left[\begin{array}{c}
H \\
:\!\overset{..}{O}\!:\!\overset{..}{P}\!:\!\overset{..}{O}\!: \\
H
\end{array}\right]^{\!-},
$$

$$
\begin{array}{c}
H \\
H\!:\!\overset{..}{P}\!:\!\overset{..}{\underset{..}{O}}\!: \\
H
\end{array},\quad
\left[\begin{array}{c}
H \\
H\!:\!\overset{..}{P}\!:\!H \\
H
\end{array}\right]^{\!+}.
$$

### Bivalent Hydrogen.

It seems to me that the most important addition to my theory of valence lies in the suggestion of what has become known as the hydrogen bond. The idea was first suggested by Dr. M. L. Huggins, and was also advanced by Latimer and Rodebush, who showed the great value of the idea in their paper to which reference has already been made.

This suggestion is that an atom of hydrogen may at times be attached to two electron pairs of two different atoms, thus acting as a loose bond between these atoms. Thus it is assumed that two molecules of water may unite as follows:

$$
\begin{array}{cc}
H\!:\!\overset{..}{\underset{..}{O}}\!:\!H\!:\!\overset{..}{\underset{..}{O}}\!: & . \\
H \qquad H &
\end{array}
$$

The atom of hydrogen attached to the two oxygen atoms represents the new type of bond. This theory of the hydrogen bond offers an immediate explanation of a large number of complexes involving water, ammonia and other such compounds, which have hitherto been inexplicable by any kind of structural formula.

For example, we know that hydrofluoric acid consists very largely of double molecules. In its acid salts the ion is $HF_2^-$, but in its neutral salts the ion contains but one atom of fluorine, $F^-$. We know nothing which would lead us to suspect that two normal fluorine ions, each of which has its completed octet, would combine with one another. The whole phenomenon, however, is very simply explained if we admit the possibility that an atom of hydrogen ties together the two fluorine atoms, as indicated in the following formulæ:

$$H : \overset{..}{\underset{..}{F}} : H : \overset{..}{\underset{..}{F}} : \, , \quad \left[ : \overset{..}{\underset{..}{F}} : H : \overset{..}{\underset{..}{F}} : \right]^-.$$

It is a striking fact that the liquids whose behavior indicates a large measure of association, and which have the high dielectric constant and ionizing power which seem to be an accompaniment of this association, are compounds which contain hydrogen as well as lone electron pairs. Such substances are water, ammonia, hydrogen peroxide, hydrocyanic acid and hydrofluoric acid. The postulate of the hydrogen bond certainly offers a very simple picture of the association of such molecules.

Ammonium hydroxide is a weak electrolyte, but tetramethyl ammonium hydroxide is a strong electrolyte. It has usually been supposed that this difference is due to the fact that ammonium hydroxide is largely dissociated according to the reaction $NH_4OH = NH_3 + H_2O$, a type of dissociation which cannot occur in the case of tetramethyl ammonium hydroxide. It was believed that the $NH_4OH$ existing as such would have all the properties of a strong base. Latimer and Rodebush offer an alternative explanation. They write the formula for ammonium hydroxide as

$$\overset{\textstyle H}{\underset{\textstyle H}{H : \overset{..}{N} : H : \overset{..}{\underset{..}{O}} : H}} \, .$$

In this picture the nitrogen is still quadrivalent, but the molecule as a whole is held together not merely by the electric force between two oppositely charged ions but by definite characteristic bonds, and the weakness of the base is due to the difficulty of breaking the hydrogen bond. On the other hand it is not assumed that the hydrogen of the methyl group is capable of acting as a bond, and therefore tetramethyl ammonium ion and hydroxide ion are held together only by virtue of their opposite charges.

In the preceding chapter I have suggested that when an atom is attached to more than four electron pairs, these are not in the first valence shell but in a secondary (or coordination) shell. The same thing may be true of hydrogen (in which the stable shell is composed of two electrons instead of the normal group of eight). Hydrogen when attached firmly to a pair of electrons, as in the hydrogen-hydrogen or hydrogen-carbon bond, shows no tendency whatsoever to become bivalent, or in other words, to form a hydrogen bond. On the other hand, when combined with an extremely negative element like nitrogen, oxygen or fluorine, toward which the electron pairs are very tightly drawn, the bonding pair may be drawn out of the first valence shell of hydrogen into a secondary shell, and it is apparently under some such circumstances that the hydrogen atom can form a loose attachment to another pair of electrons, thus forming the hydrogen bond.

## The Quadrivalence of Nitrogen.

In the older theory of valence nitrogen atoms with five bonds were a part of the regular stock in trade of the chemist. When I claimed that nitrogen is never more than quadrivalent I did not mean to deny the theoretical possibility of a compound such as $NF_5$, in which the nitrogen atom would be bonded to five other atoms, corresponding to the compound $PCl_5$ which we have already discussed. What I maintained, and still maintain, is that in any compound now known the nitrogen atom is never attached to more than four bonds. We have seen that in terms of the new valence theory the double bonds which were formerly used between nitrogen and oxygen, and which required the quinquivalence of nitrogen, are now for the most part replaced by single bonds. So also we have seen that in salts of the ammonium type, like tetramethyl ammonium chloride, the anion is not attached to the cation at all, and that if it is attached to the cation in the simple ammonium salts, it has a bond to a hydrogen but not to the nitrogen atom.

The amine oxides form a very interesting class of nitrogen compounds. The old and the new theories are represented by the formulæ $R_3N = O$, and $R_3N — O$. Such oxides when treated with an alkyl iodide form iodides which are strong electrolytes. It was shown by Meisenheimer (1913) that, when the iodide ion is replaced by an alcoholate ion, isomeric substances can be prepared, to which he assigned formulæ which are in complete accordance with our present views, namely,

$$[R_3NOR']^+ [OR']^- \text{ and } [R_3NOR']^+ [OR]^-.$$

On the other hand, L. W. Jones (1914), using the modern dualistic theory, and the idea of quinquivalent nitrogen, wrote the formulæ with both oxygens attached directly to the nitrogen, and called the two substances electromers; for he believed that one oxygen was negatively charged and the other positively charged, and that one or the other isomer is produced according as the positive atom of oxygen is attached to R or to R'. I understand, however, from Professor Jones that his prevent view of the structure of these isomers would essentially coincide with my own.

At the same time I am obliged to admit that I made privately a prediction regarding these compounds which I am now forced to retract. Regarding the positive ion $R_3NOR^+$ as analogous to tetramethyl ammonium ion, and unwilling to admit the possibility of an anion attached by a fifth bond to nitrogen, I predicted that both the salts and the hydroxide of this cation would prove to be strong electrolytes. In work by Professor T. D. Stewart and Dr. Sherwin Maeser which has not as yet been published, this question was investigated, and it was found that compounds of the type $(R_3NOR)I$ behave in aqueous solution as typical strong electrolytes, but that they hydrolyze, showing that the corresponding base is weak. It was also found that in absolute alcohol these salts absorb hydrogen ion when an acid is added. These observations which at first sight seem baffling are very simply explained on the theory of the hydrogen bond.

Let us for the sake of simplicity revert to the aqueous solutions of amine oxide itself. These oxides combine with *two* molecules of water to form very stable compounds,—a fact which obviously is not explained by assuming nitrogen to be quinquivalent. Let us assume that these two molecules of water form an "onium" compound with the oxygen rather than with the nitrogen. We may then picture the amine oxide dihydrate as follows:

$$
\begin{array}{c}
: \overset{\cdot\cdot}{\underset{\cdot\cdot}{O}} : H \\
R \quad H \\
R : \overset{\cdot\cdot}{\underset{\cdot\cdot}{N}} : \overset{\cdot\cdot}{\underset{\cdot\cdot}{O}} : \\
R \quad H \\
: \overset{\cdot\cdot}{\underset{\cdot\cdot}{O}} : H \; .
\end{array}
$$

Such a compound, in which each hydroxyl radical is held to the remainder of the molecule by a definite bond, would be expected to act as a weak base. This is in accordance·with the facts. In other words, the weakness of the base is not caused by the attachment of one of the hydroxyl groups to a fifth bond of nitrogen, but rather by attachment to oxygen through the hydrogen bond. When the amine oxide is dissolved in absolute alcohol instead of in water the formation of the oxonium complex may be presumed to be far more limited, and when acid is introduced hydrogen ion may be added directly to a lone pair of the oxygen, forming the ion.

$$
\left[
\begin{array}{c}
R \\
R : \overset{\cdot\cdot}{\underset{\cdot\cdot}{N}} : \overset{\cdot\cdot}{\underset{\cdot\cdot}{O}} : H \\
R
\end{array}
\right]^+ .
$$

Another group of substances which is particularly interesting to the theory of quadrivalent nitrogen has been obtained by Schlenck and Holtz (1917). The first of these substances has five hydrocarbon radicals to a single nitrogen atom, namely, four methyl groups and one triphenylmethyl group. This substance, however, was found to be an electrolyte, and is doubtless to be regarded as a salt with a triphenylmethyl anion, namely, $[N(CH_3)_4]^+$ $[C(C_6H_5)_3]^-$. They obtained similar compounds, in which diaryl amino groups replace the triphenylmethyl, which also gave conducting solutions in pyridine. They concluded that the combination "is of a salt-like or ionogen character." They further remark, "We thus see a confirmation of the assumption that in the ammonium compounds the fifth valence of nitrogen is under all circumstances otherwise constituted than the four other affinities." Finally they obtained a compound which according to its method of preparation and its analysis has the formula $(C_6H_5CH_2)N(CH_3)_4$. This substance may be the nearest approach yet obtained to a compound with quinquivalent nitrogen, but no solvent could be found in which the substance dissolved without decomposition, and it therefore could not be very fully investigated.

In stating that no quinquivalent compounds of carbon or nitrogen are known, we should not exclude the possibility that unstable substances of this type may appear in a transitory form during the progress of a chemical reaction, and indeed there are cases in which the mechanism of a reaction may best be interpreted by the assumption of a fleeting addition compound to an atom of carbon or nitrogen that is already quadrivalent. This is especially true when two of the bonds constitute a double bond, but may also be assumed when the central atom is attached to four other atoms. As an example let us consider very briefly the very interesting phenomenon known as the *Walden inversion*.

This phenomenon is observed when a dextro-rotary substance is passed through a cycle of processes resulting finally in the lævo-rotary form of the original substance. There seems to be but one possible way of accounting for this peculiar behavior. Let us consider a carbon attached to the four radicals $R_1$, $R_2$, $R_3$, and $R_4$, and let us assume that a fifth group $R_5$ becomes temporarily attached to the carbon atom near to the face of the tetrahedron which is opposite to $R_1$. A slight shift of the kernel might make it now the center of a new tetrahedron with corners at $R_2$, $R_3$, $R_4$, and $R_5$, while $R_1$ would become detached from the molecule. Then if the radical $R_5$ in the new molecule were to be replaced by the radical $R_1$, the resulting molecule would be the mirror image of the one with which we started. In this explanation it is not necessary to assume that the five radicals are attached to the carbon for any appreciable period of time, indeed it might be assumed that the $R_1$ leaves at the same instant that the $R_5$ becomes attached to the carbon atom.

## Valences Higher Than Four.

In substances like phosphorus pentachloride and sulfur hexafluoride we find a central atom attached to more than four other atoms. We have mentioned a similar case in per-iodic acid. Indeed iodine frequently shows evidence of holding six pairs of electrons instead of the normal four. Thus we have the group of compounds which contain what is ordinarily and I think correctly called trivalent iodine, of which the simplest example is hydrogen tri-iodide. Here we may assume that one atom of iodine is the central atom, is attached to the hydrogen and to the two other iodine atoms by bonds, and possesses altogether six electron pairs. In the same way we may interpret iodine trichloride and numerous other inorganic and organic compounds of iodine.

The majority of cases of valence higher than four are found in the complexes formed by metallic salts. One of the greatest services rendered to chemistry by Werner consisted in the classification and elucidation of such complexes. He showed that an atom such as the atom of chromium or cobalt lies in the center of a coordination zone in which a certain number of radicals are attached to the central atom, and this number he called the coordination number.

All of the radicals which enter into such coordination groups are substances which possess lone pairs of electrons, like $H_2O$, $NH_3$, $NO_2^-$, $Cl^-$ and the like, and doubtless one of these lone pairs is employed in attaching each radical to the central atom. Thus free cobaltic ion, $Co^{+++}$, has no valence electrons, and when it combines with six molecules of ammonia to form an ion of the "hexammin" type, we may consider the cobalt atom as attached to six electron pairs, probably situated at the corners of a regular octahedron. Each molecule of ammonia thus furnishes one of the bonding pairs, and by our broad definition of valence we may say that the cobalt atom has the valence of six. In other words, valence and coordination number are the same thing. So also, if we choose, we may say that the coordination number is four for sulfur in the sulfates, is four for carbon in most of its compounds, and is four for nitrogen in ammonium salts.

Whether we speak of the valence or the coordination number, there are two ideas that must be distinguished. It is sometimes customary to speak of the valence or the coordination number of an element without referring to any particular compound. The normal or maximum valence or coordination number of the element is then meant. When we are referring to a definite molecule the valence or the coordination number expresses the actual number of bonding pairs attached to the atom in question. Thus it is occasionally convenient to speak of the coordination number of carbon as four or of the cobaltic ion as six, although there are some compounds in which this maximum number of bonds is not employed.

Many of the varied phenomena shown by the complexes formed with metal salts can be ascribed to the replacement of one radical by another, and if one of the radicals is a neutral compound and the other is an ion, an interesting series of compounds results which may be illustrated by Figure 25, which is taken from Werner, and which shows the molecular conductance, at a concentration of 0.001 normal, of a series of complex platinous salts. Here the coordination number is four, and, as the ammonia molecules are replaced by chloride ion, the complex changes from a doubly charged positive ion to a doubly charged negative ion. The substance in the middle of the series is uncharged and is essentially a non-electrolyte, as shown in the diagram.

Often such complexes are held together very firmly, and the process of replacement of one atom by another is a very slow one. Nevertheless, the general character of such compounds seems to support the idea that the bonds operating in these complexes are not identical with our typical bonds, such as the one joining carbon to carbon. In other words, we may again assume that the electron pairs do not lie in the primary valence shell of the central atom, but in a secondary valence shell.

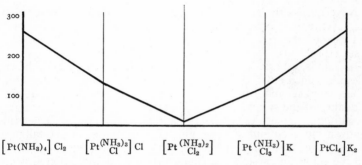

$$\left[\text{Pt(NH}_3)_4\right]\text{Cl}_2 \quad \left[\text{Pt}^{(\text{NH}_3)_3}_{\text{Cl}}\right]\text{Cl} \quad \left[\text{Pt}^{(\text{NH}_3)_2}_{\text{Cl}_2}\right] \quad \left[\text{Pt}^{(\text{NH}_3)}_{\text{Cl}_3}\right]\text{K} \quad \left[\text{PtCl}_4\right]\text{K}_2$$

FIG. 25.—Conductivity of Complex Platinous Salts (Werner).

If this idea proves to be correct, we might make a distinction between valence and coordination number. We could call a primary bond a valence bond, and a secondary bond—one in which the electron pair is not in the primary valence shell of each of the atoms which it unites—a coordination bond. But if this were to be done it would be absurd to consider that coordination bonds exist only in cases where more than four bonds are attached to a single atom. Rather it would be necessary to class as coordination bonds many that are now considered as ordinary valence bonds. I believe, however, that our present knowledge is insufficient to permit any systematic discrimination of this kind.

It will therefore suffice to point out the probability that the bonding electrons, which hold the several radicals to a central atom of a metallic element in the coordination zone, are not ordinarily in the valence shell of that atom. Nor do metals as a rule seem able to hold electrons tightly. There are, however, some exceptions, and mercuric mercury, in its salts and in its various compounds with organic radicals, seems to form a bond which is not unlike the typical bonds of organic compounds.

## Valence in Condensed Systems.

Hitherto we have been considering the molecular structure of only those substances in which the molecule is a well defined entity, or in other words, which possess a definite molecular weight. This will also be our practice in succeeding chapters, and we shall not ordinarily base our valence rules upon information concerning the stoichiometric relationships in solid substances. For example, it would be undesirable to consider that one of the atoms in cadmium sulfate has a coordination number of 8/3 merely because the hydrate has the empirical composition $CdSO_4.8/3H_2O$. Rather we must assume that in this crystal there is an arrangement of the particles in which 8 molecules of water enter to every 3 atoms of cadmium.

Nevertheless the structure of crystals and other condensed systems must eventually come within the scope of valence theory, and we shall devote the remainder of this chapter to a brief consideration of such problems.

In liquids, especially of the "sticky" kind, and in glasses, the simple molecules which exist in the gaseous state presumably become attached to one another and often form chains or groups in which the individuality of the simple molecule is partly or wholly lost. Such groups, or continuing molecules, probably have an extent which is determined by adventitious circumstances. On the other hand in crystalline substances these continuing molecules may be conceived as coterminous with the complete crystal, and characterized by a well-ordered arrangement, except where the crystal is distorted or broken.

Through the study of crystalline form, and especially through recent investigations concerning the reflection of X-rays, we have obtained important information regarding the structure of crystals. We are able to fix the positions of the heavier atoms with much certainty; the lighter atoms are located with greater difficulty, and hitherto we have been unable, except by inference, to ascertain the positions of the electron pairs which constitute the atomic valence shells.

However, we already know enough regarding crystal structure to state that there is in general a great difference in the laws of chemical combination and in the arrangement of electrons and atomic kernels, between crystalline substances on the one hand and gaseous substances on the other hand. In the latter case those forces which we know as chemical affinity must be wholly or largely satisfied within the confines of a limited molecule; in the former these forces may manifest themselves as so-called crystalline forces operating through a continuing molecule of unlimited size.

In our discussion of silicon dioxide in Chapter VII, we have shown how such a continuing molecule might arise merely through the formation of ordinary chemical bonds, and there are doubtless a number of crystals which may be adequately treated in this manner. The most striking case is furnished by diamond, in which each carbon atom is equidistant from four similar atoms, and there can be little doubt that it is joined to each by a bonding pair of electrons. Diamond may therefore be regarded as a saturated organic compound in which each carbon atom is joined by a typical bond to four other atoms, and it is not unlikely that the rigidity of the bond and the distance apart of two bonded carbon atoms are about the same as in the molecule of ethane.

As a rule, however, crystalline structures are not governed by ordinary valence rules. This problem has been discussed in a very interesting manner by Langmuir (1916). In a crystal of sodium chloride each sodium atom is positively charged and is equidistant from six negatively charged chlorine atoms; and also each chloride ion is surrounded by six sodium ions. If the molecule of sodium chloride in the gaseous state condenses upon a crystal of sodium chloride the gaseous molecule completely loses its identity and the atom of sodium belongs as much to five other chlorine atoms as to the one to which it was previously joined.

Another class of crystals is composed of molecules which are chiefly saturated internally, so that each molecule becomes the unit of a crystal, in which the several molecules are held together by only a slight residuum of chemical affinity. Solid argon, nitrogen and hexane may be taken as examples of this class. Here the same molecule that exists in the gaseous state preserves its identity in the crystal. The same two atoms of nitrogen which condense together when the gas is solidified will reappear together when the solid is vaporized. An optically active organic substance is not racemized by alternate crystallization and melting.

Presumably a substance like carbon tetrachloride would preserve its molecular identity on crystallization, but whether this would also be true of carbon tetraiodide seems less certain. There is much interesting work to be done in testing experimentally this problem of the preservation of the identity of molecules in crystals. For example, it would be very interesting to know whether solid iodine keeps together the two atoms which constitute the gaseous molecule.

There obviously must be many gradations between the two extreme types, namely, the crystal in which the primary chemical forces are largely satisfied inside the unit molecule, and the one in which the chemical bond, or something very like it, is operating as a crystalline force. On the one hand we have very soft crystals like paraffin or carbon tetrachloride, on the other extremely hard substances like diamond and quartz. Intermediate are saline substances in which there are, practically speaking, no chemical bonds, but in which the atoms are strongly held together by the electrostatic force between oppositely charged particles. The difference between the extreme types is shown also in a comparison of melting and subliming points. A small degree of thermal agitation is sufficient to destroy a crystal of paraffin or carbon tetrachloride, but a very high temperature is needed to melt or sublime substances like quartz and diamond.

A substance of the latter type, in which the chemical affinities are largely satisfied, not by the formation of small units, but by the packing together of layer upon layer of atoms, must exhibit at the crystal surface a very high degree of chemical unsaturation, and it is upon such surfaces that we must look for powerful and specific adsorption of molecules which are capable of partially relieving that condition of unsaturation. The great amount of heat which is set free when water is added to finely divided silica illustrates the magnitude of the energy changes accompanying such a process.

## Résumé

Defining valence as the number of bonds which are attached to a given atom, or the number of electron pairs which that atom shares with others, we may regard the maximum valence of four as a sort of norm. However, we find a great many cases in which an atom shares more than four pairs with other atoms and, although we suspect that in all such cases the electrons are drawn farther from the central atom than in the typical bond, we are not yet able to make a definite classification on this basis. For the present we must regard valence and coordination number as synonymous. Hence there are many elements to which must ascribe a higher valence than four and the number will doubtless be increased by further investigation. Thus Professor W. A. Noyes has called my attention to the fact that the dihydrate of perchloric acid is more stable in the vapor state than the anhydrous acid; this indicates very strongly a coordination compound in full analogy with periodic acid. Possibly also the dihydrate of sulfuric acid is not an ordinary hydrate formed through hydrogen bonds but rather has six hydroxyl groups attached to sexivalent sulfur.

# Chapter X.

# Compounds of Elements with Small Kernels.

Although the kernel of the atom usually takes no direct part in chemical combination, its size and structure must play a large part in determining the behavior of the valence electrons. The degree of complexity of the kernel determines the distance of separation of the several valence pairs, and the forces which evidently oppose the close approach of two valence shells or two kernels to one another, make it possible to speak roughly of the size of the atom.

Indeed in a crystal at low temperatures the molecules, the atoms, and the constituent parts of the atoms, may be regarded as occupying definite positions, and the structure of the unit crystal may be considered as repeated with complete regularity throughout the whole crystalline mass. From the study of the reflection of X-rays it has already become possible to ascertain the location of the several nuclei and to draw some inferences as to the location of the several electrons. Further refinements of this method will doubtless permit the complete localization of the valence electrons, and possibly the arrangement of the kernel electrons as well.

By this method, and through the aid of the known densities of substances, Bragg (1920) has made some calculations of the radii of the outer shells of various atoms. Some of the values which he thus obtained are given in the accompanying table, in which are compared the radii obtained by such a study of the several substances in their crystalline state with the radii of the corresponding molecules in the gaseous state, calculated from the gaseous viscosity by Rankine (1921).

Both methods of calculation rest on some assumptions, but the values doubtless show the approximate dimensions of the several molecules and the relative size of the light and heavy molecules. We see that the dimensions of the atom increase as the number of electron shells is increased, but the effect is partly offset by the gradual drawing in of the several shells as the positive charge of the nucleus (the atomic number) increases, so that the radius of xenon is less than twice as great as the radius of helium.

A far more accurate method of determining molecular radii is promised in the present intensive study of the ultra red spectrum of gases. I cannot enter here upon a discussion of the method of thought employed in these investigations, and shall only mention one or two of the data obtained. I am indebted to Mr. H. C. Urey for a list

TABLE.

MOLECULAR RADII IN THE CRYSTALLINE AND IN THE GASEOUS STATES.

| | Radius $(10^{-8}\text{ cm})$ Bragg | Radius $(10^{-8}\text{ cm})$ Rankine | | Radius $(10^{-8}\text{ cm})$ Bragg | Radius $(10^{-8}\text{ cm})$ Rankine |
|---|---|---|---|---|---|
| Helium .......... | .... | 0.94 | HF .............. | 0.65 | 1.17 |
| Neon ............ | 0.65 | 1.17 | HCl ............. | 1.02 | 1.43 |
| Argon ........... | 1.02 | 1.43 | HBr ............. | 1.17 | 1.58 |
| Krypton ......... | 1.17 | 1.59 | HI .............. | 1.35 | 1.75 |
| Xenon ........... | 1.35 | 1.75 | | | |

of the latest results obtained by himself and others through this method. From the work of Kratzer (1920) one-half the distance between the atoms is $0.46 \times 10^{-8}$ for HF, $0.63 \times 10^{-8}$ for HCl, and $0.70 \times 10^{-8}$ for HBr. Some other molecular dimensions obtained by this method will be mentioned later. In the meantime it will be noted that the values are considerably lower than those given in the table, although they are arranged in the same order with respect to the several substances.

A very recent paper by Bragg (1922), in which he discusses some results obtained by X-ray reflection, casts some doubt upon the arrangement of electrons in shells with eight in the outer shell, as proposed in my paper of 1916. His work leads him to believe that a smaller number of electrons than eight exist in the outer shells. I think, however, that his observations would have been otherwise interpreted if he had taken into consideration the fact that the atoms in a crystal at ordinary temperatures are in a state of motion, with amplitude sufficient to make the volume considerably greater than it would be at the absolute zero. It would be desirable if his experiments could be repeated with crystals at very low temperatures.

## Hydrogen and Helium.

The kernel of the hydrogen atom is unique in that it is composed merely of the nucleus, and therefore can be considered to have practically no volume, and this singularity is manifested in the chemical behavior of hydrogen. Unlike all other atoms which enter into chemical compounds, its stable shell is not a group of eight but a group of two. When it acquires exclusive possession of two electrons it becomes the hydride ion, $H^-$, which has the same structure as the neutral atom of helium and the positive ion of lithium. Hydride ion, as we have remarked in an earlier chapter, is to be regarded as entirely analogous to the halide ions, in each of which the stable group has been produced by the addition of one electron.

When hydrogen is attached to a bonding pair it possesses more the character of a negative than of a positive element. Thus without committing ourselves to any quantitative statement, we may safely say that methane is more like methyl chloride than it is like sodium methyl.

The hydrogen nucleus may be considered as lying very close to a bonding pair, and if we examine the figures of the above table we see that hydrofluoric acid which, except for the hydrogen nucleus, has the same structure as neon, is also given the same radius by both of the experimental methods. The same thing is true of the other acids and the corresponding rare gases. The exactness of the agreement is perhaps accidental, but it seems likely that a molecule of hydrogen halide has about the same dimensions as the halide ion alone would have.

When hydrogen loses its electron pair and becomes hydrogen ion it is altogether without electron shells and, as we have remarked, it is practically without volume. It therefore does not suffer from those "steric" effects to which all other atoms are subject, and may therefore be presumed to be capable of an exceptional degree of mobility. Indeed many types of tautomerism or rapid rearrangement, both in inorganic and in organic chemistry, may be ascribed to the movement of the hydrogen nucleus, and we shall see that in many cases the essential structure of a molecule can best be understood if we leave entirely out of consideration those atoms of hydrogen which are easily removed as hydrogen ion.

When an acid dissolves in our ordinary solvents it is to be supposed that hydrogen ion does not exist largely in the free state, but rather is held to the solvent in an "onium" complex. Nevertheless, we are tempted to explain some of the peculiar properties of acid solutions by assuming that the hydrogen ion is occasionally in the free state.

The atom of helium, which is also characterized by the stable group of two, is also electrically neutral when in exclusive possession of such a group, and chemists have found no evidence of its chemical combination with other elements. On the other hand, the band spectrum of helium is interpreted by the physicists as due to a molecule containing two helium atoms.

It was first observed by Rydberg that the spectrum of helium appears to emanate from two different substances, which were called helium and parhelium. It is now known that the different spectral series are due to a single element, presumably in different states, and it is assumed that under the excitation of electric discharge an atom of helium may assume a form in which one electron is in the first shell and one is dislodged to an outer shell. In such case the outer electron would be expected to behave as a valence electron. The atom would thus resemble the hydrogen atom and might form compounds, not only with other similar atoms, but also with a halogen or a metal. It would be interesting to see whether by exciting helium in the presence of sodium or iodine, maintained at low temperatures, it would be possible to isolate these extremely unstable compounds.

### Lithium and Beryllium.

The elements of the first period of eight are characterized by a kernel which contains a single pair of electrons. Structures built up of such kernels could hardly be expected to exhibit properties which are altogether similar to those of structures made up of kernels, possessing a complicated three-dimensional structure. In fact the properties of the elements in this first period of eight are not always predictable from those of similar elements of higher atomic number. Thus, to give a single example, the standard electrode potential, against the ion in aqueous solution, is greater for rubidium than for potassium, greater for potassium than for sodium, but the value for lithium is higher even than that for rubidium.

The great tendency of lithium and beryllium ions to form hydrates distinguishes them in degree though not in kind from other similar elements. Whether they form definite coordination complexes in the Werner sense has not as yet been ascertained.[1] This could be ascertained by a more thorough study of solutions in non-aqueous solvents. Thus through a study of the solubility of lithium salts in liquid ammonia in the presence and absence of water, or of the potential of lithium amalgam against a solution of a lithium salt in liquid ammonia, with and without added water, we might obtain the desired information.

The salts of these metals in concentrated aqueous solution show signs of hydrolysis, which lead us to suspect that their hydroxides have an amphoteric character analogous to aluminum hydroxide.

The fact has already been mentioned that beryllium chloride in the fused state is a poor conductor of electricity. This would seem to indicate the existence of more definite chemical bonds than occur in most metallic compounds. For the most part, however, the properties of lithium and beryllium compounds, like those of most metals, are due to the formation of ions, through the complete removal of the valence electrons.

### Boron.

There is a wide gulf separating the boron from the aluminum compounds, and boron is usually classified as a non-metallic element. This does not refer primarily to the properties of elementary boron which, like carbon, has one form that behaves to a small degree as a metallic conductor of electricity, but rather to the fact that boron in its compounds does not part with its valence electrons. Thus the trihalides of boron have very little of the character of electrolytes. We have seen how the molecules of a substance like boron trichloride complete the octet about the boron atom by combination, either with one another or with other molecules.

In our present discussion of the elements with kernels of the helium type we shall find a number of compounds whose structure can not yet be definitely ascertained, but which seem to depart from the usual rules of chemical combination. Of these there are none which are quite so mysterious as the two hydroborons $B_2H_6$ and $B_4H_{10}$. Using the old valence scheme one would have been tempted to write the two formulæ

$$\begin{array}{ccc} \text{H} \quad \text{H} & & \text{H} \quad \text{H} \quad \text{H} \quad \text{H} \\ | \quad | & & | \quad | \quad | \quad | \\ \text{H}-\text{B}-\text{B}-\text{H} \quad \text{and} & \text{H}-\text{B}-\text{B}-\text{B}-\text{B}-\text{H} \ , \\ | \quad | & & | \quad | \quad | \quad | \\ \text{H} \quad \text{H} & & \text{H} \quad \text{H} \quad \text{H} \quad \text{H} \end{array}$$

but there are not enough valence electrons to furnish all these bonds. Thus if we attempt to write the formula of $B_2H_6$, the number of electrons available permit only such a formula as

[1] Dr. N. V. Sidgwick has kindly called my attention to the fact that the interesting beryllium salts of the type $Be_4OA_6$ (where A is an organic acid radical) may be fully explained as coordinated compounds in which beryllium has the coordination number of 4. See his note in "Nature," June 16, 1923.

$$\begin{array}{cc} \text{H} & \text{H} \\ \text{H}:\overset{..}{\underset{..}{\text{B}}} & \overset{..}{\underset{..}{\text{B}}}:\text{H} \;, \\ \text{H} & \text{H} \end{array}$$

and there is no apparent bond between the two borons. The suggestion of Eastman, which has been discussed in Chapter VII, affords the only explanation of this molecule which has thus far been advanced.

Whatever may be the origin of the bond which joins the two halves of the molecule together, the bond is presumably a very weak one, for the corresponding alkyl compounds have the formula $BR_3$, according to the experiments of Stock. We are reminded of the similar case of ethane and hexaphenyl ethane, the latter of which breaks into two odd molecules. It is to be remarked that no bond of the hydroboron type has been found in any other compound, nor has the substance $BH_4$ been obtained.

### Nitrogen and Carbon.

The two features which chiefly distinguish the compounds of carbon and nitrogen from those of similar atoms with larger kernels are (1) the tightness and inertness of the bonds that they form, and (2) their ability to employ what we know as multiple bonds. The first characteristic permits the building up of complicated structures which are thermodynamically unstable, but which are for the most part very unreactive. The second characteristic is evidence of an ability to produce moderately stable electron arrangements by methods which are not available to atoms of large kernel. While it may possibly be desirable to assume occasionally the formation of multiple bonds in the case of elements other than those of the first period of eight, we may be sure that the idea of the multiple bond would never have been invented were it not for our study of the elements with kernels of the helium type.

Since multiply-bonded compounds are classed as unsaturated we sometimes speak of the multiple bond as the cause of unsaturation, but this seems to me to be the very opposite of the correct view. In the early stage of valence theory, when the single bond was the only means known of uniting two atoms, the unsaturated compounds were substances which could not be represented by the ordinary valence formulæ, and which might therefore have been expected to be far more abnormal in their behavior than was found to be the case. The multiple bond was invented to explain the fact that the properties of these substances did not indicate as high a degree of unsaturation as would be expected.

If the double bond had not been invented, the only ways in which we could represent the structure of ethylene would be the two following:

$$\begin{array}{cc} \text{H}\;\text{H} & \text{H}\;\text{H} \\ \text{(A)}\; \text{H}:\overset{..}{\underset{.}{\text{C}}}:\overset{..}{\underset{..}{\text{C}}}:\text{H} \;, & \text{(B)}\; \text{H}:\overset{..}{\text{C}}:\overset{}{\underset{..}{\text{C}}}:\text{H} \;. \end{array}$$

The first of these, having an odd number of electrons on each carbon atom, should have the properties which we have found to be associated with odd molecules. A substance of such a structure would presumably exhibit color, form associated molecules, and be far more reactive than ethylene in fact is. The second formula would represent a substance which would be not only unsymmetrical but also highly polarized, the right-hand portion being charged negatively and the left-hand part charged positively.

There may indeed be some dissymmetry in the normal molecule of ethylene since we shall see that when two atoms, each characterized by unsaturation, are adjacent to one another, there may be a tendency for one of the atoms to assume a very stable state while the other bears nearly the whole brunt of the unsaturation.

While it must be agreed that neither of the above formulæ A and B adequately represents the properties of ethylene, the same may be said also of the ordinary double bond formula, unless it is carefully explained that the double bond implies properties very different from those implied by two single bonds. If then we write the formula

$$\text{(C)} \quad \overset{\text{H}\ \ \text{H}}{\underset{}{\text{H} : \ddot{\text{C}} :: \ddot{\text{C}} : \text{H}}} \ .$$

we may say that the actual behavior of ethylene corresponds to something intermediate between this and the other two formulæ. Thus we may consider that, if a molecule of the form of A should at some moment be produced, the two odd electrons would approach and to some extent would conjugate with one another. But this conjugation would be by no means as complete as that which occurs when two separate odd molecules combine, with a conjugation of their two odd electrons to constitute a single bond.

The exact character of this partial conjugation or partial mutual saturation of the two atoms can at present only be guessed. In an atom with a large kernel, and consequently a large valence shell, in which the several electron pairs are separated from one another by relatively great distances, we might expect that the formation of a double bond would cause considerable distortion of the atoms concerned. On the other hand, when the nucleus is rudimentary, as is the case with the elements we are now considering, we seem justified in concluding that the octet requirements of two atoms can be met by their sharing to some extent more than one pair of electrons, and that this sharing of electron pairs occurs without very great distortion of the stable structures.

It has been suggested by Latimer and Rodebush that these atoms of small kernel can be satisfied with something less than the normal octet, namely, by a group of four, or especially by a group of six, but this does not seem to be a complete solution of the problem, for if such were the case we should expect to find monatomic carbon with its quartet of electrons, and monatomic oxygen with its sextet of electrons, to be far more stable than they are in fact.

We are therefore led to the conclusion that the properties of substances with multiple bonds are due to some sharing of two or three electron pairs, although this sharing is probably less complete than that indicated by the usual graphical formula with two or three bonds. Nevertheless the process must be assumed to have some physical reality, in order to account for the existence of those isomers which depend upon the failure of free rotation about the double bond.

Also for acetylene we might write three types of formula,

$$\text{(A)} \ \ \text{H} \colon \overset{..}{\text{C}} \colon \overset{..}{\text{C}} \colon \text{H} \ , \quad \text{(B)} \ \ \overset{\text{H}}{\text{H} \colon \overset{..}{\text{C}} \colon \overset{..}{\text{C}} \colon} \ , \quad \text{(C)} \ \ \text{H} \colon \text{C} \colon\colon\colon \text{C} \colon \text{H} \ .$$

The formula B suggests one employed by Nef. Now since acetylene acts as a weak acid, the two hydrogen atoms may be regarded as mobile, and the two forms A and B would give the same ions, namely,

$$\left[ \text{H} \colon \overset{..}{\text{C}} \colon \overset{..}{\text{C}} \colon \right] \quad \text{and} \quad \left[ \colon \overset{..}{\text{C}} \colon \overset{..}{\text{C}} \colon \right]^{--} .$$

We may therefore regard the forms A and B as belonging to that simple class of tautomers which are obtained merely by the transfer of hydrogen from one lone pair to another. On the other hand the alkyl derivatives should yield isomers, and the fact that such isomers have not been isolated is an argument against the structures A and B.

However, the formula C does not express the properties of acetylene without a good deal of explanation. Here again the behavior of acetylene seems to be intermediate between that which would be represented by the formula C and that expressed by one of the other formulæ. Indeed if, in formula A, we consider a pair of electrons from each atom drawn toward the central bond, it would be difficult to state the exact point at which the single bond would be converted into a triple bond. Of course it will be realized that in all these discussions our standardized formulæ do not very adequately represent the three-dimensional arrangement of the electrons in space.

We have already commented upon the fact that the unsaturation of a compound containing a triple bond is less, as shown by all of our best criteria, than the unsaturation of a compound with a double bond. This is entirely at variance with the strain theory of Baeyer, and we are at a loss to account for it except perhaps by the assumption that the two types of molecules do in some measure approach the two symmetrical forms represented by the formulæ A for ethylene and acetylene. In the former case the process is attended by the division of an electron pair; in the second case it is not. It is not easy to avoid the suspicion that this fact is connected with the greater unsaturation of the double bond.

A discussion of the triple bond leads us to a consideration of the interesting properties of elementary nitrogen which has generally been assigned the formula $N \equiv N$. This substance is distinguished by its very great lack of reactivity. It is also stable in a thermodynamic sense with respect to a great number of its compounds, which tend to decompose in such manner as to evolve $N_2$. For these reasons Kossel (1916) remarked: "$N_2$ is known to be very inert chemically. It is very little disposed to take on foreign electrons, and while it cannot be considered fully comparable with the noble gases, still it can for our purpose pass as a very stable structure. If one nitrogen is replaced by a carbon, a structure is obtained by which the positive charge is smaller by one unit, but also has one less electron than in the stable $N_2$. It behaves therefore with respect to $N_2$ just as a halogen, according to our assumption, behaves with respect to a noble gas. Thus CN functions chemically as a halogen."

This idea has been extended by Langmuir, who has pointed out the great similarity in physical properties between nitrogen and carbon monoxide. Each of these molecules has the same number of electrons and the same molecular weight, and it is therefore perhaps not surprising that in their boiling point and other similar properties they are closely analogous. Mr. Urey has called my attention to the fact that the distance from nucleus to nucleus, as determined by means of a study of the ultrared absorption bands, is the same for both substances, namely $1.14 \times 10^{-8}$ cm.

It is possible, however, to exaggerate the similarity between the two gases. In their chemical properties the resemblance disappears. Carbon monoxide forms many addition compounds as in the metal carbonyls, the complexes with cuprous salts and with haemoglobin. However, if we are to assume precisely the same electron structure for $N_2$ and for CO, the latter must be electrically polarized in the sense that the oxygen is positive and the carbon negative, since in the neutral state the oxygen atom has one more electron than the nitrogen atom, while the carbon atom has one less. Such polarization would probably suffice to explain the difference in chemical behavior. On the other hand if the electrons in carbon monoxide are shifted in such manner as to diminish the degree of polarization of the molecule, the distortion of valence shells so produced might equally well account for the chemical reactivity of carbon monoxide.

The particular structure which Langmuir proposed for nitrogen and carbon monoxide, and which had previously been suggested to me by Professors Bray and Branch, I do not regard as probable. Langmuir suggested what is essentially a quadruple bond, such that two atomic kernels lie together inside of a single octet. There seems to be nothing in the properties of these substances to necessitate such an *ad hoc* assumption.

On the other hand we have much reason for believing with Kossel and Langmuir that there are substances like cyanide ion and carbon monoxide which have essentially the same electronic structure as nitrogen. To these we may add also the acetylide ion, and, with the reservations regarding the meaning of the triple bond which we have already made, we may assign to these substances the formulæ

:N:::N:,    :C:::O:,    [:C:::N:]$^-$,    [:C:::C:]$^{--}$.

In accordance with this view we see that the ion CN⁻ is the same whether it comes from a cyanide or from an isocyanide. By adding hydrogen ion to a lone pair of the carbon or of the nitrogen we obtain hydrogen cyanide or hydrogen isocyanide, and these two substances therefore represent the same kind of tautomerism which we have so frequently mentioned. By employing alkyl groups in place of hydrogen the corresponding isomers may be obtained.

When we examine these four substances which have presumably approximately the same electronic structure we note that the last two are ions, that carbon monoxide on account of the difference in charge of the kernels must be polarized, but that nitrogen is neither polarized nor is it an ion, and if we bear in mind the unexpected lack of unsaturation which we have seen to be associated with the triple bond, and consider also the remarkable firmness which in general characterizes the bonds of nitrogen, we have, I believe, a sufficient explanation of the peculiar inertness of elementary nitrogen.

We may recall that Nef ascribed the isocyanides and acetylene to the class of compounds with bivalent carbon. If we interpret this statement as meaning merely that the carbon is in the same kind of structure as it is in carbon monoxide, we are now in a position to agree with his conclusions.

The oxides of nitrogen form an interesting and unusual group of compounds. Nitric oxide, NO, we have already discussed as one of the substances which have odd molecules. It has eleven valence electrons; one more than the molecule of nitrogen. Of all the substances which have odd molecules it exhibits the least degree of unsaturation. It is colorless, and at ordinary temperatures does not associate into double molecules, although this process seems to occur at low temperatures. By some method which is not yet understood, the odd electron is obviously much more firmly held in the molecule, and the molecule itself is more nearly saturated, than in the case of any other odd molecule.

Professor Branch has pointed out to me that this behavior of nitric oxide is very closely related to the anomalous properties of the nitroso compounds. When NO combines with another free radical (odd molecule) such as an alkyl group, we should expect this union of two odd molecules to produce a fully saturated compound. But this is not the case. Not only does NO in the free state behave nearly like a saturated substance, but when combined with an odd molecule like methyl it does not appear to conjugate with the odd electron of the latter. So the resulting compound, although possessing an even number of electrons, has the properties of odd molecules. The nitroso compounds in general are highly colored, and they almost invariably tend to form double molecules, as though each single molecule had an odd electron.

The first stage in the reaction between nitric oxide and oxygen appears to be as follows:

$$NO + O_2 = NO_3$$

The assumption that this reaction is reversible at ordinary temperatures, and proceeds to a very slight extent at high temperatures, accounts for the very interesting observation that the reaction between nitric oxide and oxygen, to give $NO_2$ or $N_2O_4$, diminishes in speed with increasing temperature. The intermediate substance $NO_3$, which is assumed for this reaction, can actually be isolated at low temperatures. It represents another type of odd molecule; it is intensely colored, and presumably in other ways is more unsaturated than nitric oxide.

Nitrogen dioxide is another substance with an uneven number of electrons, and it shows all the characteristic properties of the odd molecules. I believe that we are hardly in a position as yet to give definite electron structures for these odd molecules. Presumably if there is any part of the molecule which is a seat of unsaturation the odd electron seeks that position, and to some extent conjugates in such manner as to reduce as far as possible the total unsaturation.

The three remaining oxides of nitrogen, $N_2O$, $N_2O_3$ and $N_2O_5$, may be represented as multiply-bonded or by the formulæ,

$$:\overset{..}{\underset{..}{N}}:\overset{..}{\underset{..}{O}}:\overset{..}{\underset{..}{N}}: \; , \qquad :\overset{..}{\underset{..}{O}}:\overset{..}{N}:\overset{..}{\underset{..}{O}}:\overset{..}{N}:\overset{..}{\underset{..}{O}}: \; , \qquad \begin{matrix} & :\overset{..}{\underset{..}{O}}: & :\overset{..}{\underset{..}{O}}: & \\ :\overset{..}{\underset{..}{O}}: & \overset{..}{N}: & \overset{..}{\underset{..}{O}}: & \overset{..}{N}: & \overset{..}{\underset{..}{O}}: \end{matrix} \; .$$

## Oxygen and Fluorine.

Oxygen and fluorine are the two most electronegative elements. By this we mean that they are the elements which show the strongest tendency to complete their octets and to obtain as nearly as possible the exclusive possession of the eight electrons. They therefore either take electrons completely away from other atoms, forming ions, or they draw electron pairs away from other atomic centers, possibly into a secondary valence shell.

For this reason it seems at first sight surprising that water and hydrofluoric acid are weak electrolytes. This, however, is not an isolated phenomenon. Hydrofluoric acid in aqueous solution is weaker than hydrochloric acid, water is a weaker acid than hydrogen sulfide, which in turn is weaker than hydrogen selenide and hydrogen telluride, while the same phenomenon appears also in the nitrogen group. It is evident that hydrogen ion, when it adds to a lone pair of oxygen or fluorine, forms a firmer bond than when it combines with other lone pairs, and this it can do, probably because of its small size, without any great deformation of the normal octets of oxygen and fluorine atoms. The hydrogen is certainly held very close to the other atom; we have seen that the distance separating the two atoms in the molecule of hydrofluoric acid gas is probably less than $1 \times 10^{-8}$ cm.

The firmness with which the ions of these elements of small kernel hold hydrogen ion is further illustrated by the fact that neutral compounds like ammonia and water have a far greater tendency to add another hydrogen ion, forming onium compounds, than the corresponding substances, phosphine and hydrogen sulphide, respectively.

As far as we know, oxygen and fluorine do not furnish the central atoms of anions as so many other elements do. However the problem of the structure of ozone is a very interesting one in this connection. Ozone is usually given a ring formula which we may readily translate into an electron structure, but it has seemed to me that it may possibly have the form

$$: \overset{..}{O} :: \overset{..}{O} : \overset{..}{\underset{..}{O}} : \text{ , or } : \overset{..}{\underset{..}{O}} : \overset{..}{O} : \overset{..}{\underset{..}{O}} :$$

which would make it the analogue of sulfur dioxide.[1] There is some intimation in the literature that ozone is absorbed by basic substances without decomposition, and if so we should regard it as the anhydride of an acid resembling sulfurous acid. It would be interesting to obtain further experimental evidence. If this view of the structure of ozone is correct, the fact that fluorine reacts with water to produce ozone might lead us to suspect that in the reaction there are intermediate substances, which would resemble the oxyacids of chlorine, but in which the oxygen would be taking the place of the central chlorine, while fluorine would occupy the outer positions which are held by oxygen in the other halogen acids. It is possible that experiments at low temperatures might possibly lead to the isolation of such compounds between fluorine and oxygen.

The question which we have just raised regarding the constitution of ozone is of far greater consequence than the question of the constitution of hydrogen peroxide which is more frequently argued. The two formulæ for ozone, the ring formula and the one of the type of $SO_2$, are radically different in principle. On the other hand, the two formulæ which have been given to hydrogen peroxide, namely HOOH and $H_2OO$ are to all intents and purposes identical. Hydrogen peroxide is an acid whose ion is expressed by the formula

$$\left[ : \overset{..}{\underset{..}{O}} : \overset{..}{\underset{..}{O}} : \right]^{--} .$$

Whether the two mobile hydrogen atoms go to the same or different oxygen atoms is unimportant. This is the same kind of tautomerism which we have mentioned in the case of sulfuric acid, phosphoric acid, hydrocyanic acid, acetylene and hydroxylamine.

[1] I find that a similar suggestion has just been made by Lowry, Trans. Faraday Soc., 18, Part 3, page 3, 1923.

# Chapter XI.

# Elements in Positive and Negative States.

When we speak of a negative element we can only mean an element which in a neutral state will take on electrons to form stable pairs and octets. We cannot assume that a neutral atom of chlorine exerts any appreciable electrostatic force upon an electron at a distance. We can only say that when an electron is added to a chlorine atom, in such a way as to complete its group of eight, a very stable system is produced. When chloride ion is thus formed this ion will not attract but will repel negative electricity.

Our existing nomenclature is extremely misleading. We say that chlorine is a negative element because it tends to take up an electron, and we also say that in sodium chloride we have negative chlorine, because it has taken up an electron and has no tendency to acquire any more. When an atom of chlorine instead of gaining an electron has lost one, we say that we have positive chlorine, although the atom then has a great tendency to take on two electrons. I shall not, however, attempt to offer a substitute for these time-honored usages which are probably so well understood that they will cause no serious confusion. Perhaps it will somewhat clarify the situation if we agree that an element which tends to take up electrons is a negative element, that when it has taken up a sufficient number of electrons it is in a negative state, and that when its need for electrons is not fully satisfied it is in a positive state.

That the process of forming negative ions is very different from that which was assumed in the electrochemical theory is shown by the fact that a negative element, if it cannot acquire its group of eight, may often give up an electron in order at least to possess an even number of electrons in its valence shell. Thus the conductivity of pure liquid iodine indicates that one atom of iodine has acquired an electron to form iodide ion, while another has parted with an electron to become iodous ion with a group of six electrons. As a rule, however, both atoms complete their groups of eight by sharing an electron pair.

## The Problem of Electromers.

Hypoiodous acid is a very weak acid indeed. In its aqueous solution it does not increase greatly the hydrogen ion concentration due to pure water. It probably is amphoteric and dissociates to a small degree into the ions $I^+$ and $OH$ . So the compound $ICl$ may be regarded as a very weak salt, iodous chloride. Such considerations have led the proponents of the modern dualistic theory to the conclusion that all compounds of iodine can be regarded as containing either negative iodine, as represented by $I^-$, or positive iodine, as represented by $I^+$. We have seen how untenable such a hypothesis is, and that it is necessary to regard the highly polar molecules as extreme examples of the displacement of the pair of electrons which constitutes the chemical bond.

There can be no question but that iodine in hypoiodous acid is in a very different state from iodine in potassium iodide, and there is no objection to saying that it is more positive in the former substance than in the latter, but we could exhibit a whole series of compounds which are intermediate between these types, and a classification of these substances into two distinct groups, one containing positive iodine and the other containing negative iodine, would be wholly arbitrary.

We no longer therefore see any justification for the assumption that nitrogen trichloride must be either $N^{+++}Cl^-_3$, or $N^{---}Cl^+_3$. Such a pair of hypothetical substances have become known in the modern dualistic theory as electromers,—two substances which are supposed to have the same atoms in the same arrangement but with a different distribution of electronic charges. If we admit that the nitrogen in nitrogen trichloride is nearer to the state of nitrogen in ammonia than it is to nitrogen in nitrous acid, we no longer imply that we must give it the second of the above formulæ, or that it would be possible to obtain another kind of nitrogen trichloride corresponding to the first formula.

Nevertheless if we apply the quantum theory in any thoroughgoing manner to chemical combination we cannot regard the pair of electrons which serves as a bond between hydrogen and chlorine as capable of being moved in a continuous way from the one atom to the other. Rather we are led to assume that such a pair must occupy one of the finite though possibly large number of definite positions between the two atoms, and two molecules holding the bonding pair in different positions (or energy levels) might be called electromers. Thus an atom of hydrogen with its electron in the first energy level might be called an electromer of an atom which for a brief space of time holds the electron in one of the other energy levels. However, even if we assume the existence of isomeric molecules it is hardly to be expected that we shall be able to segregate and isolate the several species of molecules so as to obtain electromeric *substances*.

## Compounds Between Negative Elements.

A negative element not only tends to acquire electrons to form its stable group, but also to obtain exclusive possession of the electrons which make up its octet. In substances of the extremely polar type, such as calcium oxide, the oxygen may be considered to be in a state of oxide ion, and thus to have acquired complete and sole possession of its group of eight electrons. But in the majority of oxygen compounds in which the atoms of this element are attached by chemical bonds, one or more of its four pairs of electrons is shared with another atom, and this always produces some distortion of the valence shell. In all such cases the oxygen must be regarded as in a more positive state than it is in oxide ion.

Especially when two electronegative atoms are combined we may consider that a state of tension exists, in which each atom, so to speak, strives to obtain sole possession of the bonding pair. This pair is therefore drawn away from each atom more than it would be in the most stable form of the octet.

In such cases it has been customary in certain quarters to state that one of the atoms is in a positive condition. I would amend this by saying that whenever two electronegative atoms are united by a chemical bond *both atoms are in a more positive condition* than when they are combined with electropositive elements or are in the state of their normal ions.

As examples of compounds of this type we may consider $Cl-Cl$, $Cl-OH$, $Cl-NH_2$, $HO-OH$, $H_2N-OH$, $H_2N-NH_2$, $NCl_3$ and other similar compounds. In all such cases those who have adopted the modern **dualistic** theory have attempted to decide which of the atoms is positive and which negative. It is said that chlorine is positive in ClOH, and there is perhaps some jusification for considering that in this substance chlorine is a little farther from the state of chloride ion than the oxygen is from the state of oxide ion, but it is certainly not so positive as iodine in IOH. After all, the main thing in all such cases is to recognize that both of the atoms concerned are in the state that we call positive, and that a state of tension exists that can best be relieved by breaking the bond between the two atoms and attaching to each atom a more naturally electropositive element or radical. Such a process would be classed as a reduction, without the necessity of telling which atom is reduced.

Hitherto little has been said regarding the actual distribution of electricity within a molecule, nor would it be wise in the present state of our knowledge to attempt to speak with any definiteness in this regard. However, there are certain elementary deductions which may be safely drawn from our theory.

When two atoms of chlorine combine to form the molecule $Cl_2$, each atom contributes half of the bonding pair, and it is to be presumed that in the most stable state of the molecule the whole structure is symmetrical with respect to this bonding pair. We might then say that the pair belongs equally to the two atoms and therefore that it furnishes to each atom the equivalent of one electron, which, together with the six electrons which each atom holds by itself, makes the seven of the neutral chlorine atom.

In a purely formal way we could in other cases assign to an atom one electron from each of its bonds and thus obtain a value for the electric charge of each atom. But this would be an entirely arbitrary proceeding, taking no cognizance of the shifting of electrons which we must always consider when the two sides of the bond are not identical, and which undoubtedly occurs in some molecules even of a symmetrical type, due to thermal agitation.

Even this formal method of assigning electrons to the individual atoms would result often in ascribing charges to certain atoms. Thus in the numerous cases in which oxygen has but a single bond, as for example in the amine oxides,

$$\overset{R}{\underset{R}{R : \overset{..}{\underset{..}{N}} : \overset{..}{\underset{..}{O}} :}} ,$$

the oxygen atom furnishes neither of the electrons which constitute the bond. This atom has sole possession of the six electrons which offset the six positive charges of its kernel, and since it also has part possession of the bonding pair it must be considered to be in a negative condition. Presumably such a substance as amine oxide is therefore considerably polarized. In the same way a neutral substance like boron trifluoride may be considered to be made negative when it completes its octet by employing one of the lone pairs of water or ammonia.

In any of the numerous cases of tautomerism which consist in the passage of hydrogen ion from one lone pair of electrons to another, as in the tautomerism of hydroxyl amine, namely,

$$H : \overset{..}{\underset{\underset{H}{..}}{N}} : \overset{..}{\underset{..}{O}} : H = H : \overset{\overset{H}{..}}{\underset{\underset{H}{..}}{N}} : \overset{..}{\underset{..}{O}} : ,$$

the transfer of the positively charged nucleus of hydrogen would, formally considered, result in an increase in the positive charge of that portion of the molecule to which it goes, and probably such a change of polarity actually occurs, although it may be largely offset by some displacement of the whole electronic structure.

When hydrogen ion adds to a lone pair of electrons to form an onium ion we should expect from considerations of electric force alone that the hydrogen ion would most readily attach itself to that portion of a molecule which is negatively charged. We have seen that when one hydrogen ion or other positive radical has been attached to an atom, thus giving it a positive charge, this ordinarily prevents the formation of a second onium bond, as in the case of substances of the sulfonium type. It seems to be a universal rule that the tendency of hydrogen ion or a (positively charged) alkyl radical to add to a lone pair, in any part of a molecule, increases if that part is made more negative, and diminishes if it be made more positive.

In accordance with this rule nitrogen is less disposed to form substances of the ammonium type when it is in a positive state than when it is more negative. Thus when nitrogen is attached to chlorine, oxygen or nitrogen, it combines less readily with hydrogen ion and is said to be less basic. Thus chloramine is a weaker base than ammonia. In other words, the first of the two following reactions occurs to the least extent:

$$ClNH_2 + H^+ = ClNH_3^+$$
$$NH_3 + H^+ = NH_4^+.$$

Nitrogen trichloride is hardly basic at all. So also hydroxylamine and hydrazine are very much weaker bases than ammonia.

We have seen that univalent oxygen as it exists in an amine oxide, in spite of its attachment to another negative element, is in a negative state. It should therefore be able to add hydrogen ion. Therefore from this standpoint also we have confirmation of the view expressed in a previous chapter that an amine oxide adds hydrogen ion at the oxygen.

The strain which exists in a bond between two negative elements manifests itself in a variety of ways, and is responsible for numerous types of decomposition or rearrangement. Let us consider once more the compound formed when an amine oxide combines with methyl halide to produce the ion $R_3NOCH_3^+$. This ion very readily decomposes in alkaline solution to furnish hydrogen ion and to leave formaldehyde and free amine. It seems to me that we can form a provisional picture of the mechanism of this decomposition. Representing the ion by the structure

$$\left[ \begin{array}{ccc} R & & H \\ R\!:\!\ddot{N}\!:\!\ddot{O}\!:\!\ddot{C}\!:\!H \\ R & & H \end{array} \right]^+ ,$$

we may consider the bonding pair between nitrogen and oxygen as drawn away from the normal position of the pair in the oxygen octet. This struggle for electrons would tend to draw toward the oxygen the electrons which form the bonding pairs between carbon and hydrogen, so that the atoms of hydrogen would behave more like the hydrogen of an acid than they ordinarily do in an alkyl group. So we may consider that in the presence of an alkali one of these atoms of hydrogen occasionally is drawn off as hydrogen ion. The pair of electrons left free would then form a double bond with the oxygen, thus producing formaldehyde, and the nitrogen would take sole possession of the former bonding pair, giving trialkylamine. Such a picture of the mechanism of this decomposition seems extraordinarily satisfactory, but in the present stage of chemistry any theory as to the detailed mechanism of a reaction must be considered tentative, and it must be admitted that there are a number of quite similar decompositions known to organic chemistry which apparently cannot be explained without a far greater amount of molecular rearrangement than is assumed in this simple case.

An extremely interesting substance which is probably closely related to amine oxide is produced when ammonia reacts with an aldehyde to form the compound known as aldehyde-ammonia. We may provisionally assume that the reaction between these substances consists in the breaking of the double bond of the carbonyl group, in accordance with the following scheme:

$$\overset{:O:}{\underset{\ddot{H}}{R:\overset{..}{C}}} + \overset{..}{:N:H} = R:\overset{:\ddot{O}:}{\underset{\ddot{H}}{\overset{..}{C}}}:\overset{H}{\underset{\ddot{H}}{\overset{..}{N}}}:H$$

The formula of the compound as now written probably represents the actual structure of some of the molecules, since ammonia can be readily split off again. However, in this formula the oxygen is singly bonded as in an amine oxide, and is therefore in a negative condition. Hence one of the liable hydrogens should wander to the oxygen, resulting in the molecule

$$\begin{array}{c} H:\ddot{O}: \\ R:\overset{..}{\underset{\ddot{H}}{C}}:\overset{..}{\underset{H}{N}}:H \end{array}$$

This is probably the predominant form and accounts for the carbinol (slightly basic) properties of the aldehyde-ammonia. If in some molecules two hydrogens wander to the oxygen, we have a structure from which water could readily be split off, leaving the imide. This reaction also is characteristic of this class of substances.

By our definition of negative elements as those which show a strong tendency to acquire electrons to form a stable group, it is evident that we must regard hydrogen as a negative element. It is true, hydrogen rarely takes exclusive possession of a bonding pair to form hydride ion, but it seems to exercise a very considerable pull upon a bonding pair, especially in some inorganic acids, as we shall see in the next chapter.

# Chapter XII.

# Remnants of the Electrochemical Theory.

In our development of the new theory of valence we have found it possible to agree with Werner in many points. As the text of the present chapter we might use his statement: "The electrochemical phenomenon accompanying the saturation of principal valences is a secondary one, and quite different from the purely chemical one. It may accompany chemical change but is not a necessary consequence."

There are, however, numerous reactions the trend of which is largely determined by conditions of electric polarization within the molecule, and to these we shall now give our attention.

When a typical salt is dissolved in a solvent which is not highly polar—for example in a solvent of low dielectric constant—it often shows little evidence of electrolytic dissociation. In such cases the undissociated molecule may be regarded as held together by the electric forces between its oppositely charged parts. This is perhaps the only type of molecule in which chemical combination is the result of purely electrostatic forces, in the ordinary sense. Nevertheless there are many other cases in which the union of two chemical species is due to the formation of a chemical bond, but in which the extent to which the union occurs is largely determined by electrostatic forces.

We have seen that an element which is naturally quadrivalent does not satisfy its valence of four through the formation of an onium complex, if this requires the addition of hydrogen ion to an already positively charged ion. On the other hand, the positive hydrogen ion does not readily dissociate from an ion which is already negative. Thus hydrogen sulfide dissociates according to the equation $H_2S = H^+ + HS^-$ and the dissociation constant is $10^{-7}$, but we find a far lower dissociation constant, about $10^{-15}$ for the ionization $HS^- = H^+ + S^{--}$. A similar example is furnished by the two reactions,

$$NH_2^- + H^+ = NH_3 \ ,$$
$$NH_3 + H^+ = NH_4^+ \ .$$

While the second of these reactions is easily reversible in aqueous solutions, the first runs so nearly to an end that an amide, even when dissolved in a very alkaline solution, is completely hydrolyzed, as far as we know.

Since it is in reactions which involve the union or dissociation of ions that we might expect the clearest evidence of the influence of electrostatic forces, it is fortunate that we possess a large amount of information concerning the constants of dissociation of weak acids and bases.

## The Strength of Acids and Bases.

We are so habituated to the use of water as a solvent, and our data are so largely limited to those obtained in aqueous solutions, that we frequently define an acid or a base as a substance whose aqueous solution gives, respectively, a higher concentration of hydrogen ion or of hydroxide ion than that furnished by pure water. This is a very one-sided definition, but it will suffice for the moment while we consider those substances whose acid or basic properties are due to the presence of the hydroxyl radical.

Let us consider a substance whose structure and modes of dissociation are represented by the following schemes,

$$:\overset{..}{\underset{..}{X}}:\overset{..}{\underset{..}{O}}:H = \left[:\overset{..}{\underset{..}{X}}\right]^+ + \left[:\overset{..}{\underset{..}{O}}:H\right]^-$$

$$:\overset{..}{\underset{..}{X}}:\overset{..}{\underset{..}{O}}:H = \left[:\overset{..}{\underset{..}{X}}:\overset{..}{\underset{..}{O}}:\right]^- + H^+$$

If the dissociation occurs chiefly by the first method, the substance is called a base; if chiefly by the second method it is called an acid. Frequently both dissociations occur, and the substance is said to be amphoteric. Since the product of the concentration of hydrogen and hydroxide ions is limited by the dissociation constant of water, a substance in aqueous solution cannot be at the same time a strong acid and a strong base.

There seems, however, to be a far more fundamental opposition between acid and base than the one we have just mentioned. We frequently deal with a substance like alcohol which is so weak an acid and so weak a base that the limitation of concentration of hydrogen and hydroxide ion is of no importance, and yet in such a case we shall probably find that almost any change in the molecule which makes it a stronger acid makes it a weaker base, and vice versa.

Reverting to our type substance XOH, X may be an element or radical which may without difficulty lose electrons. In such case oxygen which strives for exclusive possession of its group of eight will break the bond with X and take possession of the bonding pair, thus forming $X^+$ and $OH^-$. On the other hand, if X is an element or radical which exerts a strong pull upon the bonding pair, all of our evidence indicates that this produces an effect upon every one of the pairs in the oxygen octet, which may be regarded as a displacement toward the left. Thus the tightening of the bond between X and O loosens the bond between O and H, and the displacement of the electrons away from the hydrogen makes the latter more free to assume the condition of hydrogen ion.

If we consider corresponding hydroxides of nitrogen, phosphorus, arsenic, antimony and bismuth, we see the effect of the diminishing pull of electrons by the central atom, as we proceed from nitrogen to bismuth. The hydroxides become progressively weaker acids and stronger bases.

Such a simple explanation accounts satisfactorily, in the main, for the observed strength of organic acids and bases. We have already discussed the case of chloracetic acid, to which we give the formula

$$\begin{array}{ccc} & \text{H} \,\colon\, \overset{\cdot\cdot}{\text{O}} \colon & \\ \colon\! \overset{\cdot\cdot}{\underset{\cdot\cdot}{\text{Cl}}} \colon \overset{}{\underset{}{\text{C}}} \colon & \overset{}{\underset{}{\text{C}}} \colon \overset{\cdot\cdot}{\underset{\cdot\cdot}{\text{O}}} \colon \text{H} \\ & \text{H} & \end{array}$$

The substitution of one methyl hydrogen by chlorine produces a greater pull upon the electrons of the methyl carbon, and this causes a displacement which seems to occur throughout the molecule, finally pulling the electrons away from the hydrogen and permitting a greater dissociation of hydrogen ion. The substitution of a second and third chlorine heightens the effect.

It is not at all certain that the whole effect is produced through the carbon chain. If we knew how to construct thoroughly satisfactory spatial models of our molecules, we might see how in certain cases there might be some more immediate steric effect which would exaggerate the effect produced through the chain. But that the latter effect, passing through the molecule atom by atom, is a real one we have no reason to doubt. One substitution of hydrogen by chlorine in propionic acid gives an acid of about the same strength as monochloracetic, when it is an alpha-hydrogen that is replaced; but β-chlorpropionic acid is much weaker. Still less marked results of the chlorine substitution are to be seen in γ-chlorbutyric and in δ-chlorvaleric acids, the latter of which is hardly stronger than valeric acid itself.

Other atoms or radicals which exert a similar pull upon the electrons give entirely parallel results when substituted for hydrogen. An apparent anomaly was found in the case of the amino-acids. The group $NH_2$ is regarded as a highly negative radical, but the amino-acids show very low electrical conductivity. This phenomenon is explained in an entirely satisfactory manner as due to the formation of inner salts. In a paper by E. Q. Adams (1916) in which he makes clear a number of important points regarding the strength of acids, it is shown that under similar circumstances hydrogen ion dissociates from the carboxyl group to a greater extent in monoaminoacetic acid than in monochloracetic acid. But the hydrogen ion which is set free recombines, forming an ammonium complex with the nitrogen. There are some cases in which hydroxyl acids have a lower conductivity than might be expected, and here too we may suspect that the hydrogen ion, which comes from the carboxyl, forms to a slight degree an oxonium complex with the hydroxyl group.

The dibasic acids make an interesting study. There has been some confusion existing as to the meaning of the first and second dissociation constants. It has occasionally been supposed that these two constants are indicative of a special difference between the hydrogens of the two carboxyls, but this is by no means the case. In a symmetrical dibasic acid the two carboxyl hydrogens may be regarded as identical in properties and the chance of dissociation is the same for one as for the other. If the dissociation of one of these hydrogens does not affect the chance of dissociation of the other hydrogen, as it may not if the two carboxyls are very far removed from one another, then it has been shown by E. Q. Adams that the second dissociation constant of the acid will be just one-fourth of the first dissociation constant. He found in fact one or two cases in which the carboxyl groups were so completely removed from one another that this proved to be the case.

Ordinarily, however, the two carboxyl groups profoundly influence one another, and since carboxyl is a negative group and exerts a pull upon electrons, the first dissociation constant of a dibasic acid is usually much higher than the dissociation constant of a corresponding monobasic acid. This effect is the more marked the nearer the two carboxyls are to one another. Thus in the series of compounds with varying numbers of carbon atoms in a chain, and with the two carboxyls at either end of the chain, the first dissociation constant varies from $10^{-(5)}$ for a chain of ten carbon atoms to $10^{-1}$ for a chain of two carbon atoms (oxalic acid).

When, however, a carboxyl group has given off a hydrogen ion and has a negative charge, it no longer exerts a pull upon neighboring electrons, but behaves rather as a strongly positive group. And thus we find, in the series of compounds which has just been mentioned, that the ratio of the second dissociation constant to the first is $\frac{1}{10}$ in the case of the ten-carbon chain, and $\frac{1}{2000}$ in the case of oxalic acid. The case of oxalic acid is therefore like that of hydrogen sulfide, but in the latter the discrepancy between the first and second dissociation constants is far greater still.

The same ideas which are useful in the interpretation of the dissociation of the weak organic acids are equally applicable to inorganic acids. Here the problem has been very ably discussed by Latimer and Rodebush. The three acids of phosphorus, namely, hypophosphorous acid, phosphorous acid, and phosphoric acid, they agree with Werner in writing

$$\begin{array}{ccc}
\text{H} & \ddot{\text{O}}\text{:} & \ddot{\text{O}}\text{:} \\
\text{:}\ddot{\text{O}}\text{:}\ddot{\text{P}}\text{:}\ddot{\text{O}}\text{:H ,} & \text{H:}\ddot{\text{O}}\text{:}\ddot{\text{P}}\text{:}\ddot{\text{O}}\text{:H ,} & \text{H:}\ddot{\text{O}}\text{:}\ddot{\text{P}}\text{:}\ddot{\text{O}}\text{:H .} \\
\text{H} & \text{H} & \text{:}\ddot{\text{O}}\text{:} \\
& & \text{H}
\end{array}$$

From the fact that these three acids are of approximately equal strength they conclude that hydrogen when attached to phosphorus behaves as a decidedly negative element and exercises at least as great a pull as the hydroxide radical, therefore causing approximately the same effect.

On the other hand, they believe, contrary to the views of Werner, that sulfurous acid is chiefly composed of molecules of the form

$$\begin{array}{c}
\text{H:}\ddot{\text{O}}\text{:}\ddot{\text{S}}\text{:}\ddot{\text{O}}\text{:H .} \\
\text{:}\ddot{\text{O}}\text{:}
\end{array}$$

In this formula sulfur possesses a lone pair of electrons, and this pair, instead of exerting a pull which would distort the oxygen octet, is mobile and tends to prevent such distortion. It behaves therefore like a positive group, and sulfurous acid is a weak acid. This distinction between a lone pair of electrons and a pair of electrons which, being attached to a negative atom, is therefore pulled away from the atom, accounts in a very simple manner for the great difference between the acids of elements in their highest state of oxidation, which have no lone pairs on their central atoms, and which are strong electrolytes, and the acids of elements in their lower stages of oxidation, which possess such lone pairs and are usually weak electrolytes. (The next to the highest acids of the halogens, such as chloric acid, seem to constitute an exception to the general rule, for which at present no explanation has been offered.) If we choose to write the formula of nitrous acid using no double bond, and assigning to nitrogen a sextet of electrons, which at least partially represents the facts, namely,

$$:\overset{..}{O}:N:\overset{..}{O}:H \ ,$$

we see that there are two possible explanations of the weakness of nitrous acid. In the first place, the lone pair on the nitrogen atom prevents that distortion of the oxygen octet which tends to set free hydrogen ion, and in the second place any hydrogen ion which does dissociate may in part be attached to the lone pair of the nitrogen, just as we have seen that the hydrogen from an amino-acid recombines with the nitrogen. It is evident that whether we write the formula with hydrogen attached to nitrogen or to oxygen, the ion $NO_2^-$ is the same, and the tautomerism is of the sort that we have so often considered. Hydrogen ion will undoubtedly attach itself in the main to that atom with which it forms the firmest bond, and therefore in general, when there is more than one possible point of union, the molecule which corresponds to the weakest acid will be formed.

## The Definition of Acids and Bases.

When we discuss aqueous solutions of substances which do not contain hydroxyl, it is simplest to define a base as a substance which adds hydrogen ion. Thus ammonia adds hydrogen ion to form ammonium ion, and the degree to which this occurs will vary as we substitute other radicals for hydrogen. Indeed if we wish, we may consider ammonium ion as an acid and say that its strength as an acid is increased when hydrogen is replaced by Cl or OH or $NH_2$. This is precisely the same as saying that ammonia is a weaker base when such substitutions are made. So we might go through a long list of organic bases and show, just as in the case of the acids, how the pull exercised upon electrons by the various negative radicals diminishes their ability to attach hydrogen ion.

Since hydrogen is a constituent of most of our electrolytic solvents, the definition of an acid or base as a substance which gives up or takes up hydrogen ion would be more general than the one that we used before, but it will not be universal. Another definition of acid and base in any given solvent would be the following: An acid is a substance which gives off the cation or combines with the anion of the solvent; a base is a substance which gives off the anion or combines with the cation of the solvent. So potassium amide is a base in ammonia, while potassium chloride would likewise be called a base in liquid hydrochloric acid.

Even this very broad definition is not entirely satisfactory. We are inclined to think of substances as possessing acid or basic properties, without having a particular solvent in mind. It seems to me that with complete generality we may say that *a basic substance is one which has a lone pair of electrons which may be used to complete the stable group of another atom,* and that *an acid substance is one which can employ a lone pair from another molecule* in completing the stable group of one of its own atoms. In other words, the basic substance furnishes a pair of electrons for a chemical bond, the acid substance accepts such a pair.

In this sense all substances which have lone pairs of electrons, capable of employment in onium formation, are basic substances. On the other hand, substances like hydrogen ion, iodous ion, silicon dioxide, sulfur trioxide and boron trichloride are acid substances, since hydrogen ion will accept a pair of electrons to form its stable group of two, and the remaining substances will accept pairs of electrons to complete their stable groups of eight. Some of these substances which we have set down as acid are obviously basic as well; the sulfur atom in sulfur trioxide is acid, but the oxygen atoms in sulfur trioxide may act in a basic manner.

## Other Factors Determining Dissociation.

We are not in a position as yet to give any quantitative measure to the pull that any given atom or radical exerts upon the electrons, and this is partly due to the fact that there are other factors which help in determining the strength of weak electrolytes. Nevertheless it is of interest to attempt in a rough way to arrange radicals according to their electronegative or electropositive character. Thus we seem to be justified in saying that hydrogen is more negative than a methyl group but more positive than a phenyl group. Methyl alcohol is a weaker acid than water, phenol is a stronger acid; on the other hand methylamine is a somewhat stronger base than ammonia, while aniline is a very much weaker base.

It is, however, necessary to exercise some caution in making these deductions. The electrolytic dissociation is important as an index to the pull exerted upon electrons by the various types of atoms, but there are doubtless a number of independent factors which help to determine the degree of dissociation of a weak electrolyte. For example, the dissociation is largely determined by the extent to which one or both of the ions of the dissolved substance form complexes with the solvent. This is a very important question when we are considering a given electrolyte in various solvents, but the extent to which hydrogen ion combines with water to form hydronium ion is not of much consequence when we are comparing a number of acids, all in aqueous solution.

Even if it is to be admitted that the displacement of the electronic structure, which is assumed to account for the strengthening or weakening of an acid, is due to the amount of pull exerted upon electrons by various atoms, it is evident that the amount of this pull cannot alone determine the displacement of electrons with respect to the positive kernels, for we must also consider the rigidity of the electronic structure. In a molecule, or in a part of a molecule, where such rigidity is small, or in other words where the electrons may be said to be mobile, a small force will produce a relatively large displacement and therefore largely influence their dissociation. Therefore we need not be surprised, when we compare two different hydroxides, to find one of them at the same time a stronger acid and a stronger base than the other.

Although this is a subject which is still obscure, we cannot doubt that there are molecules in which the framework of electrons is very rigid, and that there are other molecules that are held by less powerful constraints. Moreover we can state in general terms the criteria by which we may ascertain whether or not the electrons are mobile or are rigidly held. In any molecule or in any part of a molecule, which has those properties indicative of what we call unsaturation, the electron structure is in a mobile condition.

For example, a double bond produces such a condition of unsaturation. In an organic molecule any negative radical, such as Cl, OH, $NH_2$ and CN produces unsaturation. And this is true when two negative elements are bonded together, causing that state of strain upon which we have previously commented. Heavy radicals, such as iodine and triphenylmethyl, cause unsaturation, and this is probably due in part to the greater disruptive force in a heavy molecule which is in thermal rotation. The loosening of the bond in molecular iodine and in hexaphenylethane is shown both by the thermal and by the electrolytic dissociation of these substances.

When we say that any double bond increases the mobility of the electron structure, we do not mean merely that the electrons which produce the double bond are mobile, but rather that all electrons in the neighborhood are less rigidly held. If we consider that every condition of unsaturation is caused by some departure from the normal state of the stable pair and octet, we may suppose that the system will assume a condition in which the total unsaturation is reduced to a minimum. It is probable that this condition is best satisfied, not by leaving most of the structure in its normal state and concentrating the unsaturation at one point, but rather by distributing the necessary distortion to some extent throughout the molecule.

Let us give an example to illustrate the necessity of considering this factor of electron mobility when we are discussing the strength of electrolytes. Methyl alcohol is a weak base. By replacing the methyl hydrogens by more negative groups we should expect the alcohol to become an even weaker base. But phenyl is a negative radical and triphenylmethyl carbinol, $(C_6H_5)_3COH$, is a vastly stronger base than methyl alcohol. Here we have an extreme instance of the loosening of chemical bonds. The phenyl group, not only because of its large size and weight, but also because of its double bonds, has a large effect in loosening neighboring bonds. Three phenyls upon a single carbon atom give the very extraordinary radical triphenylmethyl, which is capable of free existence as an odd molecule, and which is never tightly held to any other radical. In the carbinol the hydroxyl group may be regarded as being held by a very loose bond.

Finally it must be pointed out that even with all these reservations the electrochemical effect of a given radical cannot be quite so simple as we have imagined it. In discussing the effect of substituted chlorine in the chain of an aliphatic acid we have seen that the influence of the chlorine becomes steadily less as the number of carbon atoms separating it from the carboxyl group increases. The action appears to be through the chain, but this view is not always tenable, as is shown clearly by the case of maleic and fumaric acids, namely,

$$\begin{array}{ccc} \text{HCCOOH} & & \text{HCCOOH} \\ \parallel & \text{and} & \parallel \\ \text{HOOCCH} & & \text{HCCOOH} \end{array}$$

Here the number of atoms separating the two carboxyl groups is the same in both acids, and we might therefore expect that the dissociation constants would be very nearly the same. As a matter of fact the first constant of the cis-acid is ten times that of the trans-acid, showing that the two groups have a much greater influence on one another in the former than in the latter. This influence is brought out still more remarkably by the second dissociation constant. The ratio of the first constant to the second is 45 in the case of the trans-acid, but in the case of the cis-acid this ratio is 50,000. It seems evident that there is an opportunity for spatial approach of the two carboxyls in the one case which is absent in the other, and that this approach enormously heightens the mutual influence of the two groups.

## The Rule of Crum Brown and Gibson.

We must not leave this subject without giving some attention to the explanations which have been offered for the very remarkable phenomena observed in connection with substitution in the benzene ring. If one of the hydrogens of benzene is replaced by a radical of a certain class comprising such groups as Cl, OH, $CH_3$, a second substituent enters the ring chiefly in the ortho and para positions. These radicals are therefore known as ortho-para-orienting groups. On the other hand, there is another class of substituents which cause the next substitution to occur in the meta position. This class comprises such radicals as $NO_2$, CN and COOH, which are known as meta-orienting groups. In one of the latest attempts to explain this phenomenon, Stieglitz (1922), in terms of the modern dualistic theory, assumed that an ortho-para-orienting group makes the carbon, to which it is attached, altogether positive. He then makes the ortho and para carbons quadrinegative and the meta carbons bipositive. He thus assumes the enormous difference of six units of charge between meta carbons on the one hand and ortho or para carbons on the other hand.

Such an extreme electrical polarization, which far exceeds any that we have been assuming, should produce startling effects upon the strength of a carboxyl hydrogen. Indeed from all that we have seen in this chapter we should expect even a relatively small difference between the charge on an ortho carbon and that on a meta carbon to affect very greatly the dissociation of hydrogen from the carboxyl attached to the atoms in these positions. In the nitro- and chlorbenzoic acids we have an opportunity of testing these deductions. Chlorine orients in ortho and para positions. The nitro group is the type of meta orienting groups. If Stieglitz' theory were correct we should expect the chlorbenzoic acid to be a very strong acid in the meta arrangement, and very weak in the ortho and para. On the other hand we should expect ortho-nitrobenzoic acid to be very strong and meta-nitrobenzoic acid to be very weak. The fact, however, is that both nitro- and chlorbenzoic acid behave almost exactly alike. The dissociation constants for nitrobenzoic acid are: ortho, $6 \times 10^{-3}$; meta, $3 \times 10^{-4}$. For chlorbenzoic acid: ortho, $1.3 \times 10^{-3}$; meta, $1.6 \times 10^{-4}$.

Whether the negative substituent in benzoic acid is an ortho or meta orienting group, its effect on the strength of the acid is entirely analogous to the effect produced by negative groups in aliphatic acids. The effect is large when the negative substituent is on the atom next to the one which has the carboxyl; the effect is much smaller when the substituent is removed by one more carbon atom in the meta arrangement; and usually the para form is the weakest of all, although in some cases it proves to be slightly stronger than the meta, which might perhaps be considered evidence that there is a very *slight* alternation of charge in the benzene carbons.

It might be argued that, in both of the acids that we have been discussing, it is the carboxyl group which determines the electronic arrangement, but this argument can be met immediately by considering benzene in which two hydrogens have been replaced by carboxyls, giving the phthalic acids. Here again we find just such a behavior as would be predicted from our knowledge of the dibasic aliphatic acids. The first dissociation constant of the ortho acid is about five times that of the meta acid, while the ratio of the first to the second dissociation constants is 10 for the meta acid and nearly 1000 for the ortho acid. (In this respect ortho-phthalic acid resembles oxalic acid; in the former, it is true, there are two more carbons between the carboxyl groups, but they are atoms in which the electron mobility is high.)

An entirely different kind of alternation in the benzene ring has been assumed by Flürscheim (1902, 1905), who considers that it is an alternation, not of electric charge, but of "residual affinity." This residual affinity corresponds to what we have called a state of unsaturation. There is much to be said in favor of this hypothesis, for indeed we see evidence not only of alternation within the ring, as shown by the fact that an ortho-orienting group is also a para-orienting group, but also in a chain directly attached to the benzene ring. Thus we see that the OH group, with oxygen attached directly to a benzene carbon, is ortho-orienting. The carboxyl radical, in which the oxygen is attached to a carbon atom once removed, is meta-orienting, while the radical $CH_2COOH$, in which the oxygen is attached to a carbon twice removed, is again ortho-orienting.

This whole problem is one of much difficulty. It may be remarked, however, that we are dealing here with a phenomenon which merely concerns rates of reaction. An ortho-orienting group increases the rate of substitution in the ortho position. There is no evidence at present that the compound produced is any more stable than one which would be produced by the corresponding substitution in the meta position.

While we may certainly conclude that electric polarization is small in benzene and its derivatives, nevertheless there is one point that must not be overlooked. All of the methods we have used to determine the degree of polarity of substances,—including the study of the dissociation of electrolytes,—give information regarding the average state of the molecules. However, when a substance enters into a reaction, it may be only molecules in a quite exceptional state that take part. At the recent conference of the Faraday Society (July, 1923) all of those who participated seemed agreed that the average organic molecule is very little polarized, but there were some who believed that polarization and indeed ionization precede every reaction. This seems too extreme a view; even when the breaking of a bond is the first step in a reaction, the electron pair may be equally divided (e. g. hexaphenyl ethane in benzene). Yet, especially in the more polar solvents, a reacting atom may often get complete possession of a bonding pair, thus causing some reaction. The momentary surge of electrons that results in such polar breaking of the bond is apparently favored in a molecule in which the successive atoms may readily acquire a large and alternating polarity. This seems to me the basis of the important theory of "induced alternating polarity" of Lapworth and Robinson.

### Résumé.

We have seen in this chapter what a pitiful residuum is left to us of the once powerful electrochemical theory. While electrostatic forces evidently play an important part in processes of ionization, and very likely also in numerous reactions which verge upon the ionic type, such forces are responsible neither for the fundamental arrangement of electrons within the molecule nor for the bonds which hold the atoms together.

# Chapter XIII.

## The Source of Chemical Affinity; a Magneto-chemical Theory.

I believe that enough has been said to show the incompetency of simple electrostatic forces to account for the essential characteristics of chemical combination. If a final argument be needed, let us compare the atom of argon, with a positive nuclear charge of 18 and its 18 electrons, with the atom of potassium which has a positive nuclear charge of 19 and 19 electrons. It might be expected that the removal of an electron would be about as easy from the one of these atoms as from the other. Instead we find that it takes but 4 volts to ionize a potassium atom, while it requires 15 volts to ionize the argon atom. An even greater disparity is found between helium, which has a nuclear charge of $+ 2$ with 2 electrons, and lithium, which has a nuclear charge of $+ 3$ with 3 electrons. The ionizing potential of lithium is 5 volts, that of helium is 25 volts.

In our previous chapters it has occasionally been hinted that in place of the electric it is the magnetic properties of the atom and the molecule which determine their essential structure. In the present chapter we shall give free rein to this idea.[1]

In Bohr's theory of the orbital electron each electronic orbit constitutes an elementary magnet or magneton. In the case of the simple hydrogen atom the electron in its first orbit, or lowest energy level, has the smallest magnetic moment; in the second circular orbit it has twice that moment; in the third it has three times that moment, and so on. It has been suggested that one of the quantum conditions of atomic structure is that in a complex atom any magnetic moment is either equal to that of the hydrogen atom in its most stable state or an integral multiple of that value. In other words, if the hydrogen atom at its lowest energy level is considered to have the unit of magnetic moment, the moment of any other atom may be expressed as an integer or zero.

If we consider two electrons in an atom, each of which has a unit magnetic moment, the two together may give a magnetic moment of 2 or 0, according to whether the two elementary magnets are so oriented as to amplify or to nullify the magnetic effect. In his remarkable treatise on atomic structure (1922) Sommerfeld discusses the determination of atomic magnetic moments from spectroscopic data. I have recently had the pleasure of a personal discussion on this subject with Professor Sommerfeld, and apparently it is safe to assert

[1] Ramsay (1916) suggested certain magnetic molecular models.

that an atom which possesses an odd number of electrons always has a magnetic moment, while atoms with an even number of electrons usually have no magnetic moment.

Here therefore we have very direct evidence that the pairing of electrons, which I have regarded as the most fundamental phenomenon in all chemistry, is some sort of conjugation of two magnetons, of such character as to eliminate mutually their magnetic moment. This conjugation does not always occur. In the elements of variable atomic kernel, such as iron, we have already seen that both chemical and magnetic properties indicate a lack of conjugation of the elementary magnets, and in such atoms Professor Sommerfeld finds that the spectroscopic evidence indicates the presence of several units of magnetic moment. There are also some molecules, like that of elementary oxygen, which indicate a failure of the magnetons to couple, and we shall see that this is probably characteristic of the double bond.

Nevertheless, we may state as the first law of chemical affinity that electrons in an atom or a molecule tend to pair with one another in such manner as to eliminate magnetic moment. The odd molecule therefore represents the highest degree of chemical unsaturation. Even the odd molecules which have been isolated in the free state show as a class the properties which we should expect of such substances. If we could work under ordinary conditions with such substances as free methyl, monatomic hydrogen and monatomic chlorine, we should find these substances to have a reactivity such as no existing substances possess.

The actual disposition of the extra electron in an odd molecule will not be an easy matter to ascertain, but it presumably seeks that portion of the molecule which possesses the highest degree of unsaturation, and there orients itself in such manner as to reduce the total unsaturation to a minimum. So also an odd molecule attaches itself readily to other molecules, even to those which we regard as least unsaturated. So, for example, triphenylmethyl forms a compound with hexane.

The odd molecule of sodium dissolves in ammonia or an amine to form a compound from which sodium ion may dissociate, leaving the odd electron attached to the solvent, as is shown by the investigations of Gibson and Argo (1918) on the absorption of light by these substances. Monatomic hydrogen attaches itself to the hydrogen molecule $H_2$ to produce the odd molecule $H_3$. It has been suggested that this molecule of "active hydrogen" is to be represented by a symmetrical ring structure, but it seems far more likely that it is a loose combination between H and $H_2$ entirely analogous to the compound between triphenylmethyl and hexane.

The fact that some odd molecules actually exist in the free state shows that there are conditions under which a molecule which has no magnetic moment may break into two molecules, each of which has a magnetic moment, as hexaphenylethane dissociates to form triphenylmethyl, and as iodine at high temperatures assumes the monatomic state. This dissociation is evidently the result of thermal agitation, but there are other more obscure factors involved in that loosening of the chemical bond which permits such dissociation. We should expect that heavy radicals would be subject to a greater centrifugal force and therefore dissociate more readily, and we find that $I_2$ dissociates more readily than $Cl_2$, and $\varphi_3CC\varphi_3$ dissociates more readily than $H_3CCH_3$. But, as has been especially pointed out to me by Professor Branch, the loosening of the bond in hexaphenylethane is not due alone to the weight of the radical, but also to the unsaturated character of the phenyl group, that we discussed in the last chapter. If in hexaphenylmethane we should replace the benzene rings by hexamethylene rings, the radicals would be slightly heavier than before, but there would be no appreciable dissociation.

When two odd molecules, each having a magnetic moment, unite by the coupling of their odd electrons to form a system in which the magnetic moment is eliminated, the energy of the separate magnetic fields may be considered as set free, manifesting itself as the heat of combination. In general we may suppose the state of minimum energy to be a state of the utmost mutual neutralization of magnetic fields, except in so far as electrostatic forces and possibly some other factors of even less significance intervene.

When all the electrons in a molecule are paired, even if we assume that the magnetic moment of a bonding pair and of every other electron pair is exactly zero, it would be neither necessary nor desirable to assume that the magnetic fields of the paired electrons completely neutralize one another. In other words, we may assume the complete disappearance of magnetic moment (although this has not yet been definitely proved), and at the same time we may assume a residual magnetic field emanating from the electron pair. This stray field we shall now consider to be equivalent to what has been called residual affinity, and to be responsible for that condition which we have spoken of as a condition of unsaturation. This residual affinity is therefore of a very different kind from that which would be due to electric polarization, where it would be necessary to assume two kinds of field, one emanating from a positive and one from a negative charge.

The several pairs of electrons in an atom may arrange themselves in such an orientation as to neutralize still further their residual fields. The second fundamental principle of chemical affinity may therefore be stated as follows: Every atom, except that of hydrogen or helium, has the smallest external magnetic field, and is therefore in a condition of maximum stability, when it possesses in its outer shell four pairs of electrons situated at the corners of a regular tetrahedron. The condition of saturation accompanying such an arrangement is best exemplified by the atoms of the argon type. The noble gases in their diamagnetic behavior and in their chemical inertness show a nearer approach to complete saturation, or lack of residual affinity, than any other known substances.

Whenever such a group of eight (or group of two in the case of hydrogen) is effected by the sharing of electron pairs, there is a less complete neutralization of the residual magnetic fields, and we may say that even a substance which contains only single bonds is not a fully saturated substance. Such single bonds as in hydrogen-hydrogen, hydrogen-carbon, and carbon-carbon seem to possess the smallest residual magnetic fields. When one of the bonded atoms is that of a negative element the residual field is greater, and becomes specially pronounced when two such elements are bonded together.

Whenever the symmetrical and stable structure is in any way distorted it leads to an increase in the residual magnetic field, and a distortion produced in one portion of a molecule will ordinarily cause some distortion in neighboring atoms in such manner that the total resultant unsaturation is reduced to a minimum. Such a distortion we find for example in the unsaturated substances with rings of three and four carbon atoms. All such distortions of the molecule, with the accompanying increase in residual magnetism, may be considered to be due to the change in the relative position or orientation of the several pairs, or to the partial "opening up" of a single pair, and probably either of these effects ordinarily accompanies the other. Such a displacement of the electrons from their most stable positions may be taken as equivalent to what we have called the loosening of bonds and the increase in electron mobility.

During the whole course of my investigations relating to the structure of molecules a very interesting question has constantly recurred to which I feel unable to give a definite answer. In our discussion of the electrochemical properties of substances we have assumed that if one pair of electrons were drawn away from an atom in a certain direction by an element striving for sole possession of the bonding pair, then the remaining pairs of that and neighboring atoms would be drawn in the same direction by electrostatic forces. This, however, would place the octet as a whole in an unsymmetrical position with respect to the atomic kernel, and the question is whether we may not occasionally meet with just the opposite phenomenon in which the drawing out of one or more pairs from the atomic center might lead to a withdrawal of the remaining pairs, in such manner as to result in a symmetrical tetrahedron about the kernel. If three of the electron pairs are drawn away from an atom through union with electronegative atoms, the two possibilities would be represented by the following scheme:

$$: \overset{\displaystyle\cdot\cdot}{\underset{\displaystyle\cdot\cdot}{X}} : \qquad\qquad : \overset{\displaystyle\cdot\cdot}{X} :$$

Thus if the three hydrogens of methyl alcohol are replaced by phenyl groups these will draw three pairs of electrons away from the carbon atom, and if we were to assume that the remaining pair, which is the bond to the hydrogen group, were forced away from the carbon atom at the same time, it might in this way be possible to account in part for the notably basic properties of triphenylmethyl carbinol which we recently considered. This question is closely connected with the possibility of alternation of properties in a chain of carbon atoms, which we discussed in the preceding chapter.

It may be that under certain circumstances two atoms which share a condition of unsaturation may reach their condition of greatest stability, not when the unsaturation is distributed between the two atoms, but rather when one of the atoms approaches its normal state and the other bears the full brunt of the unsaturation. Stieglitz has explained certain phenomena by stating that an atom tends to become wholly positive or wholly negative. While we have seen that the assumptions underlying such a statement are untenable, might we not assume that of two adjoining atoms one tends to be wholly saturated while the other carries the whole or the greater part of the residual affinity? While there are a number of facts which suggest this possibility, I have sought in vain for any definite evidence that such a phenomenon exists. We might consider the symmetrical and unsymmetrical forms of di-chlor ethane. The heat of formation as far as we can ascertain from existing data is about the same for both substances. As to their magnetic properties Pascal has shown that the symmetrical form is the more diamagnetic of the two, which seems to indicate that the unsaturation is least when it is shared between the two carbon atoms.

With the exception of the odd molecules, the molecules of organic substances which we must regard as most unsaturated are those to which we ascribe multiple bonds, and especially double bonds. Nevertheless a molecule of the ethylene type is not so unsaturated as we should expect it to be if we had to assume the two carbons to be united by a single bond, for then we should be obliged to assume either two odd electrons or a highly unsymmetrical and electrically polarized molecule with eight electrons on one carbon and six on the other. These facts, together with the existence of cis and trans isomers, lead us to assume the double bond. However, the exact physical significance of the double bond remains somewhat mysterious. It is certainly not the equivalent of two single bonds, but rather indicates a state intermediate between this and the condition which would exist if there were but a single bond and a consequent deficiency of electrons to make up the two carbon octets.

Both the chemical and the magnetic properties of substances with double bonds show a high degree of unsaturation. The extremely valuable investigations of Pascal show that the diamagnetic susceptibility is far less than would be calculated from the addition of atomic susceptibilities whenever we have a double bond between carbon and carbon, carbon and nitrogen, nitrogen and nitrogen, or carbon and oxygen. The most striking case is furnished by the double bond between oxygen and oxygen in the molecule $O_2$. Molecular oxygen is a remarkably paramagnetic substance.

While we must recognize the extraordinary parallelism between diamagnetism and chemical saturation, we cannot hope to give a complete interpretation of the latter in terms of the former until we possess a more adequate physical theory of diamagnetism. The simplest theory of this phenomenon would make the diamagnetic susceptibility of a molecule proportional to the total number of electrons in all the shells of its several atoms. This, however, is certainly not the case, although it is found that the diamagnetism of an atom increases roughly with the atomic number. Thus according to Pascal, the accompanying table gives the atomic susceptibilities of a number of elements. It is

TABLE

ATOMIC SUSCEPTIBILITIES ($\times$ 10⁻⁷).

| | | | |
|---|---|---|---|
| Hydrogen | — 30.5 | Phosphorus | — 274 |
| Carbon | — 62.5 | Sulfur | — 156 |
| Nitrogen | — 58 | Chlorine | — 209.5 |
| Oxygen | — 48 | Bromine | — 319 |
| Fluorine | — 65.5 | Iodine | — 465 |

evident that there is no simple relation between the susceptibilities and the number of electrons.

The simplest theory of paramagnetism would be that this phenomenon is non-existent except when the molecule has one or more units of magnetic moment. The susceptibility measured by the ordinary methods would be the algebraic sum of the susceptibilities due to the diamagnetic and the paramagnetic behavior of the molecule.

The idea that the magnetic moment of an atom or molecule can change only by integral steps is no essential part of our magnetochemical theory. As far as concerns the facts of chemistry and many of the facts of magnetism, it would be simpler to assume that any condition which causes unsaturation by opening up the condensed magnetic system, of electron pair or octet, produces some increase in paramagnetism, thus diminishing the diamagnetism which would be attained in the absence of any magnetic moment.

On the other hand, the assumption that the magnetic moment can occur only in discrete units would lead us to believe that diamagnetism is diminished in some unknown way whenever there is a distortion of the normal magnetic system, and that as this distortion increases a new phenomenon may suddenly appear, when the distortion reaches the point of setting up a magnetic moment.

These are questions which we ought soon to be able to decide by experiments of the type of those of Stern and Gerlach, but our present information is inadequate. It is to be noted that any experiment depending upon the observation of the average properties of a large assemblage of molecules might indicate a gradual increase or decrease in total magnetic moment without necessarily discrediting the theory of discontinuity in magnetic moments, for there might be a tautomeric equilibrium between molecules having a magnetic moment and others having none. The experiments might merely indicate a change in the relative amounts of the two tautomers.

Undoubtedly the molecule of oxygen possesses a magnetic moment, and it seems probable that this is also true in other types of double bond. We could assume the double bond of ethylene broken in such manner as to give an odd electron to each carbon atom, so that each atom would have a magnetic moment. But this is not the only way in which such moments could be set up. We have spoken several times of the possibility that the electrons in the atom may under certain circumstances be removed from the primary to a secondary valence shell. If we were to employ the analogy of the hydrogen atom as portrayed by Bohr, we might consider that a single electron in the first valence shell would have one unit of magnetic moment, but in the second shell might have two units. If one electron of each of these types were then to conjugate we might have a pair of electrons differing from an ordinary electron pair in that it possessed a resultant magnetic moment of one unit.

However, any answer to these questions must at present be speculative and need not greatly concern us, for it is sufficient to our present purpose to recognize that anything which diminishes the diamagnetism of a molecule increases the residual affinity or the condition of unsaturation.

As compared with the double bond, *a triple bond produces very little diminution in diamagnetism.* This is shown not only by the investigations of Pascal on compounds containing triple bonds between carbon and carbon, and carbon and nitrogen, but also by the diamagetism of the nitrogen molecule itself. Substances with triple bonds represent relatively saturated structures.

## Conjugation.

In the course of this book we have been using the word conjugation in what are apparently two different senses. We have spoken of that conjugation of two double bonds which diminishes the unsaturation of a molecule, and we have spoken of two odd electrons, each having a magnetic moment, conjugating to produce a couple which is largely self-contained magnetically, and possesses little residual magnetic field. We are now in a position to assert that these two meanings are identical, and may say that every process which leads to a partial neutralization of molecular magnetic fields is a process of conjugation. It probably would not be far from the truth to state that nearly every chemical process occurs in such manner as to increase the net amount of conjugation.

When two unpaired electrons combine to form an electron pair we have an extreme type of conjugation. When four of these pairs arrange themselves at the corners of a regular tetrahedron, in order to neutralize further their residual magnetic fields, this also is conjugation. When any distortion of such a symmetrical structure is relieved, there is again conjugation. When a molecule rearranges so that the loose bond between two negative elements is broken and firmer bonds are produced, there is marked conjugation. Also in the conventional sense of the organic chemist we may say that when two pairs of doubly bonded carbon atoms are separated by a single bond the molecule is able to rearrange itself, to diminish the strong residual magnetic fields and form a conjugated system.

There is every indication that the effect which we call residual affinity or stray magnetic field manifests itself but a short distance from the seat of unsaturation. We may therefore conclude that when two residual fields, which in our method of writing chemical formulæ appear to be widely separated, conjugate with one another, there is a spatial arrangement of the molecule which brings the two centers of unsaturation close together. The possibility of such approach will often determine whether or not conjugation occurs, and we see in maleic and fumaric acids, which we discussed in the last chapter, two substances which would doubtless behave alike were it not for the opportunity of conjugation afforded in the cis form.

Benzene is the typical highly conjugated system. It not only shows little chemical reactivity, but it also shows, according to Pascal, hardly any of the diminution of diamagnetism which would be expected of a system containing double bonds. From its chemical and magnetic properties, it seems to me that we can state with certainty that the unmodified Kekulé formula is not the true formula for benzene, which undoubtedly has a more compact molecule than that formula would imply.

We have seen, in Figure 24, the electron arrangement which Huggins has proposed for the benzene molecule. Whether this model is correct we cannot at present say, but it seems certain that either this or some similar structure will prove to express best the various properties of the benzene ring. Perhaps the true formula will be found to be one which is in some respects intermediate between this model and the one of Kekulé. The symmetry of the benzene structure undoubtedly permits a degree of conjugation which would not otherwise appear. Indeed we find that dihydro- and tetrahydrobenzene are far more unsaturated, chemically and magnetically, than benzene itself.

One of the most interesting types of conjugation is that which occurs in the carboxyl radical. The ordinary formula given to an organic acid,

$$O = \overset{\text{R}}{\underset{}{\text{C}}}\text{OH},$$

would indicate the existence of a typical double bond between carbon and oxygen. On the other hand we have a large amount of evidence that this is not a typical carbonyl union. Various physical methods that have been applied to organic substances indicate this. Pascal shows that the diamagnetism is much greater than would be predicted for a carbonyl compound. Certain chemical facts further support this view. We have seen that elements like silicon and sulfur rarely, if ever, exhibit the double bond, but in the carboxyl radical we may substitute silicon for carbon or sulfur for oxygen.

The conjugation apparently may occur in two ways: either two carboxyl groups may conjugate with one another, or if this does not occur, a single carboxyl group attains by itself a condition which is far more saturated than can be represented by a formula with a double bond. The conjugation between two carboxyl groups may occur when both are in the same molecule, and the facts presented in the preceding chapter indicate such a conjugation between the two carboxyls of maleic acid. It may also occur when the two carboxyls are in different molecules. A substance like acetic acid is dimolecular, not only in the liquid state, but also to a very surprising degree in the gaseous state. The union between the two molecules must almost certainly occur at the carboxyl groups, and these two groups are to be regarded as held together by a conjugation of some sort.

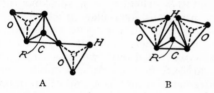

FIG. 26.—Conjugation of the Carboxyl Group (Huggins).

As to conjugation of a single carboxyl, Huggins has offered a suggestion which is interesting, and which may come very near to representing the truth. This model, with slight alterations, is shown in Figure 26B, while Figure 26A represents the structure ordinarily assumed. In both cases each black circle indicates a pair of electrons. The change consists in bending the OH group until the hydrogen is equally placed between the two oxygens, and the whole radical is symmetrical, so that there is no longer one doubly bound and one singly bound oxygen. The known facts regarding the isomers of substances of this type strongly support such a theory of conjugation. If we replace one oxygen in carboxyl by the NH group we might expect two isomers, namely,

$$\overset{R}{HN} = COH, \qquad \overset{R}{H_2NC} = O.$$

Such isomers are entirely unknown, nor would they be expected from the formula of Figure 26B, for the acid hydrogen would belong equally to the oxygen and the nitrogen. (The other hydrogen must ordinarily remain attached to the nitrogen, for its transfer to the oxygen would mean very large electric polarization.)

Conjugation in the carboxyl group seems to be closely paralleled in certain tautomeric substances containing a chain of three carbon atoms, in which the traditional method of writing organic formulæ shows a mobile hydrogen attached to one of the outer carbon atoms while the remaining two are united by a double bond. However, in an extremely convincing paper just presented by Thorpe and Ingold before the International Union of Pure and Applied Chemistry (1923), it is shown that in substances of this type, such as the glutaconic acids, the normal structure of the molecule must be a symmetrical one in which the mobile hydrogen is equally shared by the α- and γ- carbon atoms.

In all such cases of conjugation it is evident that we are dealing with conditions which cannot be adequately represented either by old-fashioned bond formulæ or by mere translation of the old formulæ into our present theory, by substituting electron pairs for bonds. Indeed even in such models as those of Figure 26, we must remember that the tetrahedra which are introduced to facilitate visualization of the model have no real existence. A true picture of a molecule would show only the positions and orientations of the atomic kernels and the electrons. It is further to be borne in mind that no one model could adequately represent the structure of a substance in which there is tautomerism between various molecular structures.

Not only may double bonds conjugate with one another, but one double bond may conjugate with any other source of residual affinity. Such a conjugation with hydroxyl we have just discussed in connection with the carboxyl group. An essentially similar conjugation is assumed by Flürscheim in his theory of substitution in the benzene ring. There it is assumed that the residual affinity of the first substituent conjugates with the adjacent double bond in such manner as to alter the original conjugation of the benzene ring. That the latter is in an extremely labile condition, is shown by the fact that the small change in residual field produced by the mere exchange of a methyl group for a hydrogen suffices to alter the state of conjugation.

Any bond between carbon and a halogen produces a large residual magnetic field, as is well shown by Pascal's discovery of the lack of additivity of the diamagnetism of organic substances containing halogens. The possibility of conjugation between a carbon-chlorine bond and a double bond is illustrated when the four hydrogens of ethylene are substituted by chlorine. The compound $Cl_2C = CCl_2$ shows a far lower degree of chemical reactivity than is usually found in molecules with double bonds. We have noticed several facts which show that what we call a triple bond is more saturated than a double bond. We are thus able to understand a peculiar form of conjugation which apparently consists in the conversion of a double bond into a triple bond. The conversion of diazo-compounds into diazonium compounds seems to belong to this category. The probable course of this reaction is indicated by the following scheme:

$$\varphi : \overset{..}{N} : : \overset{..}{N} : \quad \overset{\displaystyle : \overset{..}{O} : H}{} \quad = \left[ \varphi : N : : : N : \right]^+ + \left[ : \overset{..}{\underset{..}{O}} : H \right]^-$$

In whatever manner conjugation occurs, we must realize that if a system possesses two or more sources of unsaturation, the total unsaturation may be the sum of that due to the separate sources, *but will be less whenever there is any opportunity for such spatial rearrangement and reorientation as will serve to neutralize the residual magnetic fields*. Indeed it is the process of such rearrangement that we know as conjugation.

# Chapter XIV.

# The Discontinuity of Physico-Chemical Processes.

Attempts to apply quantum theory to chemical reactions have been largely limited to a study of reactions produced by light and of the light set free by chemical reactions. It has long been known that numerous photochemical reactions which occur in the presence of blue or violet light occur to a far more limited extent or not at all in red light. So also many reactions which are not produced by visible light take place upon exposure to ultraviolet radiation.

If one or more of the reacting molecules must receive a certain quantity of energy before it can react, then we should expect from quantum theory that no exposure to radiation, no matter how protracted, would cause the reaction to occur, unless the frequency of the radiation were high enough to make $h\nu$ as large as the energy required by the reacting molecule. It is true no case is known of a typical photochemical reaction which occurs rapidly with light of a given frequency and which does not occur at all with light of a little lower frequency. Nor perhaps is this ordinarily to be expected, since different molecules, owing to thermal agitation, would require somewhat different amounts of energy to reach a condition in which they would react.

The interesting idea has been suggested by W. C. McC. Lewis (1916) and by Perrin (1919) that all chemical reactions are photochemical in character. They assume that a molecule does not react until it becomes activated by radiant energy of a certain minimum frequency. This light may come from outside the system, as in the typical photochemical process, or it may exist in the interior of the reacting system as thermal radiation. The relative content of high frequency radiation, in general thermal radiation, increases very rapidly with the temperature, and it has been shown by Lewis that his assumption leads quantitatively to an equation which agrees with the equation that Arrhenius obtained for the change in reaction velocity with the temperature.

The assumption that every simple chemical reaction is accompanied by the absorption of light of one frequency and the emission of light of another frequency enabled Perrin to give a beautiful explanation of the phenomena of photo- and thermo-luminescence. Nevertheless in spite of the great value of this work in pointing out the influence of radiation in chemical phenomena, we cannot adopt the main contention that reactions are due solely to the influence of light and not at all to the molecular bombardment due to thermal motion.

This is perhaps sufficiently shown by a consideration of those simple phenomena which we may regard as the prototypes of all chemical processes, namely, the resonance and ionization of gases. These phenomena are known to be caused either by radiation, or by moving electrons, or by alpha particles, and they presumably can be caused by any other kind of molecular bombardment.

### The Discontinuity of Chemical Processes.

If we were to consider any one philosophic idea as the leading principle in the scientific thought of the last two generations it would be the belief in the continuity of nature. The concept of energy and of its flow through material systems and through free space, the de-

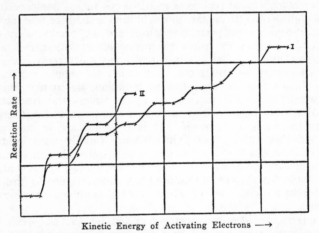

Kinetic Energy of Activating Electrons ⟶

FIG. 27.—Synthesis of Ammonia by an Electron Stream.

velopment by Maxwell of the idea of the electric and magnetic fields, with the discovery of relativity by Einstein, all contributed toward a marvellously simple picture of the universe, based upon the underlying theory of extension in a continuum.

Chemists and physicists, when they have plotted their experimental data and have obtained curves with breaks corresponding to no obvious discontinuity in the system studied, have attributed such breaks to experimental error. In nearly all cases this explanation has been justified, but there are instances, and these are now becoming more numerous, in which such broken curves are found to possess real significance even in systems which seem to possess no apparent source of discontinuity. Professor Olson and Dr. Storch have kindly permitted me to reproduce in Figure 27 some of the curves which they are about to publish, giving the results of their study of the union of nitrogen and hydrogen, to form ammonia, in the presence of a stream of electrons. The ordinate gives the rate of the reaction, and the abscissa the kinetic energy of a constant number of moving electrons. As the latter changes gradually the former changes in a manner which indicates at first sight a series of very inaccurate experiments. The successive steps in the curve, however, are real and have been reproduced at will.

Such a result is not essentially different from that which is observed in the resonance and ionization of a simple gas. The fact that electrons moving with a velocity less than a certain critical velocity, or that radiant energy with a frequency less than a certain critical frequency, produce no change in a molecule, while a slightly higher velocity or a slightly higher frequency of light produces a profound change in the molecule, must be regarded as one of the cardinal facts in all chemistry.

As far as we can see, a hydrogen atom which is in the first or lowest energy state can undergo no change whatsoever unless it can acquire a quantity of energy sufficient to raise its electron from the first to one of the other fixed energy levels, or to remove it altogether from the atom. May we not therefore conclude that a similar statement is true of any molecule, and that every reaction, no matter how complicated, takes place in one or more definite steps? Radical as such a conception is, we may show that many of the chemical ideas which have been developed and stated in terms of the continuous theory may be readily translated into the language of the discontinuous theory.

We have often had occasion to speak of tight or loose bonds, or of electron pairs which are held in position by large or small constraints. In the older theory this would imply a mechanical system in which gradual displacement from an equilibrium condition would build up a restoring force. The ratio of the restoring force to the amount of displacement would measure the magnitude of the constraint, so that a tight bond would be one in which a slight displacement would cause a large force of restitution. We could express this same idea in another way by calling an electron pair mobile when held by small constraints.

In the theory of discontinuity there would be no such thing as a gradual displacement within a molecule. The molecule must be in one or another of a series of states with finite differences in energy and in other properties. However, if we consider once more the case of the simple hydrogen atom, we note that a large energy change is required to remove the electron from the first to the second energy level, but if the electron were in the twentieth level it would take but a small amount of energy to raise it to the twenty-first, or indeed to any of the infinite number of higher levels, or to drive it completely away from the hydrogen nucleus. If we choose to employ the older phraseology we may say that the electron is held tightly in the lower energy levels and loosely in the higher levels.

In general we may conclude that when we speak of a loose bonding pair, or when we say that a molecule or a certain portion of a molecule is in a mobile condition, we mean that a state exists in which small increments of energy suffice to cause a transfer to other neighboring states. The loosening and the eventual rupture of the bond in the molecule of iodine or of hexaphenylethane may be considered analogous to the resonance and eventual ionization of the atom of hydrogen.

But while there are some molecules like the hydrogen atom, or the argon molecule, or the methane molecule, which in their most stable states are far removed in energy content from the next possible state, there are others in which even the most stable state is not very different from other possible states, so that even a mild excitation such as can be produced by light of low frequency, or by a moderate temperature, gives rise to a number of different molecular states. The molecules belonging to these several states could be called tautomeric.

Let us consider a chemical reaction which involves merely the rearrangement of a molecule, such as the conversion of one optical isomer into the other. Such racemization will occur more rapidly the looser the structure is. In other words, the reaction is rapid when a slight molecular impact, or thermal radiation of low frequency, both of which are associated with a low temperature, suffice to carry the molecule through the several energy levels to the second stable state.

Probably the majority of chemical reactions, even those which eventually lead to the evolution of large amounts of energy, require some initial excitation of the molecule, and it undoubtedly frequently happens that a system must be lifted far above its original energy level before it can fall into a still lower energy level. A *catalyst* may be regarded as any substance which, by forming a complex with one of the reacting substances, or by any other means, introduces other series of energy levels which permit a short-circuit of the normal path of the reaction, in such manner as to diminish the amount of excitation required.

### Color.

The older theory furnished an extremely happy explanation of the origin of color and its relation to the chemical properties of substances, as I attempted to show in my paper on the "Atom and the Molecule." According to that view, an electron in a position of constraint possesses, like any other elastic system, a natural period of vibration,—this frequency being proportional to the magnitude of the constraint. Light which has this same period of vibration is capable of imparting energy to the electron resonator, and thus the electron absorbs light in that part of the spectrum which corresponds to its own natural frequency. In the majority of substances the electrons are held so tightly that their natural frequency falls in the ultraviolet region, and these are therefore incapable of absorbing visible light. In other words, they are colorless. But under conditions which loosen the constraints within the molecule the frequency of the electrons is lowered until it corresponds to a visible frequency. The substance thus absorbing some part of the visible spectrum, and letting through other parts, is said to be colored.

Since those changes in the condition of a molecule, such as the substitution of one radical for another, which are known from chemical evidence to loosen the structure of the molecule, and to render it more unsaturated and more reactive, prove to be the same kind of changes that convert a colorless into a colored substance, or which convert a substance with absorption in the violet into a substance with absorption in the red, this explanation of color seemed to be eminently satisfactory. Nevertheless the idea of a vibrating electron seems to be one which is not only alien to, but essentially incompatible with, the spirit of quantum theory.

Fortunately the new theory of the discontinuity of chemical states furnishes a very similar and equally satisfactory explanation of color. When a molecule is in a state such that it may be changed to another state by a quantity of energy which, when divided by the Planck constant $h$, gives a number corresponding to the frequency of visible light, the substance is colored. Any process by which a colorless substance is converted into a colored substance may be regarded as one in which the molecule may be changed from one energy state to another state of only slightly different energy. In other words, with a new interpretation of our terms, we may still say that a colorless substance is converted into a colored substance by a loosening of the electronic structure.

If we consider the halogen group, we may assume that the color of the molecules of these elements is due to the looseness of the bond, and the pair of electrons which constitutes the bond may be considered as passing from one energy position to another during the absorption of light. The bond is weakest in the case of iodine, and here we have absorption of red light. As we pass through bromine and chlorine we see evidence of a tightening of the bond, and in fluorine, where we say that the bond is tightest, only the extreme violet end of the spectrum is absorbed.

All colored substances are highly unsaturated and correspond to a low state of conjugation. All known odd molecules, except nitric oxide, absorb light in the visible region. Most organic substances which absorb light are those which contain double bonds. The benzene ring itself is too highly conjugated to absorb visible light, but in the quinoid form, which is far less conjugated, we find a configuration which almost invariably causes color.

The great majority of compounds of the elements of variable kernel, which appear in the transition regions of the long periods of the Mendeléeff table, are colored. Here we have a case where even the levels corresponding to inner and outer shells do not differ much in energy. This is shown by the small amount of energy required to effect the oxidation or reduction of such compounds. Thus a mild oxidizing agent suffices to change a ferrous into a ferric salt, although this involves the transfer of an electron from the iron kernel.

According to the theory of discontinuity, every absorption band must consist of a series of absorption lines, except for the blurring effect due to thermal agitation; and each of these lines must correspond to the change of a molecule from one definite energy state to another.

It is evident that in many cases there must be a very large number of neighboring energy states. Only in such a way can we account for the highly complex absorption spectrum of a substance like iodine. Even in the case of the simple atom of hydrogen we are obliged to believe in the existence of an infinite number of energy levels, all of which, except the few lowest members, correspond to nearly the same energy. In a molecule containing a number of atoms, and many electrons, the complexity of the system of energy levels is presumably far greater. In a molecule which is highly unsaturated we may assume that even the most stable state is one of many states which are very near to one another in their energy content. But in the case of a highly saturated or highly conjugated system we may assume that the normal state of the molecule cannot be changed without a large addition of energy.

Just as the absorption of visible light is an index of a very loose electronic structure, so we should expect from the Einstein principle that similar conclusions could be drawn from the reaction between a molecule and a moving electron. The fact that iodine vapor absorbs visible light would lead us to predict that a slow-moving electron would be able to cause a change in the energy state of the iodine molecule. Such a reaction might involve the attachment of the electron to the iodine, forming a negative ion, or it might simply mean an inelastic collision which would deprive the electron of a part of its kinetic energy.

Both of these phenomena doubtless occur, and we are beginning to get very valuable data concerning the movement of electrons in various gases. All of these experiments indicate that moving electrons stick to, or are retarded by, those molecules which also give chemical, optical, and magnetic evidence of unsaturation. Thus by assuming that electrons stick to molecules of a halogen, Gibson and Noyes (1922) have offered a very plausible explanation of the disappearance of characteristic metallic spectra in flames when free halogens are present. The mobility of electrons has been shown by Wahlin (1922) to be greater in ethane than in ethylene and greater in ethylene than in chlorine. This is also the order in which we would place these substances with respect to their degree of saturation. Likewise we should expect the mobility of electrons to be far greater in a noble gas than in any other type of gas, and this has been proved experimentally by Townsend and Bailey (1922).

## The Future of Quantum Theory.

In that old American institution, the circus, the end of the performance finds the majority of spectators satiated with thrills and ready to return to more quiet pursuits. But there are always some who not only remain in their seats but make further payment to witness the even more blood-curdling feats of the supplementary performance.

Our own show is now over, and I trust that the majority of readers who have had the patience to reach this point will now leave the tent; for what I am about to say is no longer chemistry, nor is it physics, nor perhaps is it sense. But since we have been obliged here and there to take cognizance of the entering wedge of scientific bolshevism, which we call quantum theory, or the theory of discontinuity in nature, I cannot refrain from attempting to forecast some of the logical consequences which must follow from the new facts that have been discovered and the interpretation which they have been given. Such a forecast must of necessity be of the crudest sort, and can hardly do more than indicate the magnitude of the revolution in scientific thought which probably must occur before physical science can once more be a homogeneous whole, free from the most glaring inconsistencies and contradictions.

Two quantitative methods have been available to scientists. One consists in counting and the other consists in measuring. The former has been the basis of the theory of numbers, the latter has led to the development of geometry. The first of these sciences has been the mere plaything of abstruse mathematicians; the second has become the working tool of the scientist and the engineer. Geometry is based on the theory of the continuum, and so also is the closely related science of calculus. We have been taught that an integration of the infinitesimal elements of a continuum may be approximately replaced by a summation of finite terms, but that the former method is exact and absolute while the second gives but an approximation. Are we not now going to be obliged to reverse this decision and to recognize that the branch of mathematics which will come nearest to meeting the needs of science will be the theory of numbers, rather than a theory of extension, and that measuring must be replaced by counting?

The mathematics of hydrodynamics is based on the theory of the continuum. It is admirably suited to express the behavior of substances like water and air. Nevertheless, the method is entirely an approximate one, for water and air are not continua but are composed of discrete molecules. Hydrodynamics could not account for such a phenomenon as the Brownian movement.

The methods of hydrodynamics were taken over into the field equations of electromagnetics. An electrostatic field, regarded as a continuum, is defined by the force exerted upon an infinitesimal test charge placed within it. But an infinitesimal test charge is a concept which we can no longer hold. The smallest charge is the charge upon a single electron, and if we use the electron as a test charge to determine the properties of the simplest possible electric field, namely, the field about a hydrogen nucleus, we appear to find that this field is not a continuum but is strikingly discontinuous. As far as we are aware, the electron cannot exist except in one of a series of levels, and whether the idea of *motion* of an electron from one level to another has any meaning is somewhat doubtful. As far as we can see, it disappears from one level and appears at another. In this simple system what has become of electric force? We might get something approximating to the idea of force by dividing the energy difference between two levels by the distance between the levels, but in such a microcosmos what assurance have we that the very idea of distance has any significance? Should we not say perhaps that the distance between the first and the third levels is 2, and that the difference between the first and the seventh levels is 6?

Granting that the "field" about a positive particle has at least some elements of discontinuity, and that perhaps this may be true also of the field about an electron (provided that these two ideas are distinguishable), then since every electric field is a resultant of the fields of these elementary particles, every electric field must have properties of discontinuity. Instead of thinking then of an electric field as a continuum, we should rather regard it as an intensely complicated mesh composed of all the discontinuous elements due to the single elementary particles. Even if this view is correct, we need not for ordinary purposes hesitate to use the equations of Maxwell any more than we hesitate to employ the inexact methods of hydrodynamics in ordinary problems.

An observer, moving rapidly past an electrostatic field, finds that it is also a magnetic field, and if the electric field is discontinuous, so is the magnetic. We need not abandon the brilliant idea of Maxwell that light is an electromagnetic phenomenon, nor need we doubt the approximate validity of his equations of the propagation of electromagnetic waves, provided that we consider them to have merely statistical value. But when we consider the light emitted not from a great aggregate of atoms but from a single atom, we may be sure that this is something very different from that which is assumed in the undulatory or electromagnetic theory. It probably bears to the electromagnetic wave a similar relation to that between a molecule of water and a quart of water. On the other hand numerous attempts to return to a corpuscular theory of light have hitherto failed to account adequately for the phenomenon of interference. At present we may say that we have no adequate theory of light.

The recognition that electric and magnetic fields are essentially discontinuous leads us to suspect that there is no such thing as a continuous field of force; that a gradual acceleration accompanied by a gradual increase in kinetic energy is something which does not exist in nature. Rather we should consider that every system passes by steps, which may be small but are nevertheless finite, from one energy state to another.

Finally we might even suspect that space and time could better be treated as discontinuous than as continuous, and represented by a counting method rather than by the methods of a continuous geometry. We might still call such a mathematical representation of space a geometry, but it would be of a very different sort from any existing geometry,—whether Euclidean or non-Euclidean, metrical or non-metrical. Its elements would be nothing but points and groups of points, and a distance would always be an integral number. With relation to some one point, other points would be classified according to whether they were separated from it by one step or two steps or

$n$ steps; and we might have a certain number of points in the class removed by one step, another number in the class removed by two steps, and so on.

I hoped at one time to be able to find such a network geometry which, when the mesh was made exceedingly fine, would approximate to the properties of Euclidean geometry, but I am now convinced that such an attempt is hopeless. On the other hand, if we should consider a single atom, we might be able to state that this atom by itself determines a space which has just such properties of a network, which we might represent by 1 central point, 4 points of the class once removed, 9 points twice removed, 16 points in the third group, and 25 in the fourth. If now we should admit a pair of electrons at each of these points we should have (ignoring the sub-groups of Bohr) a representation of the shells about an atom containing respectively 2, 8, 18, 32 and 50 electrons. We should also find (once more ignoring the sub-groups) that in such a geometry the distance between two successive points would be quite without meaning, if we could consider but one atomic system.

If, in some such way as I have crudely described, we could define the space of a single atom, then general space might be regarded as the composite of all the spaces of all the atoms, and in this space we could employ the ideas of extension, of distance, and the like, which are used in Euclidean geometry; with the same sort of approximate validity that we apply the principles of hydrodynamics to a system containing a large number of molecules, or the principles of electromagnetics to a field generated by many elementary charges.

But it seems as we have proceeded that we have been getting farther and farther away from physical reality into the domain of metaphysical speculation, and it would be undesirable at present to continue. Indeed in a period of transition such as the present we must more than ever focus our attention upon our actual experimental facts, and give less heed to those conventional abstractions of the mind, such as force and fields of force, energy and the conservation of energy, or even space and time. Some of these abstractions may have to be abandoned as the conventional ether was abandoned after the acceptance of relativity. Others may have to be modified, and my chief purpose in writing the present section is not so much to predict just how these modifications are to occur as it is to emphasize the necessity of maintaining an openness of mind; so that, when the solution of these problems, which now seem so baffling, is ultimately offered, its acceptance will not be retarded by the conventions and the inadequate mental abstractions of the past.

# REFERENCES.

Abegg, 1904, *Z. anorg. Chem., 39,* 330.
Abegg and Bodländer, 1899, *Z. anorg. Chem., 20,* 453.
Adams, E. Q., 1916, *J. Am. Chem. Soc., 38,* 1503.
Arrhenius, 1887, *Z. phys. Chem., 1,* 631.
Aston, 1920, *Phil. Mag.* [6], *39,* 449, 611.

Baeyer, 1885, *Ber., 18,* 2277.
Balmer, 1885, *Wied. Ann., 25,* 80.
Bardwell, 1922, *J. Am. Chem. Soc., 44,* 2499.
Berzelius, 1819, "Essai sur la théorie des proportions chimiques et sur l'influence chimique de l'électricité." Paris.
Bohr, 1913 I, *Phil. Mag.* [6], *26,* 1.
Bohr, 1913 II, *Phil. Mag.* [6], *26,* 857.
Bohr, 1921, *Nature, 107,* 104.
Boltzmann, 1912, "Vorlesungen über Gastheorie," Barth, Leipzig.
Born and Landé, 1918, *Sitz. kg. preus. Akad., 1918,* 1048; *Verh. d. deutsch. phys. Ges., 20,* 202, 210.
Brackett, 1922, *Astrophys. J., 56,* 154.
Bragg, 1920, *Phil. Mag.* [6], *40,* 169.
Bragg, 1922, *Phil. Mag.* [6], *44,* 433.
Bray and Branch, 1913, *J. Am. Chem. Soc., 35,* 1440.
van den Broek, 1914, *Phys. Zeit., 14,* 32.
Bury, 1921, *J. Am. Chem. Soc., 43,* 1602.

Cannizarro, 1858, "Sunto di un corso di filosofia chimica." Geneva.
de Chancourtois, 1863, "Vis tellurique, classement naturel des corps simples ou radicaux obtenu au moyen d'un système de classification hélicoidal et numerique." Paris.
Crum Brown and Gibson, 1892, *J. Chem. Soc., 61,* 367.

Dalton, 1808, "A New System of Chemical Philosophy." London.
Davy, 1807, *Phil. Trans., 97,* 1.
Döbereiner, 1816, *Gilbert's Ann., 56,* 332.

Eastman, 1922, *J. Am. Chem. Soc., 44,* 438.
Einstein, 1907, *Ann. der Phys.* [4], *22,* 180.
Erlenmeyer, 1901, *Ann., 316,* 43, 71, 75.

Falk and Nelson, 1910, *J. Am. Chem. Soc., 32,* 1637.
Faraday, 1833 and 1834, *Phil. Trans., 123,* 23; *124,* 77.
Flürscheim, 1902 and 1905, *J. prakt. Chem., 66,* 321; *71,* 497.
Franck and Herz, 1913, *Verh. d. deutsch. phys. Ges., 15,* 34.
Fry, 1911, *Z. physik. Chem., 76,* 385.

Gibson and Argo, 1918, *J. Am. Chem. Soc., 40,* 1327.
Gibson and Noyes, 1922, *J. Am. Chem. Soc., 44,* 2091.
Gomberg, 1900, *J. Am. Chem. Soc., 22,* 757.

Helmholtz, 1881, *J. Chem. Soc., 39,* 277.
van't Hoff, 1875, "La chimie dans l'espace." Rotterdam.
Huggins, 1922, *Science, 40,* 679.
Hull, 1917, *Phys. Rev., 10,* 661.

Jones, L. W., 1914, *J. Am. Chem. Soc., 36,* 1268.

Kekulé, 1858, *Liebig's Ann., 106,* 129.
Kirchhoff and Bunsen, 1860 and 1861, *Pogg. Ann., 110,* 161; *113,* 337.
Körner, 1874, *Gaz. chim., 4,* 444.
Kossel, 1916, *Ann. der Phys., 49,* 229.
Kratzer, 1920, *Z. Physik., 3,* 289.

Langevin, 1904 and 1905, *Compt. rend., 139,* 1204; *Ann. Chim. Phys., 5,* 70.
Langmuir, 1916, *J. Am. Chem. Soc., 38,* 222.
Langmuir, 1919 I, *J. Am. Chem. Soc., 41,* 868.
Langmuir, 1919 II, *J. Am. Chem. Soc., 41,* 1543.
Langmuir, 1920, *J. Am. Chem. Soc., 42,* 274.
Lapworth and Robinson, 1923, *Farad. Soc.,* July meeting.

Latimer and Rodebush, 1920, *J. Am. Chem. Soc., 42*, 1419.
Le Bel, 1875, *Bull. Soc. Chim.* [2], 23, 338.
Lewis, G. N., 1913, *J. Am. Chem. Soc., 35*, ·1448.
Lewis, G. N., 1916 I, *J. Am. Chem. Soc., 38*, 762.
Lewis, G. N., 1916 II, *Proc. Nat. Acad. Sci., 2*, 586.
Lewis, G. N., 1917, *Science, 46*, 297.
Lewis, W. C. McC., 1916, *J. Chem. Soc., 109*, 796.
Lowry, 1923, *Trans. Farad. Soc. 18*, Part 3, p. 3.
Lyman, 1904 and 1906, *Astrophys. J., 19*, 263; *23*, 181.

Marignac, 1860, *Archives des sciences physiques et naturelles,* Geneva, *9*, 97.
Meisenheimer, 1913, *Ann., 397, 273.*
Mendeléeff, 1869, *J. Russ. Phys. Chem. Soc., 1*, 1.
Meyer, L., 1870, *Liebig's Ann. Suppl., 7*, 354.
Moseley, 1913 and 1914, *Phil. Mag.* [6], *26*, 1024; *27*, 703.

Nef, 1904, *J. Am. Chem. Soc., 26*, 1549.
Newlands, 1863, *Chem. News, 7*, 70.
Noyes and Lyon, 1901, *J. Am. Chem. Soc., 23*, 460.

Parson, 1915, *Smithsonian Inst. Publ., 65*, No. 11.
Pascal, 1912, *Ann. chim. phys.* [8], *25*, 289.
Paschen, 1909, *Ann. der Phys.* [4], *27*, 537.
Perrin, 1908, *Compt. rend., 147*, 967; *148*, 530.
Perrin, 1919, *Ann. de phys., 11*, 1.
Pickering, 1897, *Astrophys. J., 5*, 92.
Planck, 1901, *Ann. der Phys.* [4], *4*, 553.
Prout, 1815 and 1816, *Thomson's Ann. Phil., 6*, 321; *7*, 111.

Ramsay, 1908, *J. Chem. Soc., 93*, 774.
Ramsay, 1916, *Proc. Roy. Soc., 72A*, 451.
Rankine, 1921, *Proc. Roy. Soc.* (A), *98*, 366.
Rayleigh, 1900, *Phil. Mag.* [5], *49*, 539.
Rutherford, 1911, *Phil. Mag.* [6], *21*, 669.

Rutherford and Soddy, 1903, *Phil. Mag.* [4], *5*, 445.
Rydberg, 1890, *Compt. rend., 110*, 394.
Rydberg, 1897, *Z. anorg. Chem., 14*, 66. (See also Marignac and Clarke, "Constants of Nature," *5*, 262.)
Rydberg, 1914, *Phil. Mag.* [6], *28*, 144.

Schlenck and Holz, 1917, *Ber., 50*, 274, 276.
Sidgwick, 1923, *Nature,* June 16.
Sommerfeld, 1922, "Atombau und Spektrallinien," Vieweg und Sohn, Braunschweig.
Stark, 1915, "Prinzipien der Atomdynamik, III, Die Elektrizität im chemischen Atom," Hirzel, Leipzig.
Stern and Gerlach, 1921, *Zeit. Physik., 8*, 110.
Stieglitz, 1922, *J. Am. Chem. Soc., 44*, 1293.
Stock and others, 1912-1921, *Ber., 45*, 3539 (1912); *Z. Elektrochem., 19*, 779 (1913); *Ber., 46*, 1959, 3353 (1913); *Ber., 54* A, 142; *54* B, 531 (1921).

Thiele, 1899, *Ann., 306*, 87.
Thomson, 1904, *Phil. Mag., 7*, 237.
Thomson, 1907, "The Corpuscular Theory of Matter," Scribner, New York.
Thomson, 1913, "Rays of Positive Electricity and Their Application to Chemical Analysis," Longmans, Green & Co., London.
Thomson, 1914, *Phil. Mag.* [6], *27*, 757.
Thorpe and Ingold, 1923, *Intern. Union Pure and Appl. Chem.*
Townsend and Bailey, 1922, *Phil. Mag.* [6], *43*, 593.

Vorländer, 1922, *Z. angew. Chem., 35*, 249.

Wahlin, 1922, *Phys. Rev., 19*, 173.
Weber, 1915, *Jahrb. d. Radioakt., 12*, 74.
Werner, 1905, "Neuere Anschauungen auf dem Gebiete der anorganischen Chemie," Vieweg, Braunschweig.
Wieland, 1911 and 1914, *Ann., 381*, 200; *Ber., 47*, 2111.
Wien, 1896, *Ann. der Phys.* [3], *58*, 662.

# INDEX

CATALOGUE OF DOVER BOOKS

# PHYSICS

## General physics

**FOUNDATIONS OF PHYSICS, R. B. Lindsay & H. Margenau.** Excellent bridge between semi-popular works & technical treatises. A discussion ot methods of physical description, construction of theory; valuable tor physicist with elementary calculus who is interested in ideas that give meaning to data, tools of modern physics. Contents include symbolism, mathematical equations; space & time foundations of mechanics; probability; physics & continua; electron theory; special & general relativity; quantum mechanics; causality. "Thorough and yet not overdetailed. Unreservedly recommended," NATURE (London). Unabridged, corrected edition. List of recommended readings. 35 illustrations. xi + 537pp. 5⅜ x 8.
S377 Paperbound **$2.75**

**FUNDAMENTAL FORMULAS OF PHYSICS, ed. by D. H. Menzel.** Highly useful, fully inexpensive reference and study text, ranging trom simple to highly sophisticated operations. Mathematics integrated into text—each cnapter stands as short textbook ot field represented. Vol. 1: Statistics, Physical Constants, Special Theory of Relativity, Hydrodynamics, Aerodynamics, Boundary Value Problems in Math. Physics; Viscosity, Electromagnetic Theory, etc. Vol. 2: Sound, Acoustics, Geometrical Optics, Electron Optics, High-Energy Phenomena, Magnetism, Biophysics, much more. Index. Total of 800pp. 5⅜ x 8.     Vol. 1 S595 Paperbound **$2.00**
Vol. 2 S596 Paperbound **$2.00**

**MATHEMATICAL PHYSICS, D. H. Menzel.** Thorough one-volume treatment of the mathematical techniques vital for classic mechanics, electromagnetic theory, quantum theory, and relativity. Written by the Harvard Protessor of Astrophysics for junior, senior, and graduate courses, it gives clear explanations of all those aspects of function theory, vectors, matrices, dyadics, tensors, partial differential equations, etc., necessary tor the understanding of the various physical theories. Electron theory, relativity, and other topics seldom presented appear here in considerable detail. Scores of definitions, conversion factors, dimensional constants, etc. "More detailed than normal for an advanced text . . . excellent set of sections on Dyadics, Matrices, and Tensors," JOURNAL OF THE FRANKLIN INSTITUTE. Index. 193 problems, with answers. x + 412pp. 5⅜ x 8.     S56 Paperbound **$2.00**

**THE SCIENTIFIC PAPERS OF J. WILLARD GIBBS.** All the published papers of America's outstanding theoretical scientist (except for "Statistical Mechanics" and "Vector Analysis"). Vol I (thermodynamics) contains one of the most brilliant of all 19th-century scientific papers—the 300-page "On the Equilibrium of Heterogeneous Substances," which tounded the science of physical chemistry, and clearly stated a number of highly important natural laws. for the first time; 8 other papers complete the first volume. Vol II includes 2 papers on dynamics, 8 on vector analysis and multiple algebra, 5 on the electromagnetic theory of light, and 6 miscellaneous papers. Biographical sketch by H. A. Bumstead. Total of xxxvi + 718pp. 5⅜ x 8⅜.
S721 Vol I Paperbound **$2.50**
S722 Vol II Paperbound **$2.00**
The set **$4.50**

**BASIC THEORIES OF PHYSICS, Peter Gabriel Bergmann.** Two-volume set which presents a critical examination of important topics in the major subdivisions of classical and modern physics. The first volume is concerned with classical mechanics and electrodynamics: mechanics of mass points, analytical mechanics, matter in bulk, electrostatics and magnetostatics, electromagnetic interaction, the field waves, special relativity, and waves. The second volume (Heat and Quanta) contains discussions of the kinetic hypothesis, physics and statistics, stationary ensembles, laws of thermodynamics, early quantum theories, atomic spectra, probability waves, quantization in wave mechanics, approximation methods, and abstract quantum theory. A valuable supplement to any thorough course or text.
Heat and Quanta: Index. 8 figures. x + 300pp. 5⅜ x 8½.     S968 Paperbound **$1.75**
Mechanics and Electrodynamics: Index. 14 figures. vii + 280pp. 5⅜ x 8½.
S969 Paperbound **$1.75**

**THEORETICAL PHYSICS, A. S. Kompaneyets.** One of the very few thorough studies of the subject in this price range. Provides advanced students with a comprehensive theoretical background. Especially strong on recent experimentation and developments in quantum theory. Contents: Mechanics (Generalized Coordinates, Lagrange's Equation, Collision of Particles, etc.), Electrodynamics (Vector Analysis, Maxwell's equations, Transmission of Signals, Theory of Relativity, etc.), Quantum Mechanics (the Inadequacy of Classical Mechanics, the Wave Equation, Motion in a Central Field, Quantum Theory of Radiation, Quantum Theories of Dispersion and Scattering, etc.), and Statistical Physics (Equilibrium Distribution of Molecules in an Ideal Gas, Boltzmann statistics, Bose and Fermi Distribution, Thermodynamic Quantities, etc.). Revised to 1961. Translated by George Yankovsky, authorized by Kompaneyets. 137 exercises. 56 figures. 529pp. 5⅜ x 8½. S972 Paperbound **$2.50**

**ANALYTICAL AND CANONICAL FORMALISM IN PHYSICS, André Mercier.** A survey, in one volume, of the variational principles (the key principles—in mathematical form—from which the basic laws of any one branch of physics can be derived) of the several branches of physical theory, together with an examination of the relationships among them. Contents: the Lagrangian Formalism, Lagrangian Densities, Canonical Formalism, Canonical Form of Electrodynamics, Hamiltonian Densities, Transformations, and Canonical Form with Vanishing Jacobian Determinant. Numerous examples and exercises. For advanced students, teachers, etc. 6 figures. Index. viii + 222pp. 5⅜ x 8½.     S1077 Paperbound **$1.75**

## Acoustics, optics, electricity and magnetism, electromagnetics, magneto-hydrodynamics

**THE THEORY OF SOUND, Lord Rayleigh.** Most vibrating systems likely to be encountered in practice can be tackled successfully by the methods set forth by the great Nobel laureate, Lord Rayleigh. Complete coverage of experimental, mathematical aspects of sound theory. Partial contents: Harmonic motions, vibrating systems in general, lateral vibrations of bars, curved plates or shells, applications of Laplace's functions to acoustical problems, fluid friction, plane vortex-sheet, vibrations of solid bodies, etc. This is the first inexpensive edition of this great reference and study work. Bibliography. Historical introduction by R. B. Lindsay. Total of 1040pp. 97 figures. 5⅜ x 8.
S292, S293, Two volume set, paperbound, **$4.70**

**THE DYNAMICAL THEORY OF SOUND, H. Lamb.** Comprehensive mathematical treatment of the physical aspects of sound, covering the theory of vibrations, the general theory of sound, and the equations of motion of strings, bars, membranes, pipes, and resonators. Includes chapters on plane, spherical, and simple harmonic waves, and the Helmholtz Theory of Audition. Complete and self-contained development for student and specialist; all fundamental differential equations solved completely. Specific mathematical details for such important phenomena as harmonics, normal modes, forced vibrations of strings, theory of reed pipes, etc. Index. Bibliography. 86 diagrams. viii + 307pp. 5⅜ x 8.
S655 Paperbound **$1.50**

**WAVE PROPAGATION IN PERIODIC STRUCTURES, L. Brillouin.** A general method and application to different problems: pure physics, such as scattering of X-rays of crystals, thermal vibration in crystal lattices, electronic motion in metals; and also problems of electrical engineering. Partial contents: elastic waves in 1-dimensional lattices of point masses. Propagation of waves along 1-dimensional lattices. Energy flow. 2 dimensional, 3 dimensional lattices. Mathieu's equation. Matrices and propagation of waves along an electric line. Continuous electric lines. 131 illustrations. Bibliography. Index. xii + 253pp. 5⅜ x 8.
S34 Paperbound **$2.00**

**THEORY OF VIBRATIONS, N. W. McLachlan.** Based on an exceptionally successful graduate course given at Brown University, this discusses linear systems having 1 degree of freedom, forced vibrations of simple linear systems, vibration of flexible strings, transverse vibrations of bars and tubes, transverse vibration of circular plate, sound waves of finite amplitude, etc. Index. 99 diagrams. 160pp. 5⅜ x 8.
S190 Paperbound **$1.35**

**LIGHT: PRINCIPLES AND EXPERIMENTS, George S. Monk.** Covers theory, experimentation, and research. Intended for students with some background in general physics and elementary calculus. Three main divisions: 1) Eight chapters on geometrical optics—fundamental concepts (the ray and its optical length, Fermat's principle, etc.), laws of image formation, apertures in optical systems, photometry, optical instruments etc.; 2) 9 chapters on physical optics—interference, diffraction, polarization, spectra, the Rayleigh refractometer, the wave theory of light, etc.; 3) 23 instructive experiments based directly on the theoretical text. "Probably the best intermediate textbook on light in the English language. Certainly, it is the best book which includes both geometrical and physical optics," J. Rud Nielson, PHYSICS FORUM. Revised edition. 102 problems and answers. 12 appendices. 6 tables. Index. 270 illustrations. xi +489pp. 5⅜ x 8½.
S341 Paperbound **$2.50**

**PHOTOMETRY, John W. T. Walsh.** The best treatment of both "bench" and "illumination" photometry in English by one of Britain's foremost experts in the field (President of the International Commission on Illumination). Limited to those matters, theoretical and practical, which affect the measurement of light flux, candlepower, illumination, etc., and excludes treatment of the use to which such measurements may be put after they have been made. Chapters on Radiation, The Eye and Vision, Photo-Electric Cells, The Principles of Photometry, The Measurement of Luminous Intensity, Colorimetry, Spectrophotometry, Stellar Photometry, The Photometric Laboratory, etc. Third revised (1958) edition. 281 illustrations. 10 appendices. xxiv + 544pp. 5½ x 9¼.
S319 Clothbound **$10.00**

**EXPERIMENTAL SPECTROSCOPY, R. A. Sawyer.** Clear discussion of prism and grating spectrographs and the techniques of their use in research, with emphasis on those principles and techniques that are fundamental to practically all uses of spectroscopic equipment. Beginning with a brief history of spectroscopy, the author covers such topics as light sources, spectroscopic apparatus, prism spectroscopes and graphs, diffraction grating, the photographic process, determination of wave length, spectral intensity, infrared spectroscopy, spectrochemical analysis, etc. This revised edition contains new material on the production of replica gratings, solar spectroscopy from rockets, new standard of wave length, etc. Index. Bibliography. 111 illustrations. x + 358pp. 5⅜ x 8½.       S1045 Paperbound **$2.25**

**FUNDAMENTALS OF ELECTRICITY AND MAGNETISM, L. B. Loeb.** For students of physics, chemistry, or engineering who want an introduction to electricity and magnetism on a higher level and in more detail than general elementary physics texts provide. Only elementary differential and integral calculus is assumed. Physical laws developed logically, from magnetism to electric currents, Ohm's law, electrolysis, and on to static electricity, induction, etc. Covers an unusual amount of material; one third of book on modern material: solution of wave equation, photoelectric and thermionic effects, etc. Complete statement of the various electrical systems of units and interrelations. 2 Indexes. 75 pages of problems with answers stated. Over 300 figures and diagrams. xix +669pp. 5⅜ x 8.
S745 Paperbound **$2.75**

**MATHEMATICAL ANALYSIS OF ELECTRICAL AND OPTICAL WAVE-MOTION, Harry Bateman.** Written by one of this century's most distinguished mathematical physicists, this is a practical introduction to those developments of Maxwell's electromagnetic theory which are directly connected with the solution of the partial differential equation of wave motion. Methods of solving wave-equation, polar-cylindrical coordinates, diffraction, transformation of coordinates, homogeneous solutions, electromagnetic fields with moving singularities, etc. Index. 168pp. 5⅜ x 8. S14 Paperbound **$1.75**

**PRINCIPLES OF PHYSICAL OPTICS, Ernst Mach.** This classical examination of the propagation of light, color, polarization, etc. offers an historical and philosophical treatment that has never been surpassed for breadth and easy readability. Contents: Rectilinear propagation of light. Reflection, refraction. Early knowledge of vision. Dioptrics. Composition of light. Theory of color and dispersion. Periodicity. Theory of interference. Polarization. Mathematical representation of properties of light. Propagation of waves, etc. 279 illustrations, 10 portraits. Appendix. Indexes. 324pp. 5⅜ x 8. S178 Paperbound **$2.00**

**THE THEORY OF OPTICS, Paul Drude.** One of finest fundamental texts in physical optics, classic offers thorough coverage, complete mathematical treatment of basic ideas. Includes fullest treatment of application of thermodynamics to optics; sine law in formation of images, transparent crystals, magnetically active substances, velocity of light, apertures, effects depending upon them, polarization, optical instruments, etc. Introduction by A. A. Michelson. Index. 110 illus. 567pp. 5⅜ x 8. S532 Paperbound **$2.45**

**ELECTRICAL THEORY ON THE GIORGI SYSTEM, P. Cornelius.** A new clarification of the fundamental concepts of electricity and magnetism, advocating the convenient m.k.s. system of units that is steadily gaining followers in the sciences. Illustrating the use and effectiveness of his terminology with numerous applications to concrete technical problems, the author here expounds the famous Giorgi system of electrical physics. His lucid presentation and well-reasoned, cogent argument for the universal adoption of this system form one of the finest pieces of scientific exposition in recent years. 28 figures. Index. Conversion tables for translating earlier data into modern units. Translated from 3rd Dutch edition by L. J. Jolley. x + 187pp. 5½ x 8¾. S909 Clothbound **$6.00**

**ELECTRIC WAVES: BEING RESEARCHES ON THE PROPAGATION OF ELECTRIC ACTION WITH FINITE VELOCITY THROUGH SPACE, Heinrich Hertz.** This classic work brings together the original papers in which Hertz—Helmholtz's protegé and one of the most brilliant figures in 19th-century research—probed the existence of electromagnetic waves and showed experimentally that their velocity equalled that of light, research that helped lay the groundwork for the development of radio, television, telephone, telegraph, and other modern technological marvels. Unabridged republication of original edition. Authorized translation by D. E. Jones. Preface by Lord Kelvin. Index of names. 40 illustrations. xvii + 278pp. 5⅜ x 8½. S57 Paperbound **$1.75**

**PIEZOELECTRICITY: AN INTRODUCTION TO THE THEORY AND APPLICATIONS OF ELECTRO-MECHANICAL PHENOMENA IN CRYSTALS, Walter G. Cady.** This is the most complete and systematic coverage of this important field in print—now regarded as something of scientific classic. This republication, revised and corrected by Prof. Cady—one of the foremost contributors in this area—contains a sketch of recent progress and new material on Ferroelectrics. Time Standards, etc. The first 7 chapters deal with fundamental theory of crystal electricity. 5 important chapters cover basic concepts of piezoelectricity, including comparisons of various competing theories in the field. Also discussed: piezoelectric resonators (theory, methods of manufacture, influences of air-gaps, etc.); the piezo oscillator; the properties, history, and observations relating to Rochelle salt; ferroelectric crystals; miscellaneous applications of piezoelectricity; pyroelectricity; etc. "A great work," W. A. Wooster, NATURE. Revised (1963) and corrected edition. New preface by Prof. Cady. 2 Appendices. Indices. Illustrations. 62 tables. Bibliography. Problems. Total of 1 + 822pp. 5⅜ x 8½.
S1094 Vol. I Paperbound **$2.50**
S1095 Vol. II Paperbound **$2.50**
Two volume set Paperbound **$5.00**

**MAGNETISM AND VERY LOW TEMPERATURES, H. B. G. Casimir.** A basic work in the literature of low temperature physics. Presents a concise survey of fundamental theoretical principles, and also points out promising lines of investigation. Contents: Classical Theory and Experimental Methods, Quantum Theory of Paramagnetism, Experiments on Adiabatic Demagnetization. Theoretical Discussion of Paramagnetism at Very Low Temperatures, Some Experimental Results, Relaxation Phenomena. Index. 89-item bibliography. ix + 95pp. 5⅜ x 8. S943 Paperbound **$1.25**

**SELECTED PAPERS ON NEW TECHNIQUES FOR ENERGY CONVERSION: THERMOELECTRIC METHODS; THERMIONIC; PHOTOVOLTAIC AND ELECTRICAL EFFECTS; FUSION, Edited by Sumner N. Levine.** Brings together in one volume the most important papers (1954-1961) in modern energy technology. Included among the 37 papers are general and qualitative descriptions of the field as a whole, indicating promising lines of research. Also: 15 papers on thermoelectric methods, 7 on thermionic, 5 on photovoltaic, 4 on electrochemical effect, and 2 on controlled fusion research. Among the contributors are: Joffe, Maria Telkes, Herold, Herring, Douglas, Jaumot, Post, Austin, Wilson, Pfann, Rappaport, Morehouse, Domenicali, Moss, Bowers, Harman, Von Doenhoef. Preface and introduction by the editor. Bibliographies. xxviii + 451pp. 6⅛ x 9¼. S37 Paperbound **$3.00**

**SUPERFLUIDS: MACROSCOPIC THEORY OF SUPERCONDUCTIVITY, Vol. I, Fritz London.** The major work by one of the founders and great theoreticians of modern quantum physics. Consolidates the researches that led to the present understanding of the nature of superconductivity. Prof. London here reveals that quantum mechanics is operative on the macroscopic plane as well as the submolecular level. Contents: Properties of Superconductors and Their Thermodynamical Correlation; Electrodynamics of the Pure Superconducting State; Relation between Current and Field; Measurements of the Penetration Depth; Non-Viscous Flow vs. Superconductivity; Micro-waves in Superconductors; Reality of the Domain Structure; and many other related topics. A new epilogue by M. J. Buckingham discusses developments in the field up to 1960. Corrected and expanded edition. An appreciation of the author's life and work by L. W. Nordheim. Biography by Edith London. Bibliography of his publications. 45 figures. 2 Indices. xviii + 173pp. 5⅜ x 8⅜. S44 Paperbound **$1.45**

**SELECTED PAPERS ON PHYSICAL PROCESSES IN IONIZED PLASMAS, Edited by Donald H. Menzel, Director, Harvard College Observatory.** 30 important papers relating to the study of highly ionized gases or plasmas selected by a foremost contributor in the field, with the assistance of Dr. L. H. Aller. The essays include 18 on the physical processes in gaseous nebulae, covering problems of radiation and radiative transfer, the Balmer decrement, electron temperatures, spectrophotometry, etc. 10 papers deal with the interpretation of nebular spectra, by Bohm, Van Vleck, Aller, Minkowski, etc. There is also a discussion of the intensities of "forbidden" spectral lines by George Shortley and a paper concerning the theory of hydrogenic spectra by Menzel and Pekeris. Other contributors: Goldberg, Hebb, Baker, Bowen, Ufford, Liller, etc. viii + 374pp. 6⅛ x 9¼. S60 Paperbound **$2.95**

**THE ELECTROMAGNETIC FIELD, Max Mason & Warren Weaver.** Used constantly by graduate engineers. Vector methods exclusively: detailed treatment of electrostatics, expansion methods, with tables converting any quantity into absolute electromagnetic, absolute electrostatic, practical units. Discrete charges, ponderable bodies, Maxwell field equations, etc. Introduction. Indexes. 416pp. 5⅜ x 8. S185 Paperbound **$2.00**

**THEORY OF ELECTRONS AND ITS APPLICATION TO THE PHENOMENA OF LIGHT AND RADIANT HEAT, H. Lorentz.** Lectures delivered at Columbia University by Nobel laureate Lorentz. Unabridged, they form a historical coverage of the theory of free electrons, motion, absorption of heat, Zeeman effect, propagation of light in molecular bodies, inverse Zeeman effect, optical phenomena in moving bodies, etc. 109 pages of notes explain the more advanced sections. Index. 9 figures. 352pp. 5⅜ x 8. S173 Paperbound **$1.85**

**FUNDAMENTAL ELECTROMAGNETIC THEORY, Ronold P. King,** Professor Applied Physics, Harvard University. Original and valuable introduction to electromagnetic theory and to circuit theory from the standpoint of electromagnetic theory. Contents: Mathematical Description of Matter—stationary and nonstationary states; Mathematical Description of Space and of Simple Media—Field Equations, Integral Forms of Field Equations, Electromagnetic Force, etc.; Transformation of Field and Force Equations; Electromagnetic Waves in Unbounded Regions; Skin Effect and Internal Impedance—in a solid cylindrical conductor, etc.; and Electrical Circuits—Analytical Foundations, Near-zone and quasi-near zone circuits, Balanced two-wire and four-wire transmission lines. Revised and enlarged version. New preface by the author. 5 appendices (Differential operators: Vector Formulas and Identities, etc.). Problems. Indexes. Bibliography. xvi + 580pp. 5⅜ x 8½. S1023 Paperbound **$2.75**

# Hydrodynamics

**A TREATISE ON HYDRODYNAMICS, A. B. Basset.** Favorite text on hydrodynamics for 2 generations of physicists, hydrodynamical engineers, oceanographers, ship designers, etc. Clear enough for the beginning student, and thorough source for graduate students and engineers on the work of d'Alembert, Euler, Laplace, Lagrange, Poisson, Green, Clebsch, Stokes, Cauchy, Helmholtz, J. J. Thomson, Love, Hicks, Greenhill, Besant, Lamb, etc. Great amount of documentation on entire theory of classical hydrodynamics. Vol I: theory of motion of frictionless liquids, vortex, and cyclic irrotational motion, etc. 132 exercises. Bibliography. 3 Appendixes. xii + 264pp. Vol II: motion in viscous liquids, harmonic analysis, theory of tides, etc. 112 exercises, Bibliography. 4 Appendixes. xv + 328pp. Two volume set. 5⅜ x 8.
S724 Vol I Paperbound **$1.75**
S725 Vol II Paperbound **$1.75**
The set **$3.50**

**HYDRODYNAMICS, Horace Lamb.** Internationally famous complete coverage of standard reference work on dynamics of liquids &. gases. Fundamental theorems, equations, methods, solutions, background, for classical hydrodynamics. Chapters include Equations of Motion, Integration of Equations in Special Gases, Irrotational Motion, Motion of Liquid in 2 Dimensions, Motion of Solids through Liquid-Dynamical Theory, Vortex Motion, Tidal Waves, Surface Waves, Waves of Expansion, Viscosity, Rotating Masses of liquids. Excellently planned, arranged; clear, lucid presentation. 6th enlarged, revised edition. Index. Over 900 footnotes, mostly bibliographical. 119 figures. xv + 738pp. 6⅛ x 9¼. S256 Paperbound **$3.75**

**HYDRODYNAMICS, H. Dryden, F. Murnaghan, Harry Bateman.** Published by the National Research Council in 1932 this enormous volume offers a complete coverage of classical hydrodynamics. Encyclopedic in quality. Partial contents: physics of fluids, motion, turbulent flow, compressible fluids, motion in 1, 2, 3 dimensions; viscous fluids rotating, laminar motion, resistance of motion through viscous fluid, eddy viscosity, hydraulic flow in channels of various shapes, discharge of gases, flow past obstacles, etc. Bibliography of over 2,900 items. Indexes. 23 figures. 634pp. 5⅜ x 8.                               S303 Paperbound **$2.75**

# Mechanics, dynamics, thermodynamics, elasticity

**MECHANICS, J. P. Den Hartog.** Already a classic among introductory texts, the M.I.T. professor's lively and discursive presentation is equally valuable as a beginner's text, an engineering student's refresher, or a practicing engineer's reference. Emphasis in this highly readable text is on illuminating fundamental principles and showing how they are embodied in a great number of real engineering and design problems: trusses, loaded cables, beams, jacks, hoists, etc. Provides advanced material on relative motion and gyroscopes not usual in introductory texts. "Very thoroughly recommended to all those anxious to improve their real understanding of the principles of mechanics." MECHANICAL WORLD. Index. List of equations. 334 problems, all with answers. Over 550 diagrams and drawings. ix + 462pp. 5⅜ x 8.
S754 Paperbound **$2.00**

**THEORETICAL MECHANICS: AN INTRODUCTION TO MATHEMATICAL PHYSICS, J. S. Ames, F. D. Murnaghan.** A mathematically rigorous development of theoretical mechanics for the advanced student, with constant practical applications. Used in hundreds of advanced courses. An unusually thorough coverage of gyroscopic and baryscopic material, detailed analyses of the Coriolis acceleration, applications of Lagrange's equations, motion of the double pendulum, Hamilton-Jacobi partial differential equations, group velocity and dispersion, etc. Special relativity is also included. 159 problems. 44 figures. ix + 462pp. 5⅜ x 8.
S461 Paperbound **$2.25**

**THEORETICAL MECHANICS: STATICS AND THE DYNAMICS OF A PARTICLE, W. D. MacMillan.** Used for over 3 decades as a self-contained and extremely comprehensive advanced undergraduate text in mathematical physics, physics, astronomy, and deeper foundations of engineering. Early sections require only a knowledge of geometry; later, a working knowledge of calculus. Hundreds of basic problems, including projectiles to the moon, escape velocity, harmonic motion, ballistics, falling bodies, transmission of power, stress and strain, elasticity, astronomical problems. 340 practice problems plus many fully worked out examples make it possible to test and extend principles developed in the text. 200 figures. xvii + 430pp. 5⅜ x 8.                                                              S467 Paperbound **$2.00**

**THEORETICAL MECHANICS: THE THEORY OF THE POTENTIAL, W. D. MacMillan.** A comprehensive, well balanced presentation of potential theory, serving both as an introduction and a reference work with regard to specific problems, for physicists and mathematicians. No prior knowledge of integral relations is assumed, and all mathematical material is developed as it becomes necessary. Includes: Attraction of Finite Bodies; Newtonian Potential Function; Vector Fields, Green and Gauss Theorems; Attractions of Surfaces and Lines; Surface Distribution of Matter; Two-Layer Surfaces; Spherical Harmonics; Ellipsoidal Harmonics; etc. "The great number of particular cases . . . should make the book valuable to geophysicists and others actively engaged in practical applications of the potential theory," Review of Scientific Instruments. Index. Bibliography. xiii + 469pp. 5⅜ x 8.                    S486 Paperbound **$2.50**

**THEORETICAL MECHANICS: DYNAMICS OF RIGID BODIES, W. D. MacMillan.** Theory of dynamics of a rigid body is developed, using both the geometrical and analytical methods of instruction. Begins with exposition of algebra of vectors, it goes through momentum principles, motion in space, use of differential equations and infinite series to solve more sophisticated dynamics problems. Partial contents: moments of inertia, systems of free particles, motion parallel to a fixed plane, rolling motion, method of periodic solutions, much more. 82 figs. 199 problems. Bibliography. Indexes. xii + 476pp. 5⅜ x 8.            S641 Paperbound **$2.50**

**MATHEMATICAL FOUNDATIONS OF STATISTICAL MECHANICS, A. I. Khinchin.** Offering a precise and rigorous formulation of problems, this book supplies a thorough and up-to-date exposition. It provides analytical tools needed to replace cumbersome concepts, and furnishes for the first time a logical step-by-step introduction to the subject. Partial contents: geometry & kinematics of the phase space, ergodic problem, reduction to theory of probability, application of central limit problem, ideal monatomic gas, foundation of thermo-dynamics, dispersion and distribution of sum functions. Key to notations. Index. viii + 179pp. 5⅜ x 8.
S147 Paperbound **$1.50**

**ELEMENTARY PRINCIPLES IN STATISTICAL MECHANICS, J. W. Gibbs.** Last work of the great Yale mathematical physicist, still one of the most fundamental treatments available for advanced students and workers in the field. Covers the basic principle of conservation of probability of phase, theory of errors in the calculated phases of a system, the contributions of Clausius, Maxwell, Boltzmann, and Gibbs himself, and much more. Includes valuable comparison of statistical mechanics with thermodynamics: Carnot's cycle, mechanical definitions of entropy, etc. xvi + 208pp. 5⅜ x 8.                                  S707 Paperbound **$1.45**

**PRINCIPLES OF MECHANICS AND DYNAMICS, Sir William Thomson (Lord Kelvin) and Peter Guthrie Tait.** The principles and theories of fundamental branches of classical physics explained by two of the greatest physicists of all time. A broad survey of mechanics, with material on hydrodynamics, elasticity, potential theory, and what is now standard mechanics. Thorough and detailed coverage, with many examples, derivations, and topics not included in more recent studies. Only a knowledge of calculus is needed to work through this book. Vol. I (Preliminary): Kinematics; Dynamical Laws and Principles; Experience (observation, experimentation, formation of hypotheses, scientific method); Measures and Instruments; Continuous Calculating Machines. Vol. II (Abstract Dynamics): Statics of a Particle—Attraction; Statics of Solids and Fluids. Formerly Titled "Treatise on Natural Philosophy." Unabridged reprint of revised edition. Index. 168 diagrams. Total of xlii + 1035pp. 5⅜ x 8½.
Vol. I: S966 Paperbound **$2.35**
Vol. II: S967 Paperbound **$2.35**
Two volume Set Paperbound **$4.70**

**INVESTIGATIONS ON THE THEORY OF THE BROWNIAN MOVEMENT, Albert Einstein.** Reprints from rare European journals. 5 basic papers, including the Elementary Theory of the Brownian Movement, written at the request of Lorentz to provide a simple explanation. Translated by A. D. Cowper. Annotated, edited by R. Fürth. 33pp. of notes elucidate, give history of previous investigations. Author, subject indexes. 62 footnotes. 124pp. 5⅜ x 8.
S304 Paperbound **$1.25**

**MECHANICS VIA THE CALCULUS, P. W. Norris, W. S. Legge.** Covers almost everything, from linear motion to vector analysis: equations determining motion, linear methods, compounding of simple harmonic motions, Newton's laws of motion, Hooke's law, the simple pendulum, motion of a particle in 1 plane, centers of gravity, virtual work, friction, kinetic energy of rotating bodies, equilibrium of strings, hydrostatics, sheering stresses, elasticity, etc. 550 problems. 3rd revised edition. xii + 367pp. 6 x 9. S207 Clothbound **$4.95**

**THE DYNAMICS OF PARTICLES AND OF RIGID, ELASTIC, AND FLUID BODIES; BEING LECTURES ON MATHEMATICAL PHYSICS, A. G. Webster.** The reissuing of this classic fills the need for a comprehensive work on dynamics. A wide range of topics is covered in unusually great depth, applying ordinary and partial differential equations. Part I considers laws of motion and methods applicable to systems of all sorts; oscillation, resonance, cyclic systems, etc. Part 2 is a detailed study of the dynamics of rigid bodies. Part 3 introduces the theory of potential; stress and strain, Newtonian potential functions, gyrostatics, wave and vortex motion, etc. Further contents: Kinematics of a point; Lagrange's equations; Hamilton's principle; Systems of vectors; Statics and dynamics of deformable bodies; much more, not easily found together in one volume. Unabridged reprinting of 2nd edition. 20 pages of notes on differential equations and the higher analysis. 203 illustrations. Selected bibliography. Index. xi + 588pp. 5⅜ x 8. S522 Paperbound **$2.45**

**A TREATISE ON DYNAMICS OF A PARTICLE, E. J. Routh.** Elementary text on dynamics for beginning mathematics or physics student. Unusually detailed treatment from elementary definitions to motion in 3 dimensions, emphasizing concrete aspects. Much unique material important in recent applications. Covers impulsive forces, rectilinear and constrained motion in 2 dimensions, harmonic and parabolic motion, degrees of freedom, closed orbits, the conical pendulum, the principle of least action, Jacobi's method, and much more. Index. 559 problems, many fully worked out, incorporated into text. xiii + 418pp. 5⅜ x 8.
S696 Paperbound **$2.25**

**DYNAMICS OF A SYSTEM OF RIGID BODIES (Elementary Section), E. J. Routh.** Revised 7th edition of this standard reference. This volume covers the dynamical principles of the subject, and its more elementary applications: finding moments of inertia by integration, foci of inertia, d'Alembert's principle, impulsive forces, motion in 2 and 3 dimensions, Lagrange's equations, relative indicatrix, Euler's theorem, large tautochronous motions, etc. Index. 55 figures. Scores of problems. xv + 443pp. 5⅜ x 8. S664 Paperbound **$2.50**

**DYNAMICS OF A SYSTEM OF RIGID BODIES (Advanced Section), E. J. Routh.** Revised 6th edition of a classic reference aid. Much of its material remains unique. Partial contents: moving axes, relative motion, oscillations about equilibrium, motion. Motion of a body under no forces, any forces. Nature of motion given by linear equations and conditions of stability. Free, forced vibrations, constants of integration, calculus of finite differences, variations, precession and nutation, motion of the moon, motion of string, chain, membranes. 64 figures. 498pp. 5⅜ x 8. S229 Paperbound **$2.45**

**DYNAMICAL THEORY OF GASES, James Jeans.** Divided into mathematical and physical chapters for the convenience of those not expert in mathematics, this volume discusses the mathematical theory of gas in a steady state, thermodynamics, Boltzmann and Maxwell, kinetic theory, quantum theory, exponentials, etc. 4th enlarged edition, with new material on quantum theory, quantum dynamics, etc. Indexes. 28 figures. 444pp. 6⅛ x 9¼.
S136 Paperbound **$2.65**

**THE THEORY OF HEAT RADIATION, Max Planck.** A pioneering work in thermodynamics, providing basis for most later work, Nobel laureate Planck writes on Deductions from Electrodynamics and Thermodynamics, Entropy and Probability, Irreversible Radiation Processes, etc. Starts with simple experimental laws of optics, advances to problems of spectral distribution of energy and irreversibility. Bibliography. 7 illustrations. xiv + 224pp. 5⅜ x 8.
S546 Paperbound **$1.75**

**FOUNDATIONS OF POTENTIAL THEORY, O. D. Kellogg.** Based on courses given at Harvard this is suitable for both advanced and beginning mathematicians. Proofs are rigorous, and much material not generally avaliable elsewhere is included. Partial contents: forces of gravity, fields of force, divergence theorem, properties of Newtonian potentials at points of free space, potentials as solutions of Laplace's equations, harmonic functions, electrostatics, electric images, logarithmic potential, etc. One of Grundlehren Series. ix + 384pp. 5⅜ x 8.
S144 Paperbound **$1.98**

**THERMODYNAMICS, Enrico Fermi.** Unabridged reproduction of 1937 edition. Elementary in treatment; remarkable for clarity, organization. Requires no knowledge of advanced math beyond calculus, only familiarity with fundamentals of thermometry, calorimetry. Partial Contents: Thermodynamic systems; First & Second laws of thermodynamics; Entropy; Thermodynamic potentials: phase rule, reversible electric cell; Gaseous reactions: van't Hoff reaction box, principle of LeChatelier; Thermodynamics of dilute solutions: osmotic & vapor pressures, boiling & freezing points; Entropy constant. Index. 25 problems. 24 illustrations. x + 160pp. 5⅜ x 8.
S361 Paperbound **$1.75**

**THE THERMODYNAMICS OF ELECTRICAL PHENOMENA IN METALS and A CONDENSED COLLECTION OF THERMODYNAMIC FORMULAS, P. W. Bridgman.** Major work by the Nobel Prizewinner: stimulating conceptual introduction to aspects of the electron theory of metals, giving an intuitive understanding of fundamental relationships concealed by the formal systems of Onsager and others. Elementary mathematical formulations show clearly the fundamental thermodynamical relationships of the electric field, and a complete phenomenological theory of metals is created. This is the work in which Bridgman announced his famous "thermomotive force" and his distinction between "driving" and "working" electromotive force. We have added in this Dover edition the author's long unavailable tables of thermodynamic formulas, extremely valuable for the speed of reference they allow. Two works bound as one. Index. 33 figures. Bibliography. xviii + 256pp. 5⅜ x 8. S723 Paperbound **$1.65**

**TREATISE ON THERMODYNAMICS, Max Planck.** Based on Planck's original papers this offers a uniform point of view for the entire field and has been used as an introduction for students who have studied elementary chemistry, physics, and calculus. Rejecting the earlier approaches of Helmholtz and Maxwell, the author makes no assumptions regarding the nature of heat, but begins with a few empirical facts, and from these deduces new physical and chemical laws. 3rd English edition of this standard text by a Nobel laureate. xvi + 297pp. 5⅜ x 8.
S219 Paperbound **$1.75**

**THE MATHEMATICAL THEORY OF ELASTICITY, A. E. H. Love.** A wealth of practical illustration combined with thorough discussion of fundamentals—theory, application, special problems and solutions. Partial Contents: Analysis of Strain & Stress, Elasticity of Solid Bodies, Elasticity of Crystals, Vibration of Spheres, Cylinders, Propagation of Waves in Elastic Solid Media, Torsion, Theory of Continuous Beams, Plates. Rigorous treatment of Volterra's theory of dislocations, 2-dimensional elastic systems, other topics of modern interest. "For years the standard treatise on elasticity," AMERICAN MATHEMATICAL MONTHLY. 4th revised edition. Index. 76 figures. xviii + 643pp. 6⅛ x 9¼.
S174 Paperbound **$3.25**

**STRESS WAVES IN SOLIDS, H. Kolsky,** Professor of Applied Physics, Brown University. The most readable survey of the theoretical core of current knowledge about the propagation of waves in solids, fully correlated with experimental research. Contents: Part I—Elastic Waves: propagation in an extended elastic medium, propagation in bounded elastic media, experimental investigations with elastic materials. Part II—Stress Waves in Imperfectly Elastic Media: internal friction, experimental investigations of dynamic elastic properties, plastic waves and shock waves, fractures produced by stress waves. List of symbols. Appendix. Supplemented bibliography. 3 full-page plates. 46 figures. x + 213pp. 5⅜ x 8½.
S1098 Paperbound **$1.75**

## Relativity, quantum theory, atomic and nuclear physics

**SPACE TIME MATTER, Hermann Weyl.** "The standard treatise on the general theory of relativity" (Nature), written by a world-renowned scientist, provides a deep clear discussion of the logical coherence of the general theory, with introduction to all the mathematical tools needed: Maxwell, analytical geometry, non-Euclidean geometry, tensor calculus, etc. Basis is classical space-time, before absorption of relativity. Partial contents: Euclidean space, mathematical form, metrical continuum, relativity of time and space, general theory. 15 diagrams. Bibliography. New preface for this edition. xviii + 330pp. 5⅜ x 8.
S267 Paperbound **$2.00**

**ATOMIC SPECTRA AND ATOMIC STRUCTURE, G. Herzberg.** Excellent general survey for chemists, physicists specializing in other fields. Partial contents: simplest line spectra and elements of atomic theory, building-up principle and periodic system of elements, hyperfine structure of spectral lines, some experiments and applications. Bibliography. 80 figures. Index. xii + 257pp. 5⅜ x 8.
S115 Paperbound **$2.00**

**THE PRINCIPLE OF RELATIVITY, A. Einstein, H. Lorentz, H. Minkowski, H. Weyl.** These are the 11 basic papers that founded the general and special theories of relativity, all translated into English. Two papers by Lorentz on the Michelson experiment, electromagnetic phenomena. Minkowski's SPACE & TIME, and Weyl's GRAVITATION & ELECTRICITY. 7 epoch-making papers by Einstein: ELECTROMAGNETICS OF MOVING BODIES, INFLUENCE OF GRAVITATION IN PROPAGATION OF LIGHT, COSMOLOGICAL CONSIDERATIONS, GENERAL THEORY, and 3 others. 7 diagrams. Special notes by A. Sommerfeld. 224pp. 5⅜ x 8.
S81 Paperbound **$1.75**

**EINSTEIN'S THEORY OF RELATIVITY, Max Born.** Revised edition prepared with the collaboration of Gunther Leibfried and Walter Biem. Steering a middle course between superficial popularizations and complex analyses, a Nobel laureate explains Einstein's theories clearly and with special insight. Easily followed by the layman with a knowledge of high school mathematics, the book has been thoroughly revised and extended to modernize those sections of the well-known original edition which are now out of date. After a comprehensive review of classical physics, Born's discussion of special and general theories of relativity covers such topics as simultaneity, kinematics, Einstein's mechanics and dynamics, relativity of arbitrary motions, the geometry of curved surfaces, the space-time continuum, and many others. Index. Illustrations, vii + 376pp. 5⅜ x 8. S769 Paperbound **$2.00**

**ATOMS, MOLECULES AND QUANTA, Arthur E. Ruark and Harold C. Urey.** Revised (1963) and corrected edition of a work that has been a favorite with physics students and teachers for more than 30 years. No other work offers the same combination of atomic structure and molecular physics and of experiment and theory. The first 14 chapters deal with the origins and major experimental data of quantum theory and with the development of conceptions of atomic and molecular structure prior to the new mechanics. These sections provide a thorough introduction to atomic and molecular theory, and are presented lucidly and as simply as possible. The six subsequent chapters are devoted to the laws and basic ideas of quantum mechanics: Wave Mechanics, Hydrogenic Atoms in Wave Mechanics, Matrix Mechanics, General Theory of Quantum Dynamics, etc. For advanced college and graduate students in physics. Revised, corrected republication of original edition, with supplementary notes by the authors. New preface by the authors. 9 appendices. General reference list. Indices. 228 figures. 71 tables. Bibliographical material in notes, etc. Total of xxiii + 810pp. 5⅜ x 8⅜.
S1106 Vol. I Paperbound **$2.50**
S1107 Vol. II Paperbound **$2.50**
Two volume set Paperbound **$5.00**

**WAVE MECHANICS AND ITS APPLICATIONS, N. F. Mott and I. N. Sneddon.** A comprehensive introduction to the theory of quantum mechanics; not a rigorous mathematical exposition it progresses, instead, in accordance with the physical problems considered. Many topics difficult to find at the elementary level are discussed in this book. Includes such matters as: the wave nature of matter, the wave equation of Schrödinger, the concept of stationary states, properties of the wave functions, effect of a magnetic field on the energy levels of atoms, electronic spin, two-body problem, theory of solids, cohesive forces in ionic crystals, collision problems, interaction of radiation with matter, relativistic quantum mechanics, etc. All are treated both physically and mathematically. 68 illustrations. 11 tables. Indexes. xii + 393pp. 5⅜ x 8½. S1070 Paperbound **$2.25**

**BASIC METHODS IN TRANSFER PROBLEMS, V. Kourganoff,** Professor of Astrophysics, U. of Paris. A coherent digest of all the known methods which can be used for approximate or exact solutions of transfer problems. All methods demonstrated on one particular problem—Milne's problem for a plane parallel medium. Three main sections: fundamental concepts (the radiation field and its interaction with matter, the absorption and emission coefficients, etc.); different methods by which transfer problems can be attacked; and a more general problem—the non-grey case of Milne's problem. Much new material, drawing upon declassified atomic energy reports and data from the USSR. Entirely understandable to the student with a reasonable knowledge of analysis. Unabridged, revised reprinting. New preface by the author. Index. Bibliography. 2 appendices. xv + 281pp. 5⅜ x 8½.
S1074 Paperbound **$2.00**

**PRINCIPLES OF QUANTUM MECHANICS, W. V. Houston.** Enables student with working knowledge of elementary mathematical physics to develop facility in use of quantum mechanics, understand published work in field. Formulates quantum mechanics in terms of Schroedinger's wave mechanics. Studies evidence for quantum theory, for inadequacy of classical mechanics, 2 postulates of quantum mechanics; numerous important, fruitful applications of quantum mechanics in spectroscopy, collision problems, electrons in solids; other topics. "One of the most rewarding features . . . is the interlacing of problems with text," Amer. J. of Physics. Corrected edition. 21 illus. Index. 296pp. 5⅜ x 8. S524 Paperbound **$2.00**

**PHYSICAL PRINCIPLES OF THE QUANTUM THEORY, Werner Heisenberg.** A Nobel laureate discusses quantum theory; Heisenberg's own work, Compton, Schroedinger, Wilson, Einstein, many others. Written for physicists, chemists who are not specialists in quantum theory, only elementary formulae are considered in the text; there is a mathematical appendix for specialists. Profound without sacrifice of clarity. Translated by C. Eckart, F. Hoyt. 18 figures. 192pp. 5⅜ x 8. S113 Paperbound **$1.25**

# PHYSICS, HISTORIES AND CLASSICS

**A HISTORY OF PHYSICS: IN ITS ELEMENTARY BRANCHES (THROUGH 1925), INCLUDING THE EVOLUTION OF PHYSICAL LABORATORIES, Florian Cajori.** Revised and enlarged edition. The only first-rate brief history of physics. Still the best entry for a student or teacher into the antecedents of modern theories of physics. A clear, non-mathematical, handy reference work which traces in critical fashion the developments of ideas, theories, techniques, and apparatus from the Greeks to the 1920's. Within each period he analyzes the basic topics of mechanics, light, electricity and magnetism, sound, atomic theory and structure of matter, radioactivity, etc. A chapter on modern research: Curie, Kelvin, Planck's quantum theory, thermodynamics, Fitzgerald and Lorentz, special and general relativity, J. J. Thomson's model of an atom, Bohr's discoveries and later results, wave mechanics, and many other matters. Much bibliographic detail in footnotes. Index. 16 figures. xv + 424pp. 5⅜ x 8. T970 Paperbound **$2.00**

**A HISTORY OF THE MATHEMATICAL THEORIES OF ATTRACTION AND THE FIGURE OF THE EARTH: FROM THE TIME OF NEWTON TO THAT OF LAPLACE, I. Todhunter.** A technical and detailed review of the theories concerning the shape of the earth and its gravitational pull, from the earliest investigations in the seventeenth century up to the middle of the nineteenth. Some of the greatest mathematicians and scientists in history applied themselves to these questions: Newton ("Principia Mathematica"), Huygens, Maupertuis, Simpson, d'Alembert, etc. Others discussed are Poisson, Gauss, Plana, Lagrange, Boit, and many more. Particular emphasis is placed on the theories of Laplace and Legendre, several chapters being devoted to Laplace's "Mécanique Céleste" and his memoirs, and several others to the memoirs of Legendre. Important to historians of science and mathematics and to the specialist who desires background information in the field. 2 volumes bound as 1. Index. xxxvi + 984pp. 5⅜ x 8. S148 Clothbound **$7.50**

**OPTICKS, Sir Isaac Newton.** In its discussions of light, reflection, color, refraction, theories of wave and corpuscular theories of light, this work is packed with scores of insights and discoveries. In its precise and practical discussion of construction of optical apparatus, contemporary understandings of phenomena it is truly fascinating to modern physicists, astronomers, mathematicians. Foreword by Albert Einstein. Preface by I. B. Cohen of Harvard University. 7 pages of portraits, facsimile pages, letters, etc. cxvi + 414pp. 5⅜ x 8. S205 Paperbound **$2.25**

**TREATISE ON LIGHT, Christiaan Huygens.** The famous original formulation of the wave theory of light, this readable book is one of the two decisive and definitive works in the field of light (Newton's "Optics" is the other). A scientific giant whose researches ranged over mathematics, astronomy, and physics, Huygens, in this historic work, covers such topics as rays propagated in straight lines, reflection and refraction, the spreading and velocity of light, the nature of opaque bodies, the non-spherical nature of light in the atmosphere, properties of Iceland Crystal, and other related matters. Unabridged republication of original (1912) English edition. Translated and introduced by Silvanus P. Thompson. 52 illustrations. xii + 129pp. 5⅜ x 8. S179 Paperbound **$1.50**

**FARADAY'S EXPERIMENTAL RESEARCHES IN ELECTRICITY.** Faraday's historic series of papers containing the fruits of years of original experimentation in electrical theory and electrochemistry. Covers his findings in a variety of areas: Induction of electric currents, Evolution of electricity from magnetism, New electrical state or condition of matter, Explication of Arago's magnetic phenomena, New law of electric conduction, Electro-chemical decomposition, Electricity of the Voltaic Pile, Static Induction, Nature of the electric force or forces, Nature of electric current, The character and direction of the electric force of the Gymnotus, Magneto-electric spark, The magnetization of light and the illumination of magnetic lines of force, The possible relation of gravity to electricity, Sub-terranean electrotelegraph wires, Some points of magnetic philosophy, The diamagnetic conditions of flame and gases, and many other matters. Complete and unabridged republication. 3 vols. bound as 2. Originally reprinted from the Philosophical Transactions of 1831-8. Indices. Illustrations. Total of 1463pp. 5⅜ x 8. S783-4, Clothbound **$17.50** (tentative)

**REFLECTIONS ON THE MOTIVE POWER OF FIRE, Sadi Carnot,** and other papers on the 2nd law of thermodynamics by E. Clapeyron and R. Clausius. Carnot's "Reflections" laid the groundwork of modern thermodynamics. Its non-technical, mostly verbal statements examine the relations between heat and the work done by heat in engines, establishing conditions for the economical working of these engines. The papers by Clapeyron and Clausius here reprinted added further refinements to Carnot's work, and led to its final acceptance by physicists. Selections from posthumous manuscripts of Carnot are also included. All papers in English. New introduction by E. Mendoza. 12 illustrations. xxii + 152pp. 5⅜ x 8. S661 Paperbound **$1.50**

**DIALOGUES CONCERNING TWO NEW SCIENCES, Galileo Galilei.** This classic of experimental science, mechanics, engineering, is as enjoyable as it is important. A great historical document giving insights into one of the world's most original thinkers, it is based on 30 years' experimentation. It offers a lively exposition of dynamics, elasticity, sound, ballistics, strength of materials, the scientific method. "Superior to everything else of mine," Galileo. Trans. by H. Crew, A. Salvio. 126 diagrams. Index. xxi + 288pp. 5⅜ x 8. S99 Paperbound **$1.75**

# CHEMISTRY AND PHYSICAL CHEMISTRY

**ORGANIC CHEMISTRY, F. C. Whitmore.** The entire subject of organic chemistry for the practicing chemist and the advanced student. Storehouse of facts, theories, processes found elsewhere only in specialized journals. Covers aliphatic compounds (500 pages on the properties and synthetic preparation of hydrocarbons, halides, proteins, ketones, etc.), alicyclic compounds, aromatic compounds, heterocyclic compounds, organophosphorus and organometallic compounds. Methods of synthetic preparation analyzed critically throughout. Includes much of biochemical interest. "The scope of this volume is astonishing," INDUSTRIAL AND ENGINEERING CHEMISTRY. 12,000-reference index. 2387-item bibliography. Total of x + 1005pp. 5⅜ x 8. Two volume set.
S700 Vol I Paperbound **$2.00**
S701 Vol II Paperbound **$2.00**
The set **$4.00**

**THE MODERN THEORY OF MOLECULAR STRUCTURE, Bernard Pullman.** A reasonably popular account of recent developments in atomic and molecular theory. Contents: The Wave Function and Wave Equations (history and bases of present theories of molecular structure); The Electronic Structure of Atoms (Description and classification of atomic wave functions, etc.); Diatomic Molecules; Non-Conjugated Polyatomic Molecules; Conjugated Polyatomic Molecules; The Structure of Complexes. Minimum of mathematical background needed. New translation by David Antin of "La Structure Moleculaire." Index. Bibliography. vii + 87pp. 5⅜ x 8½.
S987 Paperbound **$1.00**

**CATALYSIS AND CATALYSTS, Marcel Prettre,** Director, Research Institute on Catalysis. This brief book, translated into English for the first time, is the finest summary of the principal modern concepts, methods, and results of catalysis. Ideal introduction for beginning chemistry and physics students. Chapters: Basic Definitions of Catalysis (true catalysis and generalization of the concept of catalysis); The Scientific Bases of Catalysis (Catalysis and chemical thermodynamics, catalysis and chemical kinetics); Homogeneous Catalysis (acid-base catalysis, etc.); Chain Reactions; Contact Masses; Heterogeneous Catalysis (Mechanisms of contact catalyses, etc.); and Industrial Applications (acids and fertilizers, petroleum and petroleum chemistry, rubber, plastics, synthetic resins, and fibers). Translated by David Antin. Index. vi + 88pp. 5⅜ x 8½.
S998 Paperbound **$1.00**

**POLAR MOLECULES, Pieter Debye.** This work by Nobel laureate Debye offers a complete guide to fundamental electrostatic field relations, polarizability, molecular structure. Partial contents: electric intensity, displacement and force, polarization by orientation, molar polarization and molar refraction, halogen-hydrides, polar liquids, ionic saturation, dielectric constant, etc. Special chapter considers quantum theory. Indexed. 172pp. 5⅜ x 8.
S64 Paperbound **$1.50**

**THE ELECTRONIC THEORY OF ACIDS AND BASES, W. F. Luder and Saverio Zuffanti.** The first full systematic presentation of the electronic theory of acids and bases—treating the theory and its ramifications in an uncomplicated manner. Chapters: Historical Background; Atomic Orbitals and Valence; The Electronic Theory of Acids and Bases; Electrophilic and Electrodotic Reagents; Acidic and Basic Radicals; Neutralization; Titrations with Indicators; Displacement; Catalysis; Acid Catalysis; Base Catalysis; Alkoxides and Catalysts; Conclusion. Required reading for all chemists. Second revised (1961) eidtion, with additional examples and references. 3 figures. 9 tables. Index. Bibliography xii + 165pp. 5⅜ x 8.
S201 Paperbound **$1.50**

**KINETIC THEORY OF LIQUIDS, J. Frenkel.** Regarding the kinetic theory of liquids as a generalization and extension of the theory of solid bodies, this volume covers all types of arrangements of solids, thermal displacements of atoms, interstitial atoms and ions, orientational and rotational motion of molecules, and transition between states of matter. Mathematical theory is developed close to the physical subject matter. 216 bibliographical footnotes. 55 figures. xi + 485pp. 5⅜ x 8.
S95 Paperbound **$2.55**

**THE PRINCIPLES OF ELECTROCHEMISTRY, D. A. MacInnes.** Basic equations for almost every subfield of electrochemistry from first principles, referring at all times to the soundest and most recent theories and results; unusually useful as text or as reference. Covers coulometers and Faraday's Law, electrolytic conductance, the Debye-Hueckel method for the theoretical calculation of activity coefficients, concentration cells, standard electrode potentials, thermodynamic ionization constants, pH, potentiometric titrations, irreversible phenomena, Planck's equation, and much more. "Excellent treatise," AMERICAN CHEMICAL SOCIETY JOURNAL. "Highly recommended," CHEMICAL AND METALLURGICAL ENGINEERING. 2 Indices. Appendix. 585-item bibliography. 137 figures. 94 tables. ii + 478pp. 5⅝ x 8⅜.
S52 Paperbound **$2.45**

**THE PHASE RULE AND ITS APPLICATION, Alexander Findlay.** Covering chemical phenomena of 1, 2, 3, 4, and multiple component systems, this "standard work on the subject" (NATURE, London), has been completely revised and brought up to date by A. N. Campbell and N. O. Smith. Brand new material has been added on such matters as binary, tertiary liquid equilibria, solid solutions in ternary systems, quinary systems of salts and water. Completely revised to triangular coordinates in ternary systems, clarified graphic representation, solid models, etc. 9th revised edition. Author, subject indexes. 236 figures. 505 footnotes, mostly bibliographic. xii + 494pp. 5⅜ x 8.
S91 Paperbound **$2.45**

**THE SOLUBILITY OF NONELECTROLYTES, Joel H. Hildebrand and Robert L. Scott.** The standard work on the subject; still indispensable as a reference source and for classroom work. Partial contents: The Ideal Solution (including Raoult's Law and Henry's Law, etc.); Nonideal Solutions; Intermolecular Forces; The Liquid State; Entropy of Athermal Mixing; Heat of Mixing; Polarity; Hydrogen Bonding; Specific Interactions; "Solvation" and "Association"; Systems of Three or More Components; Vapor Pressure of Binary Liquid Solutions; Mixtures of Gases; Solubility of Gases in Liquids; of Liquids in Liquids; of Solids in Liquids; Evaluation of Solubility Parameters; and other topics. Corrected republication of third (revised) edition. Appendices. Indexes. 138 figures. 111 tables. 1 photograph. iv + 488pp. 5⅜ x 8½.
S1125 Paperbound **$2.50**

**TERNARY SYSTEMS: INTRODUCTION TO THE THEORY OF THREE COMPONENT SYSTEMS, G. Masing.** Furnishes detailed discussion of representative types of 3-components systems, both in solid models (particularly metallic alloys) and isothermal models. Discusses mechanical mixture without compounds and without solid solutions; unbroken solid solution series; solid solutions with solubility breaks in two binary systems; iron-silicon-aluminum alloys; allotropic forms of iron in ternary system; other topics. Bibliography. Index. 166 illustrations. 178pp. 5⅝ x 8⅜.
S631 Paperbound **$1.50**

**THE KINETIC THEORY OF GASES, Leonard B. Loeb,** University of California. Comprehensive text and reference book which presents full coverage of basic theory and the important experiments and developments in the field for the student and investigator. Partial contents: The Mechanical Picture of a Perfect Gas, The Mean Free Path—Clausius' Deductions, Distribution of Molecular Velocities, discussions of theory of the problem of specific heats, the contributions of kinetic theory to our knowledge of electrical and magnetic properties of molecules and its application to the conduction of electricity in gases. New 14-page preface to Dover edition by the author. Name, subject indexes. Six appendices. 570-item bibliography. xxxvi + 687pp. 5⅜ x 8½.
S942 Paperbound **$2.95**

**IONS IN SOLUTION, Ronald W. Gurney.** A thorough and readable introduction covering all the fundamental principles and experiments in the field, by an internationally-known authority. Contains discussions of solvation energy, atomic and molecular ions, lattice energy, transferral of ions, interionic forces, cells and half-cells, transference of electrons, exchange forces, hydrogen ions, the electro-chemical series, and many other related topics. Indispensable to advanced undergraduates and graduate students in electrochemistry. Index. 45 illustrations. 15 tables. vii + 206pp. 5⅜ x 8½.
S124 Paperbound **$1.50**

**IONIC PROCESSES IN SOLUTION, Ronald W. Gurney.** Lucid, comprehensive examination which brings together the approaches of electrochemistry, thermodynamics, statistical mechanics, electroacoustics, molecular physics, and quantum theory in the interpretation of the behavior of ionic solutions—the most important single work on the subject. More extensive and technical than the author's earlier work (IONS IN SOLUTION), it is a middle-level text for graduate students and researchers in electrochemistry. Covers such matters as Brownian motion in liquids, molecular ions in solution, heat of precipitation, entropy of solution, proton transfers, dissociation constant of nitric acid, viscosity of ionic solutions, etc. 78 illustrations. 47 tables. Name and subject index. ix + 275pp. 5⅜ x 8½.
S134 Paperbound **$1.75**

**CRYSTALLOGRAPHIC DATA ON METAL AND ALLOY STRUCTURES, Compiled by A. Taylor and B. J. Kagle,** Westinghouse Research Laboratories. Unique collection of the latest crystallographic data on alloys, compounds, and the elements, with lattice spacings expressed uniformly in absolute Angstrom units. Gathers together previously widely-scattered data from the Power Data File of the ATSM, structure reports, and the Landolt-Bornstein Tables, as well as from other original literature. 2300 different compounds listed in the first table, Alloys and Intermetallic Compounds, with much vital information on each. Also listings for nearly 700 Borides, Carbides, Hydrides, Oxides, Nitrides. Also all the necessary data on the crystal structure of 77 elements. vii + 263pp. 5⅜ x 8.
S1013 Paperbound **$2.25**

**MATHEMATICAL CRYSTALLOGRAPHY AND THE THEORY OF GROUPS OF MOVEMENTS, Harold Hilton.** Classic account of the mathematical theory of crystallography, particularly the geometrical theory of crystal-structure based on the work of Bravais, Jordan, Sohncke, Federow, Schoenflies, and Barlow. Partial contents: The Stereographic Projection, Properties Common to Symmetrical and Asymmetrical Crystals, The Theory of Groups, Coordinates of Equivalent Points, Crystallographic Axes and Axial Ratios, The Forms and Growth of Crystals, Lattices and Translations, The Structure-Theory, Infinite Groups of Movements, Triclinic and Monoclinic Groups, Orthorhombic Groups, etc. Index. 188 figures. xii + 262pp. 5⅜ x 8½.
S1058 Paperbound **$2.00**

**CLASSICS IN THE THEORY OF CHEMICAL COMBINATIONS. Edited by O. T. Benfey.** Vol. I of the Classics of Science Series, G. Holton, Harvard University, General Editor. This book is a collection of papers representing the major chapters in the development of the valence concept in chemistry. Includes essays by Wöhler and Liebig, Laurent, Williamson, Frankland, Kekulé and Couper, and two by van't Hoff and le Bel, which mark the first extension of the valence concept beyond its purely numerical character. Introduction and epilogue by Prof. Benfey. Index. 9 illustrations. New translation of Kekulé paper by Benfey. xiv + 191pp. 5⅜ x 8½.
S1066 Paperbound **$1.85**

**THE CHEMISTRY OF URANIUM: THE ELEMENT, ITS BINARY AND RELATED COMPOUNDS, J. J. Katz and E. Rabinowitch.** Vast post-World War II collection and correlation of thousands of AEC reports and published papers in a useful and easily accessible form, still the most complete and up-to-date compilation. Treats "dry uranium chemistry," occurrences, preparation, properties, simple compounds, isotopic composition, extraction from ores, spectra, alloys, etc. Much material available only here. Index. Thousands of evaluated bibliographical references. 324 tables, charts, figures. xxi + 609pp. 5⅜ x 8. S757 Paperbound **$2.95**

**THE STORY OF ALCHEMY AND EARLY CHEMISTRY, J. M. Stillman.** An authoritative, scholarly work, highly readable, of development of chemical knowledge from 4000 B.C. to downfall of phlogiston theory in late 18th century. Every important figure, many quotations. Brings alive curious, almost incredible history of alchemical beliefs, practices, writings of Arabian Prince Oneeyade, Vincent of Beauvais, Geber, Zosimos, Paracelsus, Vitruvius, scores more. Studies work, thought of Black, Cavendish, Priestley, Van Helmont, Bergman, Lavoisier, Newton, etc. Index. Bibliography. 579pp. 5⅜ x 8. S628 Paperbound **$2.45**

*Prices subject to change without notice.*

*Dover publishes books on art, music, philosophy, literature, languages, history, social sciences, psychology, handcrafts, orientalia, puzzles and entertainments, chess, pets and gardens, books explaining science, intermediate and higher mathematics, mathematical physics, engineering, biological sciences, earth sciences, classics of science, etc. Write to:*

*Dept. catrr.*
*Dover Publications, Inc.*
*180 Varick Street, N.Y. 14, N.Y.*